CORNISH STUDIES

Second Series

SEVEN

INSTITUTE OF CORNISH STUDIES

Sardinia Pilchardus
(The Pilchard)

EDITOR'S NOTE

Cornish Studies (second series) exists to reflect current research conducted internationally in the inter-disciplinary field of Cornish Studies. It is edited by Dr Philip Payton, Reader in Cornish Studies and Director of the Institute of Cornish Studies at the University of Exeter, and is published by the University of Exeter Press. The opinions expressed in *Cornish Studies* are those of individual authors and are not necessarily those of the editor or publisher. The support of Cornwall County Council is gratefully acknowledged.

Cover illustration: reproduced courtesy of South Devon Railway Trust.

CORNISH STUDIES

Second Series

SEVEN

Edited by

Philip Payton

UNIVERSITY
of
EXETER
PRESS

First published in 1999 by
University of Exeter Press
Reed Hall, Streatham Drive
Exeter, Devon EX4 4QR
UK
www.ex.ac.uk/uep/

© Philip Payton 1999

British Library Cataloguing in Publication Data
A catalogue record for this book is
available from the British Library

ISBN 0 85989 644 7
ISSN 1352-271X

Typeset in 10/12pt Times by Kestrel Data, Exeter

Printed and bound in Great Britain by
Short Run Press Ltd, Exeter

Contents

REVIEW ARTICLE

INTRODUCTION

The increasing maturity of Cornish Studies as an area of academic endeavour has been reflected, as this series is fond of reminding its readers, in both a 'new Cornish historiography' and a 'new Cornish social science', evidence of a concern to construct interdisciplinary perspectives and to engage with wider scholarly discourses. For many practitioners, this has required considerable personal and academic courage, whether in venturing a Cornish perspective in major international debates such as 'Who are the Celts?' and 'What is Celtic Studies?', or in entering the fray closer to home in contests such as those that have surrounded the development of the Revived Cornish language. Indeed, at least part of the audience for Cornish Studies presumes the existence of a normative project designed to bolster the claims of 'the Cornish movement' (and its political, cultural and economic objectives) and is occasionally dismayed when Cornish Studies practitioners offer an overtly critical assessment of its shibboleths. That is not to deny that much of the concern of Cornish Studies is with contemporary issues of identity, or with current socio-economic conditions, or with the politics of 'difference', nor is it to conceal that individual practitioners do themselves hold their own personal views on a range of Cornish matters. But it is to insist that Cornish Studies, as a component of mainstream academic activity, should guard its own academic freedom and, crucially, maintain a critical edge in its research and writing.

This edition of *Cornish Studies*, number *Seven* in the series, exhibits both courage and critical edge in the contributions of a range of scholars who tackle subjects as disparate as the influence of landscape on cultural activity in Cornwall to the methodologies adopted by Cornish language revivalists, sometimes unwittingly and sometimes by design challenging the several 'sacred cows' that roam west of the Tamar. The aim, however, is not merely to challenge but to advance the contribution to knowledge that Cornish Studies can make, not least by pressing ever further into new and fruitful fields of enquiry. In this volume, for example, *gender* makes a welcome entry into the 'new Cornish historiography'; and not before time, Cornish history having been in the past so often pre-occupied with male-oriented themes. There is also important new work in the realms of 'cultural studies', itself an interdisciplinary activity which draws upon a range of subjects from literature to anthropology and geography and thus sits happily within the new approaches to Cornish Studies that have been developed in recent years.

This collection begins with Sharron Schwartz's ground-breaking analysis of women's struggles in nineteenth-century Cornwall in defence of 'customary rights', an article which not only places gender centre-stage in Cornish Studies but engages with recent work on the nature of the 'Industrial Revolution' in Cornwall, particularly the process of 'proto-industrialization'. She notes, for example, the changing role of the 'independent bal maiden' (female mine worker), a role—like others—that declined in the face of technological, structural and social change, concluding that by the late nineteenth century 'For many Cornish labouring women, the gradual shift from proto-industrialism culminated in domestic hardship and misery'. A student too of the Great Emigration, Schwartz also notes the impact of male emigration on those women left behind in Cornwall: 'For those whose husbands were overseas, women had control of the family budget, but ironically, they had become increasingly isolated within the domestic sphere.'

William A. Morris continues the theme of nineteenth-century Cornish emigration but, in contrast to recent attempts to set that emigration in its global context (see Philip Payton, *The Cornish Overseas*, Fowey, 1999), he employs techniques of micro-analysis to examine the migration patterns of one specific parish (Zennor) in the years after 1850. Perhaps surprisingly, he finds that, despite the isolated nature of Zennor and the generally distinctive characteristics of Cornish emigration, patterns of in-migration and out-migration did not vary significantly from those for England and Wales elucidated in the well-known studies of E.G. Ravenstein.

The nineteenth century is also the concern of Brian Elvins, but this time the theme is politics, using the experience of the Lemon 'family interest' to re-examine Norman Gash's view of the Cornish political scene in the years leading up to and immediately after the Great Reform Act of 1832. Gash argued that Cornish politics were distinctive in this period because geographical peripherality insulated Cornwall from the metropolitan party-political contests of reformers and anti-reformers, the deciding factor in Cornish allegiances and elections being the influence of prominent families—notably the Lemons who allegedly played a major role in the decline of the Conservatives after 1832. Elvins concludes, however, that the Lemon connection was already in decline by then, and that the failure of the Conservatives in West Cornwall in particular was more a function of the increasing effectiveness of Liberal organization in the area, heralding amongst other things the growth of Cornwall's Radical tradition.

Elvins' article helps to illuminate the emergence of the Radical tradition but Garry Tregidga's brings the story forward another hundred years to the inter-war period, the 'Age of Alignment' in British politics when the Liberals went into near terminal decline, the principal contest becoming increasingly that of Labour versus Conservative. Tregidga reminds us, however, that Cornwall failed to participate in this Alignment, the dominant contest remaining that between the Liberals and the Conservatives, but in a careful and sensitive handling of the sources he shows that the situation was in fact more complex than at first appears. Not only had Labour made good progress in Cornwall after the First World War but in the aftermath of the extreme poverty of the 1920s the Labour Party, under the leadership of A.L. Rowse, made a concerted effort to penetrate and establish itself within Cornish political culture. By the end of the 1930s, however, this effort was already failing, the Liberals having effectively reinforced their continuing credentials as the Radical alternatives to the Conservatives in Cornwall.

Labour failure was in part a result of Cornwall's early and traumatic experience of de-industrialization. Other consequences of this phenomenon were the rise of tourism as an economic alternative, and the emergence of the Celto-Cornish Revival as a response to the cultural crisis precipitated by the loss of industrial prowess. Ronald Perry brings these two factors together in an examination of 'Celtic Tourism' in Cornwall in the century 1875–1975. He argues that, despite the growth of the Revival in the years before the First World War, it was not until the slump of the 1920s and 1930s that Celtic themes were adopted by the holiday industry with any enthusiasm, and then largely through the publicity activity of external organizations such as the Great Western Railway. Perry agrees (with Payton and Thornton) that in this inter-war period there was some evidence of collusion between these external image-makers and the enthusiasts of the Celto-Cornish Revival but he goes on to argue that, after 1945, when Cornwall was faced by widespread socio-economic and demographic change, this relationship changed. Revivalists became more hostile to the tourist industry, although, by the 1970s, when Cornwall's eagerly anticipated economic resurgence had already proved a false dawn, Celtic tourism did once again find favour in at least some quarters.

Perry's approach highlights the significance of contrasting, conflicting and sometimes contested constructions or 'imaginings' of Cornwall, a process by no means restricted to the marketing strategies of the holiday industry but present in a most profound manner in the activities of artists and writers. Patrick Laviolette addresses himself to the iconography of landscape images in Cornish art and prose in a cerebral article designed to reveal the relationship between creativity, landscape and identity. He doubts whether there is something in-herently creative in Cornwall itself but he does accept that much of the Cornish countryside is revealed through its human landscape features. This environment is multi-faceted and beyond the range of 'normal' southern British countryside, a landscape that is instead a 'rather exotic and intimidating territory' and has led to some key portrayals by artists and writers drawn to specific localities in which 'Cornish communities are immortalized vicariously by the creation of numerous works of art that encompass a sense of Cornishness'.

Catherine Brace, in her article, focuses on one such writer, Arthur Caddick, and one such locality, Nancledra (near St Ives), exploring the relationship between Cornish identity and landscape in Caddick's work in the years between 1945 and 1981. As Brace argues, Caddick made explicit the link between Cornish identity and landscape, in particular the West Penwith countryside around his adopted home at Nancledra. Caddick felt himself deeply rooted in this landscape, almost an integral part of it in the manner described by Laviolette, a spiritual attachment that he celebrated in verse. But Caddick was not Cornish-born (he came from Yorkshire), and an ever-present tension in his personal identification with the Cornish landscape, and thus in his work, was his resistance to what he saw (erroneously) as a Cornish exclusivity promoted by the Gorsedd and Mebyon Kernow in which Cornishness was somehow a function of racial inheritance. Yet Caddick could also identify with Cornish causes, notably the continual loss of young Cornish people and their replacement by 'complacent up-country folk'. As Brace concludes, Caddick occupies a paradoxical position as part-outsider, part-insider, a paradox caught by Cornish poet Frank Ruhrmund who declared that, although Caddick was an Englishman, he was nevertheless 'one of us'.

In contrast to Caddick, there is no doubting the Cornish creden-tials of Charles Causley, a Cornishness with which Causley has always felt at ease and over which he has not had occasion to agonize. But, like Caddick, there is also a strong identification with locality, for while Causley's poetry and prose range widely across Cornwall and elsewhere, he is nonetheless deeply rooted in his Cornish hometown of Launceston. And yet, John Hurst notes that 'This even surface may not, however, tell the whole story', and he delves beyond the published work to the 'remarkable collection of manuscripts and documents' held (like those of Arthur Caddick examined by Catherine Brace) in the University of Exeter Library. Here Hurst is able to discern a deeper Causley 'between the lines', a Causley of 'dark sounds' behind the apparent simplicity of words, as well as gaining an insight into his literary life and working methods. Hurst singles out for particular attention Causley's well-known poem, 'A Short Life of Nevil Northey Burnard', the tale of the poor lad from Altarnun (but 'a handful of miles to the west of Launceston', as Hurst remarks) who went from obscurity to fame and back again, a poem which—in Hurst's phrase—exemplifies 'not only his [Causley's] rootedness in the environment of East Cornwall, but also the deep link between that rootedness and work'.

The 'cultural studies' approach that has informed the contributions of Laviolette, Brace and, to a degree, Hurst, is made plain in Jim Hall's article 'Maximilla, the Cornish Montanist: The Final Scenes of *Origo Mundi*', an innovative analysis of part of the medieval miracle play, the *Ordinalia*. With refreshing candour, Hall admits that it is the objections and interjections of his own cultural studies students that have sent him down these new pathways of discovery, allowing him to suggest that 'The relationship of religion and culture in medieval Cornwall . . . informs us about a time before ideology and might also be instructive in an era [today] that is considered by some to be post-ideological'. Rather like the recent interpretations of the later play *Beunans Meriasek*, the *Ordinalia*, Hall argues, should be read in the context of a struggle for political power, a multi-layered conflict at a time when Cornwall was being drawn closer to England and where 'The cycle's careful ambiguities speak of an unstable and fractious audience whose faith . . . was often heavily compromised with persistent superstition and pagan vestiges'.

The *Ordinalia*, of course, is in the Cornish language, an important reminder (if one were needed) of the distinctive qualities of medieval Cornwall but an important icon too for present-day Celto-Cornish Revivalists. Indeed, amongst the most fascinating aspects of contemporary Cornwall is not only the enduring determination to revive the Cornish language but the cultural contestation that has attended this process. In addition to the sometimes conflicting ideological motivations of the various revivalist groups, is the extended debate concerning methodology and linguistics, a debate that has been pursued with dogged persistence over the years by its several protagonists. In the 1980s, Ken George, with considerable courage and not a little ingenuity, devised a new orthography for Revived Cornish, called 'Kernewek Kemmyn' (Common Cornish), an event known sometimes as the 'phonemic revision'. Although embraced enthusiastically by the Cornish Language Board and many Cornish speakers and learners, Kernewek Kemmyn has also attracted sustained criticism from at least part of the academic community of linguists and Celticists.

In this volume Jon Mills, a linguist at the University of Luton, adds his voice to those academic critics, taking as his text for deconstruction the 1993 *Gerlyver Kernewek Kemmyn*, a new Cornish dictionary devised by Ken George. Mills insists that this dictionary is 'linguistically naïve' and 'not a suitable pedagogical basis for Revived Cornish', and, taking his cue from the work of Richard Gendall, concludes that

> While it is not possible to recover the actual sounds of medieval Cornish, there are no significant grounds for rejecting Late Cornish as being corrupted by English, and Lhuyd provides us with the clearest record of how Cornish was pronounced. Lhuyd should . . . provide the basis for recommendations on pronunciation.

N.J.A. Williams, meanwhile, a familiar detractor of Kernewek Kemmyn, returns to the debate in his discussion of ' "Saint' in Cornish', an article which he uses as a vehicle for criticizing the process by which Kernewek Kemmyn alternatives for Cornish place-names have been devised and suggested for use. He is especially critical of the publication *Henwyn Tylleryow Kernewek* ('Cornish Place-names') produced by the magazine *An Gannas*, deciding that 'it is very unsatisfactory and cannot be recommended'. A newcomer to the debate, Michael Everson, a linguist and director of a Dublin-based company which specializes in minority-language software localization, fonts and publishing, adds his voice to Williams' objections. In a Review Article which examines Ken George's very recent 1998 dictionary, the *Gerlyver Kres*, Everson echoes the familiar objections to Kernewek Kemmyn but he also addresses the form and content of the 1998 dictionary, couching his criticisms in the firm tones so characteristic of the Cornish language debate.

To the external observer, the conviction, indeed passion, of the Cornish language debate may sometimes appear baffling but, stripping aside the complexities and intricacies of linguistic dispute, the debate is in some respects an exemplar of the condition of modern (or postmodern) Cornwall. As the United Kingdom slowly re-invents itself at the end of this millennium, as 'Britishness' is increasingly open to doubt and dispute, so Cornwall is increasingly an enigma—not falling neatly or happily into the new categories that are appearing, a battle-ground perhaps for conflicting visions, constructions, imaginings of Cornishness and Celticity. For all its uncertainty, it is an exciting process, and one that will continue to demand the attention of Cornish Studies practitioners.

Philip Payton,
Reader in Cornish Studies and
Director,
Institute of Cornish Studies,
University of Exeter.

IN DEFENCE OF CUSTOMARY RIGHTS: LABOURING WOMEN'S EXPERIENCE OF INDUSTRIALIZATION IN CORNWALL, c1750–1870

Sharron P. Schwartz

INTRODUCTION

In recent years a growing number of feminist historians has challenged E.P Thompson's attempt to 'rescue the poor labourer from the enormous condescension of posterity',[1] by focusing attention on women. Historical scholarship, they argued, was far from 'subjective' or 'universal', because it was based on male experience, placed men at the centre and as a measure of all things human, thereby leaving out half of mankind.[2] As a result, labouring women's experience of the Industrial Revolution is now regarded as being of deep significance.[3]

Very recently, practitioners of the new Cornish historiography have attempted to offer a more sophisticated critique of the notion of industrial revolution, looking in particular at the process of industrialization in Cornwall. As Payton explains, this has been at two levels, attempting first of all to contextualize the Cornish industrial experience within a wider explanation of Cornwall's history, and then setting that experience within broader models of regional economic specialization.[4] Deacon has offered us a revised narrative for the social and industrial history of Cornwall in the nineteenth century,[5] but labouring women's experience of industrialization in Cornwall has surprisingly remained a neglected field. This article revisits a familiar territory— Cornwall in the age of the Industrial Revolution—but seeks to infuse gender into an analysis of this period in order to achieve a more comprehensive picture of the Cornish industrial experience.

WOMEN, PROTO-INDUSTRIALIZATION AND PATRIARCHY

The main problem in attempting to analyse women's work before the mid-nineteenth century is the absence of census materials which would enable us to construct aggregate indices of women's activity. And unfortunately, it is this very period in which many of the changes affecting Cornwall's working women took place. Nevertheless, this article attempts to bridge the gap in current historiography which largely omits labouring women's experience of industrialization, by focusing firstly upon the period of development which preceded and paved the way for industrialism proper. This important transitional period, spanning much of the eighteenth century and the beginning of the nineteenth, witnessed the development of the precursors of many modern industries, and has been identified as 'proto-industrialism', (a merchant-dominated, family wage economy, where workers had significant access to non-commodity production).

To what extent Cornwall might be described as a proto-industrial region in solely economic terms is debatable.[6] But instead of focusing exclusively on economic criteria, Deacon has made a convincing case for describing Cornwall as a proto-industrial region with his argument that proto-industrialism refers more to a social formation marked by strongly 'traditional' aspects than to a particular division of labour.[7] And it is within this 'traditional' social model that we can fully appreciate the importance of women's work.

Women have always worked, be it wage-earners or otherwise, but it was the nature of their work which changed with the advent of industrialism. Prior to the rise of a formal wage economy, women's work was mainly centred on the home, where their labour has been described as 'the vanguard of the peasant household industries'.[8] The nature of such 'cottage industry' allowed women to combine their duties as mothers and wives, for they could undertake the work at their own pace, and at the time they chose. Furthermore, cottage industry offered a strategy of survival in times when male wage-earners suffered periods of unemployment. However, some historians argue that because women often worked within a family group and probably did not see their earnings as individuals, their work was subsumed within a patriarchal framework, and was low waged and deemed as of low status.[9] But Valenze has argued that women's labour, both waged and non-waged, played an indispensable economic role by making a valid contribution to the family economy which helped to keep working-class families above the subsistence threshold.[10]

A variety of cottage industries—basket making, straw plaiting and straw bonnet manufacture—had been carried on to some extent in many Cornish parishes for some time, as noted by the seventeenth-century commentator, Richard Carew. But it is domestic textile manufacture which immediately comes to mind when we think of proto-industry. Of greater importance was the carding of wool which was then spun on a 'turn' (spinning wheel) into wool for knitting a variety of garments. This classic example of proto-industry once provided valuable income for labouring women throughout Cornwall, but so too did spinning thread for weaving.

For example, at Sennen, the weaving industry attained great importance and kept many women busy spinning thread for the workers who operated the hand looms. Indeed, Bottrell mentions the numerous women in the Zennor vicinity who eked out a slender livelihood by spinning yarn or thread, whilst Henry Quick, the Zennor poet, (1792–1857), throws light on the symbiosis of his parents' proto-industrial lifestyle:

> My father laboured underground,
> Mother the spinning wheel put round.[11]

Even though this industry was evident in West Penwith in the late eighteenth century, it was by no means as high profile as it had been in earlier times. Using probate inventories, Callum has shown that domestic textile production in West Penwith was an industry already well in decline by the mid-eighteenth century.[12] Nevertheless, we find in other areas of Cornwall that spinning also clung on: vestry meetings in the Parish of Stoke Climsland in 1797 and 1801 provide proof of the importance of the spinning industry to the labouring population, chiefly women, who manufactured thread for yarn jobbers.[13] And realizing the importance of women's contribution to the family economy through domestic industries, eighteenth-century parish vestry books, such as that of Gwennap, sometimes make mention of the granting of 'cards' for combing wool, and more frequently of 'turns', given to impoverished women in lieu of financial disbursements.[14]

Women's work also included small-scale farming. Hamilton Jenkin has alerted us to the role women once played in the annual harvest, noting that 'in earlier times, the actual reaping was done for the most part by women with the 'hook' (sickle), an occupation in which many of them were extraordinarily expert'.[15] In the winter months, women helped with threshing, and performed winnowing. And it was usually women who made full use of time-honoured rights of turbary and pasture for access to wastes and common land for grazing and to gather fuel in the form of peat, furze, and 'gloys' (dried cow pats). They also helped to collect the hearth ashes and the dung from the family livestock, used to fertilize the land which underpinned the success of the allotment system. Women also played an important role in small-scale dairying. In West Cornwall, many households rented a cow from local farmers, which was grazed on wastes or common land for the provision of milk. Milking was customarily women's work, who then 'unreamed' (skimmed) the milk and made it into butter, clotted cream and occasionally cheese. Such dairy produce, along with surplus vegetables or eggs, were taken to the local market and traded for pin money which was a vital component of the family income. Sometimes such home-produced dairy goods were bartered locally. Therefore, access to land meant that labouring families as well as widows and single women could eke out a living and avoid dependence on the parish pay.

Women's labour was important in coastal areas too, where they played an indispensable role in the seasonal pilchard industry, employed in large numbers in the fish cellars where the pilchards were bulked, washed and packed, earning several shillings in one night.[16] This income, combined with that of their men folk, helped to ensure the family's survival above subsistence level.[17]

Although in proto-industrial times work was often allotted according to gender, sometimes subsistence necessitated a maximum of familial co-operation which helped to erase the traditional division of labour between the sexes and age groups. Bottrell provides an illuminating example of the working life of a St Buryan woman living in the early nineteenth century, which clearly shows that in this area of West Penwith, men and women worked cheek by jowl at harvest time, with women performing many of the tasks which today we tend to associate with men:

> I did outdoor work and helped old mistress besides, when there was extra housework such as great brewings, cheese-making, the baking and roasting at feasten-tides, and spinning for the weavers, besides the regular spinning of winter's nights . . . there was no woman and but a few men that could beat me in shaking liners (threshed wheaten sheaves), leading trusses, branding turves, raking tabs (roots, grass etc.), reaping, rulling, aye, or building either on a push; and I could make an arish mow as well as any man . . . there wasn't an equal at the windan-sheet (winnowing-sheet), there wasn't my equal in the parish for handling the sieve and kayer (coarse sieve), and I made a better sample of corn, and not half so much after-winding and waste.[18]

We find in the coastal regions too (it was noted in the fish cellars of St Ives for example) that during the pilchard season male workers as well as every variety of the 'female type', from old women of sixty to girls of sixteen, worked side by side.[19]

As eighteenth-century Cornwall underwent a transformation, through deep-lode mining, into an early industrial region, farming and smallholding subsidized the production costs of Cornish mining by reducing real labour costs. Deacon has added to our understanding of the importance of access to collateral aid in the form of the informal potato plot, and customary access to non-commodity food supplies.[20] But the role of women in this important period, when proto-industrialism was gradually giving way to early large-scale industrialization, has been overlooked. For it was labouring women in the mining districts who often undertook the main responsibility of cultivating allotments for growing wheat, potatoes and vegetables, keeping a cow, pigs, goats or poultry, as well as spinning or other handicraft production, thereby providing valuable support to their husbands who could only spend time on the land outside normal working hours.

Indeed, Tremenheere states that the attempt to combine the cultivation of a farm of several acres with regular mining engagements was seldom successful, and men so situated were less likely to be considered eligible for employment.[21] Therefore, for mining families leasing a smallholding, the responsibility for cultivating crops and maintaining livestock often lay with their women folk. And this was magnified after the decline in tribute work in favour of contract employment on the mines increased the length of mining cores, which lessened the independence of men who had formerly decided, by and large, what hours they worked. The Reverend Pascoe's wife in her walks around St Hilary commented on the plight of a woman who through necessity had been forced to leave her sick bed prematurely to work in the fields in order to supplement her miner-husband's wages.[22] However, from the latter half of the eighteenth century, the quickening pace of industrialization, Acts of Enclosure and agricultural mechanization began to restrict women's opportunities for work in the agricultural world, and also limited the opportunities for gleaning, grazing and gathering on common lands and wastes. And the change from the hook to the heavier scythe, deemed a tool suitable only for male labourers, meant that women's role at harvest time was severely reduced.[23]

We find, too, that in the spinning and weaving industries, gradual mechanization allowed male workers to monopolise the more complicated machinery, leaving women with the less skilled, more onerous tasks. Moreover, many weaving enterprises were sited in the growing towns, not the scattered villages in which many of the female spinners lived. Indeed, the most skilled male weavers from Escols left Sennen to set up the first looms worked by machinery at Alverton, Penzance, in 1823.[24] And Truro was the centre of a large mechanized carpet manufactory, established in 1792, capable of producing a thousand yards of carpet weekly.[25] The trend of single female workers quitting rural areas for more 'modern' urban centres in search of employment in town workshops and factories was therefore established, raising questions about a possible lapse in female morality coupled with the breakdown of the traditional family unit.

It must be stressed, however, that these changes did not happen overnight. Cornwall in the late eighteenth and early nineteenth centuries was a complex mix of tradition and change, which differed greatly from one area to another. But the gradual cessation in the first half of the nineteenth century of the varied traditional forms of women's labour in domestic manufacture, small-scale dairying and gleaning created a surplus pool of female job seekers, who were slowly pushed into formal waged employment. For many this led to jobs in domestic service, or sweated labour in town workshops, but for some it took the form of work in the more visible mining and china clay industries. The watershed came in the late 1840s with the calamity of the potato blight, which Deacon has shown marked the final breakdown of a proto-industrial way of life in Cornwall.[26]

INDUSTRIAL ADVANCE: WOMEN AND A FORMAL WAGE ECONOMY

The rise of formal waged employment undoubtedly witnessed a sharpening in the sexual division of labour. Many historians have argued that women's work was always viewed as low status and at the bottom of the wages hierarchy, and that this attitude was merely extended to cover new employment opportunities for females on mines and in manufactories, resulting in women becoming crowded into badly paid and insecure sectors of the labour market, thus making them still partially dependent on their fathers, husbands and sons.[27] But other historians stress the emancipating effect of mine and factory work for women, who, they argued, were freed from the patriarchal framework of proto-industrialism to enjoy the fruits of being independent wage earners.[28] Yet perhaps things are not as clear cut as this. Empirical evidence is vital to a clearer understanding of the effects of industrialization on women, which differed from region to region and were compounded by a variety of fashionable opinions within early to mid nineteenth-century society.

One of the most visible forms of formal waged employment for labouring women in industrial Cornwall was offered by the mines, where females had been working since the early eighteenth century as bal maidens, receiving wages up to about one shilling a day. Indeed, in 1736, Borlase was grumbling about the difficulty of obtaining decent female domestic servants because of the competition from mining. In Cornwall the mine produced a greater female income than was usual in the metalliferous mining districts of the north of England, where convention restricted female labour at the mines.[29] The larger numbers of female labourers on Cornish mines might, therefore, help to explain the diminishing importance of domestic textile manufacture noted by Callum in West Penwith.[30]

By the eighteenth century a sexual division of labour had emerged peculiar to Cornwall, with women working only at the mine's surface, so that in the early nineteenth century Cornwall's bal maidens, in their characteristic white aprons and gooks, made up a large sector of the surface labour force. Here they processed the ore as spallers, cobbers and buckers (job descriptions which referred to the reduction of copper minerals using a variety of hammers and anvils: spallers broke the lumps of ore into smaller pieces with large hammers; cobbers chipped off the good ore from its waste matrix; buckers ground the chipped ore into a coarse powder). In 1841, forty-one mines throughout the Cornwall were employing over 2,500 females from 13 years of age.[31] And in the china clay industry too, numerous women scraped the green growth, straw and sand from the blocks of clay prior to shipment, for which they were paid a similar amount to their counterparts on the mines. This disposable income was the woman's to spend in which ever way she chose. Her wages, therefore, gave her a degree of independence not found in many classes of Victorian females, which, historians have argued, provided the opportunity of emancipation from the patriarchy of the pre-capitalist household.[32]

Many nineteenth-century commentators noted the degree of independence enjoyed by bal maidens, who appeared to have much freedom over their working hours on the mines, and as independent wage earners. Bal maidens' working hours undoubtedly contrasted with the independence of another far larger, but less visible, section of female labour—domestic servants—whose freedom was often restricted by employers who dictated what hours they could work and closely regulated their free time to suit the changing requirements of their households. Indeed, on many mines bal maidens were usually free to go when they had completed the task set them for the day. Barham's Report noted some young women expressing a preference for mine labour over that of domestic service, which they claimed to have been more arduous. However, there were limits to the independence enjoyed by women working on the mines; at times it was necessary to work overtime. At Tresavean Mine, in Gwennap, this occurred about once a month during 'sampling' and sometimes in winter when the days were short. The women were then required to remain behind until about 8.30 p.m. The working was considered voluntary, but an agent at Tresavean commented, 'a girl might be considered lazy and lose her place if she declined'. Women were, therefore, tied to the mines in a way which was not at first apparent.[33] And as far as wages were concerned, although their earnings allowed them a degree of economic and social freedom compared to the unskilled male surface workers, whose wages were double those of the bal maidens, women's employment on the local mines can undoubtedly be defined as being of low status, 'acknowledged by low wages and lack of recognition that acquiring skill could lead to promotion'.[34]

Such female financial independence caused concern, resulting in the notion of single women working in factories and mines being frequently attacked because it did not fit the ideal of the dependent wife and mother. As the centre of gravity for female employment shifted from predominantly home-based industries to a wage earned outside the home, this began to challenge and break down the middle-class maxim that a woman's place was in the home.[35] For in the Victorian period, the ideal of 'separate spheres' had taken root, which championed the male breadwinner, who alone should undertake waged work to maintain his family, while his wife's vocation in life was to remain wholly within the domestic sphere in her capacity as nurturer, child-carer and housewife—an 'Angel in the House'.[36] This mindset closely paralleled the rise of masculinist politics of Chartism with its message of male citizenship and the trade-unionist view of a male breadwinner wage, which ultimately led to the passing of legislation to limit women's participation in many industries.[37]

Therefore, the presence of women working on Cornwall's mines created important implications for gender relationships. Bal maidens who worked alongside men over time probably lost some of their deference to them, and their behaviour was often noted as being forthright and cheeky. Single, independent women, many living in towns or industrial villages, were feared to have been acquiring 'ideas above their station'. Sex antagonism on the mines heightened. Bal maidens were noted for their brightly coloured and often pretentious display of clothing, and were accused of frivolity and wasting money, features well-commented on in the Victorian press. Indeed, George Henwood, a Cornish journalist whose articles appeared in the *Mining Journal*, joined the debate. In his 'observations' about Cornwall's bal maidens, particularly in their 'out of core time', he echoed the typical fears of middle-class professional men.

> Their being associated in such numbers and before men, a spirit of rivalry in dress . . . is soon engendered . . . To see the 'bal maidens' on Sunday would astonish a stranger; whilst at their work the pendant earrings and showy bead necklaces excite the pity as well as the surprise of the thoughtful. All desire to save a few shillings for after life is discarded, and nothing but display is thought of. This is carried on to an incredible extent and all the preaching in the world will never interfere with the wearing of a fine bonnet.[38]

Henwood's attack on the bal maidens' attire had important class connotations. Working-class women who were well-dressed were becoming indistinguishable from the class above them, so much so that a clergyman unacquainted with 'Cornish ways' was totally unaware that his congregation in a mining district was completely that of the labouring class. To him, they appeared to be the very epitome of ladies and gentlemen. This extravagant love of clothes amongst bal maidens thus challenged the social order, as it threatened to erode accepted class divisions.[39]

Doubtless many of Cornwall's bal maidens at their work appeared to be quite masculine, swinging their long-handled hammers as they broke up the ore and carted the mineral around in wheelbarrows. And many Victorian middle-class commentators, both male and female, seemed uncomfortable with the manly nature of the bal maidens' work, and perhaps compensated for this by describing them in glowing terms, either by referring to their spotless, feminine working attire, or by drawing attention to their singing, one poet describing them as the 'sweet thrushes of our Cornish isle'.[40] But there was no disguising the fact that Cornwall's bal maidens hardly appeared to be the model of genteel womanhood which had become highly prized by middle-class Victorian England; indeed, Henwood described them as 'Amazons' in the *Mining Journal*. And confirming this observation of their manly nature is the following rhyme, reputed to have been sung by Gwennap's bal maidens:

> I can buddy and I can rocky,
> And I can walk like a man.
> I can lobby and shaky,
> And please the Old Jan.[41]

Clarke has argued that the migration of women from the domestic sphere to places of industry—mines and factories—created a fear among men of the potential for female labour to undercut their economic privileges and skills, which went hand in hand with artisanal misogyny.[42] By the 1840s, many Cornish mines had introduced labour-saving machinery—crushing machines and mechanized jiggers—often operated by men, which reduced the bal maidens' role in the hand reduction of ore. Numbers of women employed on the mines were therefore already falling. It was possibly the belief of the threat posed by female mine labour which led to men like Henwood arguing that the logical result of the continuing association of the sexes at the mines, coupled with the bal maidens' financial independence and flamboyant manner of dress, much degeneracy, and by implication, immorality. Indeed, instances in which the paternity of illegitimate children was due to mine agents under whom young girls were employed were not rare, the *Cornubian* of 1868 citing such a case, stating that a local judge had 'intimated' that he should very much like to expose by name any mine agents 'who had so abused the trust reposed in them'.[43]

In reality this appeared a forlorn hope, for later that month a grass captain at Penhale Wheal Vor Mine, one Samuel Scaddon, a married man, was accused of raping Mary Harvey, a bal maiden at the mine.[44] A protracted hearing followed, but at the Summer Assizes the judge decreed that the charge was one easy to make, but difficult to refute, and instructed the jury to be guided and influenced by the 'demeanour' of the prosecutrix when she appeared before them. He also noted that Scaddon had previously taken liberties with her, but that she had not complained about his conduct. Furthermore, he suggested that the bal maiden might not have offered every 'resistance in her power' to prevent Scaddon's advances, in effect discrediting Mary Harvey and leaving her little chance of a fair hearing.[45] It appears the case was thrown out.

Underlying the debate about women on the mines was really the burning issue of whether women should undertake paid labour at all and whether this should be in the industrial sphere—at a metal mine—which evidently did not entirely please all their men folk. And this sentiment may be detected in the following comment by a Gwennap man: 'I have four daughters, but if I had fifty I would never allow one of them to go on to a mine; they are exposed to be corrupted by bad conversation.'[46] In fact it appears that this was not always the case on all the mines, as an agent who had been employed on the Gwennap mines remarked that,

there is a great improvement with regard to decency in this
neighbourhood, both old and young; they take example from
the agents, and where they hear an agent using oaths they do
the same. I take care to check swearing or bad language in
this mine, threatening discharge if the offence is repeated.
The result is, I hear very little of it.[47]

The era of the bal maiden, coming as it did during a period of
transition from a proto-industrial society to one which manifested
many of the features associated with other industrial regions, inevitably
called for an evaluation of labouring women's role in Cornwall's
industrializing society. In Cornwall, as in other parts of Britain, a
challenging dichotomy of opinion emerged as the factory girl, or mine
girl, was condemned for her immoral behaviour, her coarse language,
and a propensity for frivolously wasting money on worldly trifles,
whilst being pitied for her long and arduous workday. The new
masculinist working-class politics which had emerged, supporting the
ideal of separate spheres, which sought to effectively curtail female
activity outside the home, undoubtedly explains the attitude of the man
from Gwennap, quoted above.

From the evidence thus assembled, it is possible to conclude that
the advent of industrialization at first appeared to open up new employment possibilities on the mines for women in Cornwall, and to
have given them a new kind of independence, albeit an independence
with limitations. Yet this gain was of relatively short duration, for, as
Deacon has shown, Cornwall's convergence with other industrial parts
of Britain was interrupted by the collapse of the Cornish copper and
tin mining industries in the 1860s and 70s.[48] The services of large
numbers of female mine surface workers were dispensed with. We
might adopt Valenze's argument that at this time women's work was
thus 'relegated in principle to the invisibility of domestic housework
or, even worse, to a unique sub-proletarian purgatory of domestic
service'.[49]

But for many Cornish women the collapse of the mining industry
was doubly devastating, as their men were forced to migrate in ever
greater numbers in search of work throughout the second half of the
nineteenth century, and as wives, they became increasingly dependent
on remittances from overseas. Paradoxically, women then had control
over the whole family budget, but they had also become increasingly
isolated within the domestic sphere.

A SISTERHOOD OF RECIPROCITY: WOMEN AND COTTAGE RELIGION

The late eighteenth and early nineteenth centuries witnessed great changes. As the rhythm of life began to move to a different beat, struck on the drums of industrialization, labouring women found their position in society less and less influential. Within a pre-capitalist framework, women occupied an important place, and not just through their ability to keep their families above subsistence level. Whilst public economic activity was set firmly within the domestic realm, they were closely involved in every facet of life within their communities and acquired respect.[50] As basic educators, it was women who often kept the Dame Schools and taught their children basic literacy. They were sometimes respected as 'pellars' and fortune tellers, attaining positions which inspired fear and awe within their communities. And it was usually women who introduced their sons and daughters to the Bible and took them to prayer meetings and love-feasts.

But large population shifts, parliamentary legislation and increased mechanization underlay the social and political changes which were breaking down established custom and tradition. Public policy increasingly took over functions of authority and decision-making which had earlier resided with institutions which were local, familial and private, rather than public.[51] Labouring women lost out heavily as the customary way of life began to break down, for with the shift from the private to the public sphere, their influence within their communities as basic educators in local schools and as preachers and itinerants in local chapels waned. The question of why the authority of working-class women was lessened is intricately bound up with the polarization between the public, and male-dominated sphere and the private, or female, domestic sphere, and the rise of masculinist legislation which arose out of the industrial experience.

Indeed, as Valenze has noted, through the medium of sectarian religion labouring women were able to consciously address the problems arising from the growth of a liberal industrial society. Cottage industry obscured the division between public and private, and affirmed a particular combination of domestic and community concerns, values labouring women found threatened and which were only indirectly addressed in other working-class organizations. As Valenze has argued, this is borne out by the blossoming of female preaching within the context of cottage religion, which lasted from the 1790s to the 1860s, suggesting that it was intimately related to the economic instability and political and social unrest that marked the first half of the nineteenth century in Britain.[52] Women found in cottage religion an intellectual outlet denied them in politics. Indeed, religion made possible the redefinition of private, domestic concerns as public and political issues.[53] And Clark argues that radical religion imbued the common people, especially women, with a sense of spiritual equality.[54] But women's ability to achieve active participation in cottage religion was dependent, to a certain extent, on a degree of sex equality.

In the early days of Cornish Methodism, cottage-based meetings and preaching services favoured the active participation of labouring women in religious affairs. For it was women who often seized the initiative in opening their homes for meetings. Ann Arthur of White-cross was one of the first to open her cottage at Tregunna for Bible Christian preaching, and in the Penzance circuit 'Pious Grandmother' Joan Baynard allowed the Bible Christians to preach in her cottage in the early days.[55] Such women gained support and increased member-ship for Methodism at grass-roots level, by visiting and assisting their neighbours with gifts, advice, work and support, and sharing the word of the Lord. Helen Sandercock of North Hill was visited by a woman from her village who was delivering tracts for the Wesleyans. She persuaded her to attend a class meeting, which initiated a life-long interest and devotion to Methodism.[56] Through the medium of cottage-based religion, women were able to channel their collective frustrations at the quickening pace and changes brought by industrialization, in-terpreting their trials and tribulations through the Scriptures. Some women attained a high-profile role in religious life, as class leaders, exhorters, preachers and even itinerants. This was remarkable, since the privilege of *public* speaking was almost unprecedented for women at this time.[57]

The Bible Christians were quick to take advantage of the drawing force of their female members who were busy entering towns, villages and hamlets 'with flaming zeal, holding the burning torches of the Gospel in field, moor or meadow; in barns, cottages or halls'.[58] In 1826 the Bible Christians printed a poster which displayed the words, 'A FEMALE' in heavy type to attract attention to the service she was to conduct, and at Twelveheads in about 1821 a female preacher attracted much public attention and, it was said, multitudes flocked to hear,[59] which was made all the more remarkable when set against the back-ground of their time: 'The sheer novelty of their appearance should be remembered when contrasted against the age which confined women to their homes, or menial agricultural or industrial employment'.[60] Many were converted through their preaching, including Abraham Bastard, a hardy wrestler, who heard the words of preacher Betsy Reed in about 1817. Indeed, Catherine, the wife of William O'Bryan, founder of the Bible Christians, Johanna Brooks, Eliza Jew, Mary Billing and Elizabeth Dart, a member of the former Methodist society at Poundstock, comprised an astonishing sisterhood of powerful, remarkably talented women.

The Bible Christians were the most predisposed to female preachers, William O'Bryan noted as commenting, 'If women have the gift of the Holy Spirit they have the power from on high. Christ makes no exception anywhere in the Bible against women publishing the glad tidings of the Gospel'.[61] And there were women, such as Elizabeth Dart, who became itinerants. In 1821, eighteen such women were identified in circuits covering Cornwall and South Devon; by 1829 there were twenty-nine.[62] Female preachers among the Wesleyan Church (which was closest to the Established Church which forbade women to preach) were, however, very rare. Yet one remarkable woman, Betsy Tonkin, a native of Gwinear, began preaching at a Wesleyan house meeting in Feock in 1782. But this irregularity was entirely at the discretion of the superintendent, Joseph Taylor, who was reputed to have told her 'I did not open your mouth and I will not shut it'.[63] This closely mirrors the comments made by Wesley, who, although not particularly at ease about female preachers, did not desire to discourage them entirely: 'But it will not permit you to be silent when God commands you to speak, yet I would have you give as little offence as possible; and therefore I would advise you not to speak at any place where a preacher is speaking at the same time, lest you should draw away his hearers.'[64]

Yet as the nineteenth century wore on, the influence exercised by women in Methodism began to wane. Why was this? The answer is multi-faceted, and lies partly in the divorce of religion from the domestic sphere. Methodism began to lose its character as a radical sect, gaining larger membership, more wealth and institutionalizing itself as a church, with worship becoming increasingly centred on purpose-built chapels, some colossal in size. Religion was moving away from domestic surroundings—the humble cottage with thatched roof and earthen floor—which diminished the influence women had on religious affairs. Sectarianism resulted in more chapels, some with smaller memberships, which affected the numbers of women who, for example, were class leaders, usually only found at the larger chapels which had separate classes for women led by women. It has also been argued that the decrease in female preaching was due to the fact that women itinerants were expected to give up 10 shillings of their salaries, which fell heavily upon women from a labouring background, who could not afford to live on a reduced income. Numbers fell after this.[65]

But the decline in female participation in Methodism is also attributable to the invasion of masculinist policies in religious life. Shaw claims that Joseph Taylor was some fifty years ahead of his time in allowing Betsy Tonkin to preach, but this misses the point entirely. If anything, Taylor was very much in tune with his time, a period when women could exercise far more influence in society than their counterparts over half a century later, when the idea of separate spheres was resulting in women's withdrawal from public life.

Clark draws our attention to the fact that in 1803 (after Wesley's death) and again in 1810, the Wesleyan Methodist Connexion forbade female preaching, which incited the more radical Primitive Methodist Connexion to secede in 1812.[66] And in the Bible Christian Church, the right of female preaching was being challenged by the early nineteenth century. Indeed, Thorne and O'Bryan were kept busy marshalling the arguments in favour of female preachers, Thorne stating, 'I query whether these men who speak against female preaching could exceed it'.[67] But while both championed the right of women to preach, neither saw the need to give them a vote in the business meetings of the Connexion. And to parallel the attacks on the flamboyant clothing of the bal maidens, women within the Bible Christian Church were increasingly questioned over their attire, Mary O'Bryan noting in her diary of 1825 that 'Our male preachers, it seems, are not above employing hours disputing about women's bonnets, cloaks, and even the colour of their gowns, kerchiefs, &c'. She continued:

> My mother and others have taught me, that single females have only to please the Lord, but those who are married, their husbands; now it seems the case is altered; those bachelors are endeavouring to lord it over us, tyrannically dictating even the colour of our garments; what husband could do more? And having public discussions about our very petticoats![68]

At the same time, the memoirs of women increasingly began to stress their domestic credentials and their retirement into semi-public activities of charity, an example being that of the Memoir of Mrs Jane Treffry:

> My mother was eminently a domestic woman; she laboured to make her home a happy one . . . visiting the sick, particularly of their own sex, becoming agents of charitable institutions generally, are employments confessedly suited to the female character . . . Few women of ordinary intellect and education have contributed more largely to promote and enhance the religious character of that social intercourse, into the sphere of which she was admitted.[69]

By 1840, the number of female itinerants on the Cornish and South Devon Circuits had fallen to eight. Indeed, after 1890, women whose names appeared in the minutes of the Bible Christian Church were more accurately described as deaconesses than as women in the ministry and they were not publicly received into full Connexion as were the men, nor had they the same status.[70]

Yet it must be noted that many women from a labouring background chose not to participate publicly in religious affairs. Methodism was noted for its championing of self-help and independence, which engendered a desire for upward social mobility. By the mid-nineteenth century, the wives of prosperous tradesmen, mine agents and artisans were increasingly adopting the fashionable middle-class ideology of separate spheres, leading more leisurely lifestyles and grounding their lives more firmly within their homes and families. Many were content to involve themselves in semi-public work of charity and fund raising for auxiliary, missionary societies and the poor, the Dorcas Society (set up to provide clothing to needy women and their families) being a good example of the latter. With the withdrawal of women from active participation in religious affairs, men came to control the positions of power within the chapels. This is exemplified by the lists of mid to late Victorian chapel stewards and trustees, which were almost exclusively male.[71]

The rise of masculinist politics which increasingly championed the male wage earner and relegated women to a sphere of domesticity largely precluded labouring women from public life. As a result, they were gradually marginalized in matters of religion, and took little part in public institutions of trade unions, friendly societies, co-operative societies and political organizations of mid-Victorian Britain. In the chapels, labouring women were gradually confined to semi-public activities such as Sunday Schools and philanthropic and charitable institutions, which were commonly organized by men, or women from a higher social class.

Labouring women had been slowly denied a voice to register their indignation over the loss of common rights, customary aid and reciprocity, which had often been vented through democratic forms of worship. But their anger at the indignities which came to afflict them with the rise of industrialization was to manifest itself in a far more volatile manner: through women's participation in collective acts of rioting.

IN DEFENCE OF CUSTOMARY RIGHTS: LABOURING WOMEN AND RIOTING

For many commentators, the labouring woman was cast as an aggressive, shrewish creature, in need of suppression and control. 'Woman are more disposed to be mutinous,' wrote Robert Southey in 1808, 'they stand in less fear of the law, partly from ignorance, partly because they presume upon the privilege of their sex, and therefore in all public tumults they are foremost in violence and ferocity'.[72] Historians have argued that such mutinous behaviour was a manifestation of the political aspirations of the working classes, who engaged in collective bargaining by rioting to protest at changes which were threatening to undermine a moral economy.[73] And women often initiated food riots by encouraging their husbands to create disorder, and risked their reputations and safety in order to satisfy the needs of their families and communities.

For with the rise of a formal wage economy within a liberal industrial society, coupled with Acts of Enclosure and the New Poor Law of 1834, the aspects of rural life which permitted women to labour in the margins were systematically destroyed. Deprived of access to various meagre means of subsistence, such as regular employment in agriculture, the opportunity to own and graze a cow, or sources of free fuel, labouring women had to resort to limited forms of employment, almost all underpaid and irregular, even resorting to pilfering to make ends meet. But more importantly, women, who had often been proactive in rioting, began to play a more prominent role in public disturbance in defence of their customary rights.

The 1760s were a time when market prices for pilchards and oil were very depressed. Women who worked in the pilchard cellars of Mousehole customarily took the 'druggs' (dregs and scum train oil) from the washing troughs and the 'mund' (small or damaged fish), which helped to keep their families above subsistence level. However, hard times called for extreme measures, and the Mousehole cellar women were up in arms when the Reverend Thomas Carlyon, the agent of the rectory of Paul, attempted to end such practices, in league with his brother-in-law, William Veale of Trevaylor in Gulval.[74] In 1762, the rectors had summoned Dorothy Stevens for 'clandestinely taking salt' from the lower tithe cellar. She was found guilty and made to pay the overseers five shillings for use of the poor of the parish of Paul.[75] Stevens' arrest probably focused attention on the petty pilfering from the cellars which was doubtless commonplace, prompting Veale and Carlyon to carry out an inspection of the cellars, stock and equipment in 1768. The result was their decision to entirely abolish 'those bad customs' which undermined the rectory's profits, so that the women could then have 'no pretence of going into the cellars . . . for embezzling things to which they have not the least right', in order that everything would be disposed in the rectory's favour.[76] A remarkable stand-off ensued, in which the Mousehole women formed themselves into a makeshift combination, demanded higher wages and refused to work under conditions which took away their customary rights. But Carlyon refused to give in to the women, and made plans to break their resolve by drafting in workers from nearby Newlyn, even if this incurred extra expense in the short term.[77]

This event was merely a harbinger of what was to come half a century later. In 1830 the townsfolk of Newlyn and Mousehole took affairs into their own hands when the new rector, William Hitchens of St Ives, demanded tithe for fish caught in drift nets, which had customarily been exempt. This demand came at a time when fishing families were suffering greatly after a poor drifting season. The bailiff who came to Mousehole to serve writs on the defaulters met stiff resistance from the people of Mousehole. Upon drawing a pistol he was attacked by the village women, and escaped battered and bedraggled, only to be mobbed and beaten by the women of neighbouring Newlyn who pelted him with stinking fish offal. The tithe owners were forced to accept defeat, and tithe was never again collected in the parish of Paul.[78]

But such scenes of defiance and unrest were not restricted to the coastal regions. As the march of industrialization gathered pace, price rises and shortages compounded by the unsettled Napoleonic period prompted labouring women throughout Cornwall to openly participate in food riots in response to times of widespread poverty. At Launceston in 1801, 200 women were reported to have seized corn from a farmer who was attempting to sell it to a commercial agent. They 'put him to flight' and proceeded to sell the corn at 10 shillings at Winchester.[79] And at Falmouth in the same year, women in the market-place insisted on having potatoes at a reduced price. When refused, they proceeded to help themselves until order was restored by the magistrates.[80] In 1818 at Penzance, a large crowd of men, women and children prevented a supply of potatoes from being exported in response to the rapid rise in local prices. The export only went ahead after the Riot Act was read.[81] The spectacle of rioting was repeated in 1831 when some corn was being carried through Breage to Penzance. A great number of persons, chiefly female, thought that it was ear-marked for export and unloaded the cart. But on realizing that it was instead destined for a local miller for the use of the immediate district, the grain was reloaded and the cart continued on its way.[82]

By far the worse rioting was that which occurred in 1847. As

Deacon has observed, the late 1840s were a period of great change in which a number of pressures combined to ensure that older survival strategies became less applicable and the appeal to custom and tradition a less rational or relevant strategy.[83] The calamitous potato blight, coupled with a depression in the mining industry due to falling metal prices as a result of the unsettled state of the Continent, translated into low wages, temporary unemployment and great distress among the labouring classes. The result was widespread food rioting as mining communities resorted to the age-old response to the moral economy, in which Cornish women assumed their highest-ever profile. In 1847 a man buying corn in Helston market was driven out by women. And at the following weekly market, about twenty discontented women, backed by hundreds of miners armed with bludgeons, attempted to have the corn sold at the prices they chose and a scuffle ensued.[84] At Redruth, where the local press had reported that most main staples were almost unobtainable, and that families had been forced to fry turnips in the tallow of miners' candles, the worst was expected. Special constables were sworn in as disturbances commenced at nearby Pool. The most active of the mob were described as women, who were reported to have beaten on the door of a Pool flour dealer with large stones. One 'Amazon' found a sledge hammer from a smithy and broke the door in. In the mêlée which ensued, women, covered in flour, were reported to have emerged from the stores with flour, tea, coffee, pins and saffron all mixed up in their aprons. Yet another woman was caught waving a tool for cutting weeds menacingly above her head and when confronted by a constable, threatened to 'stick it in his mouth if he did not hold his tongue'. Another woman, seen making off with various goods, was heard to threaten the flour merchant's female servant not to inform on the rioters, or they would 'beat her brains against the wall'. At nearby Redruth, women confronted two market gardeners over the price of cabbages, demanding they be sold at a lower price. The noise drew a large crowd, and the market was soon in uproar.

In the trial which followed, three women were charged with rioting and stealing. Prudence Thomas, 37, received six months' hard labour, Ann Roberts, 45, and Mary Ann Craze, age not given, both got three months' hard labour. At the trial great incredulity and shock was expressed at the behaviour of the women, one of whom was said to have been of a respectable family.[85] Although accepting the degree of local hardship and distress, contemporary opinion saw this as no excuse for rioting. Moreover, local people disowned the main female perpetrators of the riot, claiming that they were strangers who had fled to parts unknown. For by the mid 1840s this form of communal protest was being rapidly discredited when it collided with the representations of female piety and goodness gaining credence in the Victorian period. Yet through their participation in riots, labouring women increasingly expressed themselves as active agents who struggled to maintain and uphold imperatives and principles related to community, family and survival.[86] But the riots of 1847 were to be the last, the final battle in the war to maintain a traditional, customary way of life.

CONCLUSION

In proto-industrial times, women had performed a multitude of economic activities, founded on a household-based economy which was organized within a patriarchal structure of authority. Yet women's work was acknowledged as having an invaluable economic role and was not subsumed within this patriarchal framework. For in their communities labouring women were often to be found working side by side with their men folk, a subsistence way of life outweighing gender concerns. And in the proto-industrial society, labouring women were empowered through participation in cottage religion and were respected within their communities for their role as basic educators.

But the advent of a liberal industrial society began to break down this traditional, customary way of life. The rise of formal waged employment in the eighteenth century did create new job opportunities for labouring women, on the mines, in manufactories and workshops. This resulted in a degree of independence never before experienced, for two, perhaps three generations of young women, before the changes of the late 1840s. Moreover, the pattern of giving up paid employment upon marriage meant that there was a rapid turnover of work in the mining districts, which in turn meant that a model of independence was probably available to a larger number of women than the actual numbers employed suggest.

However, it is questionable just how real this independence was, as women's work was characterized as of low status, was low paid accordingly, and there was little opportunity for promotion even if a woman showed a high level of skill or initiative. Henwood's questioning of the propriety of allowing women to work at Cornwall's mines coincided with the masculinist policies gaining credence in middle-class Victorian England which meant that certain types of female labour did not accord with standards and definitions of femininity and morality. The 'Amazons' who toiled at the mines' surface simply did not concur with the ideal of domesticity and separate spheres then gaining credence.

Scope for independent female economic activity rapidly narrowed as protective legislation for women in the visible 'public' and therefore

'masculine' domains such as mines and factories came into force from
the mid nineteenth century. As Lown argues, 'protective' legislation
can be seen, in fact, as a form of paternalism.[87] Therefore, the changes
in work patterns associated with the emergence of deep mining in the
late eighteenth century which resulted in an opening out of new roles
and increased independence for young women can be described as of
relatively short duration—spanning two or three generations.

The changes which affected women's position within society were
equally marked. State legislation mirroring paternalistic thought
reduced women's role in public. In Cornwall, where labouring women
had played a valuable part in cottage religion and the spread of
Methodism at grass-roots level, the ideology of separate spheres and
the institutionalization of the Methodist churches undermined and
reduced women's active participation in religious life. Yet Cornwall's
labouring women did not accept the changes passively. In times of
shortage and hardship, it was the labouring women who appealed to
the moral economy, campaigning in the streets and market-place for
fair prices. Things came to a head in the late 1840s in Cornwall, with
some of the worst rioting ever seen here, in which women played a
dominant part. This can be seen in the light of a reaction to change—a
last ditch appeal to tradition and continuity in the face of modernization in line with other regions of the British Isles. As Deacon has
noted, the 1840s marked a period when Cornwall decisively moved
from a proto-industrial to an industrial society, one which was partially
urbanized, partially industrial.

Women's struggle in defence of customary rights can be placed in
perspective by looking at the outcome of the convergence with other
industrial regions of Britain. For many Cornish labouring women, the
gradual shift away from proto-industrialism culminated in domestic
hardship and misery. Numerous Cornish families found it difficult to
live up to the ideal of separate spheres, particularly when Cornwall
entered a period of de-industrialization in the last quarter of
the nineteenth century, following the collapse of the copper and tin
mining industries. This created significant unemployment and mass
emigration, compounded by greater reliance on inadequate male wages
which contributed to domestic tension. Many labouring women used
to 'getting by and making do' on their husbands' meagre earnings
were ultimately financially forced into having to toil as charwomen or
washerwomen (both deemed socially demeaning occupations), or take
in a lodger, so as not to lose face by applying for the parish pay. For
those whose husbands were overseas, women had control of the family
budget, but ironically, they had become increasingly isolated within the
domestic sphere.[88]

NOTES AND REFERENCES

1. See E.P. Thompson, *The Making of the English Working Class*, London, 1980.
2. G. Bock, 'Challenging Dichotomies: Perspectives on Women's History', in Karen Offen, Ruth Roach Pierson and Jane Randall (eds), *Writing Women's History International Perspectives*, London, 1991, p. 1.
3. J. Humphries, 'Women and Paid Work', in Jane Purvis (ed.), *Women's History: Britain 1850–1945, An Introduction*, London, 1995, p. 86.
4. P. Payton, 'Cornwall in Context: The New Cornish Historiography', in Philip Payton (ed.), *Cornish Studies: Five*, Exeter, 1997, pp.13–14.
5. See Bernard Deacon, 'Proto-Industrialization and Potatoes', in Payton (ed.), 1997, p. 60ff.
6. D. Callum,, 'Society and Economy in West Cornwall, c1588–1750', unpub. Ph.D., University of Exeter, 1993.
7. Deacon, 1997, pp. 63–4.
8. W. Putney, 'Account of a Cottager', *Annals of Agriculture*, 44, 1806, pp. 21, 108.
9. I. Pinchbeck, *Women Workers and the Industrial Revolution*, London, 1981, see Chapters 6, 7 and 8.
10. D. Valenze, *The First Industrial Woman*, Oxford, 1995, pp. 13–28.
11. A.K. Hamilton Jenkin, *Cornwall and Its People*, Newton Abbot, 1983, p. 329.
12. Callum, 1993.
13. Jenkin, 1983, p. 330.
14. Cornwall Record Office (CRO), P79/81/2.
15. Jenkin, 1983, p. 406.
16. There was a long history of this work—Carew noting in 1602 that work in the pilchard cellars 'setteth almost an infinite number of women to work, to their great advantage . . . a lusty housewife may earn three shillings in a night'. See R.E. Halliday, (ed.), *Richard Carew's The Survey of Cornwall, 1602*, London, 1953, p. 118.
17. C. Noall, *Cornish Seines and Seiners*, Truro, 1872, pp. 43–4.
18. W. Bottrell, *Traditions and Hearthside Stories of West Cornwall*, Penzance, 1873, p. 24.
19. W. Collins, *Rambles Beyond Railways*, London, 1861, New Edition, p. 132.
20. See Deacon, 1997.
21. 1841 Children's Commission, *British Parliamentary Papers*, p. 753.
22. C.C. Pascoe, *Walks Around St. Hilary, Chiefly Among the Poor*, Penzance, 1879, p. 174.
23. Jenkin, 1983, pp. 406–7.
24. Bottrell, 1873, p. 196; CRO J/ 264/28.
25. H.L. Douch, *The Book of Truro*, Truro, 1977, pp. 46–7.
26. See Deacon, 1997.
27. See for example, P. Mathias, *First Industrial Nation. An Economic History of Britain 1700–1914*, London, 1983, pp. 175–6.
28. See S.O. Rose, 'Proto-Industry, Women's Work and the Household Economy in the Transition to Industrial Capitalism', *Journal of Family*

Industry, 13, 1988, pp. 181–93; J. Lown, *Women and Industrialisation: Gender at Work in Nineteenth Century England*, Cambridge, 1990; Pinchbeck, 1981.

29. R. Burt, *The British Lead Mining Industry*, Redruth, 1984, pp. 166–7.
30. Callum, 1993.
31. The 1841 Children's Employment Commission, Dr Barham's Report, *British Parliamentary Papers (BPP)*, p. 799.
32. G. Burke, 'The Decline of the Independent Bâl Maiden', in Angela V. John (ed.), *Unequal Opportunities—Women's Employment in England 1800–1918*, Oxford, 1986.
33. See S.P. Schwartz and R. Parker, *Lanner, A Cornish Mining Parish*, Tiverton, 1998, p. 88.
34. Burke, 1984, p. 184.
35. J. Wallach Scott, *Gender and the Politics of History*, (especially Chapter 7), Colombia (USA), 1988.
36. The term 'Angel in the House', was taken from a poem by Coventry Patmore, written in 1854. See Jane Randall, *Women in an Industrialising Society: England 1750–1880*, Oxford, 1990, pp. 2–3.
37. A. Clark, *The Struggle For the Breeches: Gender and the Making of the British Working Class*, Berkeley, 1995, pp. 220–63.
38. R. Burt, *Cornwall's Mines and Miners*, Truro, 1972, p. 120.
39. *West Briton*, 30 June 1870.
40. *Cornubian*, 7 January 1887.
41. C.C. James, *History of Gwennap*, nd, privately published, p. 242.
42. Clark, 1995, pp. 11–157. Collins, in *Observations on the West of England Mining Region*, Truro, 1912, p. 268, notes that it was John Taylor, founder of the company John Taylor and Sons, who improvised the first mechanized crusher on occasion of a strike by bal maidens.
43. *Cornubian*, 12 June 1868.
44. *Cornubian*, 26 June 1868.
45. *West Briton*, 6 August 1868.
46. *BPP*, 1841, p. 824.
47. *BPP*, 1841, p. 821.
48. See Deacon, 1997, pp. 75–9.
49. Valenze, 1995, op. cit., pp. 3–12.
50. R.M. Zimbalist, 'Women, Culture and Society: A Theoretical Overview', in R.M. Zimblast and A. Lamphere (eds), *Women, Culture and Society*, Stanford (CA), 1974, p. 36.
51. D. Thompson, 'Women, Work and Politics in Nineteenth Century England: The Problem of Authority', in *Equal or Different: Women's Politics 1800–1914*, Oxford, 1987, p. 58.
52. For an expanded version of this argument, see Deborah Valenze, *Prophetic Sons and Daughters: Female Preaching and Popular Religion in Industrial England*, Princeton, 1985, pp. 17–73.
53. D. Valenze, 'Cottage Religion and the Politics of Survival', in *Equal or Different: Women's Politics 1800–1914*, 1987, p. 37.
54. Clark, 1995, p. 93.

55. See *Bible Christian Magazine*, 1863, pp. 39, 50b and 401.
56. *Memoir of Mrs. Bendle*, London, 1872.
57. Clark, 1995, p. 96.
58. S. Thorne, *The Converted Life of Abraham Bastard*, London, 1877.
59. 'Memoir of Joyce Bray', *Bible Christian Magazine*, 1849, p. 421.
60. M.J.L. Wickes, *The Westcountry Preachers: A History of the Bible Christians, 1815–1907*, Bideford, 1987, p. 31.
61. MR/L/121/1, *Armenian Magazine*, 1822–1823, p. 41.
62. Minutes of the First Conference of the Preachers in Connexion, 1819, Devon.
63. T. Shaw, *A History of Cornish Methodism*, Truro, 1967, p. 58.
64. G. Milburn and M. Batty, *Workday Preachers*, London, 1995, p. 172.
65. M. Mitcheson, 'Women in Cornish Methodism', unpub. B.A. Hons. dissertation, College of St Mark and St John, Plymouth, 1996, p. 36.
66. Clark, 1995, p. 98
67. Wickes, 1987, p. 31.
68. T. Shaw, *The Bible Christians, 1815–1907*, London, 1965, pp. 110–1.
69. R. Treffry, *Memoirs of Mrs. Jane Treffry*, London, 1830.
70. Shaw, 1965, p. 69.
71. This was not the case at Torpoint, where four out of seven trustees were women, probably women of means. But it would be fair to say that few labouring women had the financial means to become chapel trustees.
72. Valenze, 1987, p. 36.
73. P. Hudson, *The Industrial Revolution*, London, 1992, p. 205.
74. T. Pawlyn, 'The Cornish Pilchard Fishery in the Eighteenth Century', *Journal of the Royal Institute of Cornwall*, 1998, pp. 79–80. Veale and Carlyon had married the Gwavas sisters who were the heirs to the Rectory of Paul which owned the income from tithe fish.
75. CRO ML/464.
76. CRO ML/798.
77. CRO ML/793.
78. J. Rowe, *Cornwall in the Age of the Industrial Revolution*, Liverpool, 1953, pp. 296–7.
79. *Royal Cornwall Gazette*, 4 March 1801.
80. *Royal Cornwall Gazette*, 11 March 1801.
81. J.G. Rule, 'The Labouring Miner in Cornwall, *c.* 1740–1844, A Study in Social History', unpub. Ph.D. thesis, University of Warwick, 1971, p. 146.
82. *Royal Cornwall Gazette*, 26 February 1831.
83. Deacon, 1997, p. 73.
84. A. Rowe, 'The Food Riots of the 1840s in Cornwall', *Report of the Royal Polytechnic Society*, 1942, p. 57; *West Briton*, 4 June 1847.
85. F. Michell, *Annals of an Ancient Cornish Town, Redruth*, Redruth, 1978, pp. 129–31.
86. Valenze, 1987, p. 35.
87. J. Lown, *Women and Industrialisation: Gender at Work in Nineteenth Century England*, Cambridge, 1990, p. 217.
88. Schwartz and Parker, 1998, pp. 39, 163.

AN INVESTIGATION INTO MIGRATION PATTERNS FOR THE PARISH OF ZENNOR IN CORNWALL DURING THE SECOND HALF OF THE NINETEENTH CENTURY

William A. Morris

INTRODUCTION

Zennor during the second half of the nineteenth century was an isolated moorland parish in West Cornwall with a population falling from 1,025 in 1851 to 491 in 1891[1] and an area of 4,229 acres, three-quarters of which comprised waste land of moor, heath, and rocky carns.[2] It was surrounded by rural parishes to the west, south and east, and by the Atlantic Ocean to the north. The working population was mainly involved in two of the traditional Cornish industries, farming and mining. Two small tin mines, Carn Galver and Carnelloe, were working in the parish in 1871[3] and a very important mine, Ding Dong Tin Mine employing 194 people, lay just to the south outside the parish boundary.[4] Farms in the parish were small, the average acreage in 1871 being 19.7 acres (8 hectares),[5] and produced dairy products, such as butter and cheese, which were sold in the market towns of St Ives and Penzance. They were almost all worked by farmers with the help of their families, so agricultural labourers were not an important part of the workforce. Only three hired farm labourers were recorded at Zennor in 1871, two of whom worked on the 75-acre farm at Porthmeor, the largest in the parish at the time. The third traditional Cornish industry of fishing was hardly possible because the high cliffs allowed no good place for a harbour.

Despite the isolation of the area a noticeable amount of migration took place both into and out of the parish, and the question arises as to whether the pattern of this in-migration and out-migration was substantially similar to the general pattern in England and Wales as a whole at the period, or whether the 'isolation factor' might have caused a substantial distortion of this general pattern.

In order to answer this question an investigation was made, based principally on the 1871 and 1881 Census Enumerators' Books for the parish of Zennor, in line with similar investigations carried out by E.G. Ravenstein,[6] who used the census records of these same years to determine the general pattern of migration for England and Wales as a whole.

DISTANCE TRAVELLED BY IN-MIGRANTS

The chart in Figure 1, calculated from the 1871 census returns for the parish, shows the flow of in-migrants of all ages to Zennor broken down according to the distance they travelled. The figures for migration flow have been standardized to account for the fact that the respective sending areas successively increase with distance from Zennor over the migration field.[7]

From Figure 1 it is seen clearly that the majority of in-migrants to Zennor had moved over only a short distance. This is in agreement with Ravenstein's general finding for England and Wales as a whole, so the isolation factor does not seem to have caused any distortion here. In fact, 55 per cent of all in-migrants had a place of origin in the four parishes adjoining Zennor, which corresponded to a migration distance of less than 5 kilometres, the largest group, some

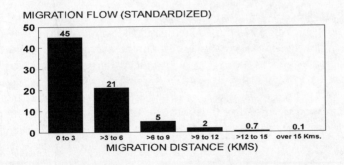

Figure 1: Migration flow for Zennor 1871 of all in-migrants

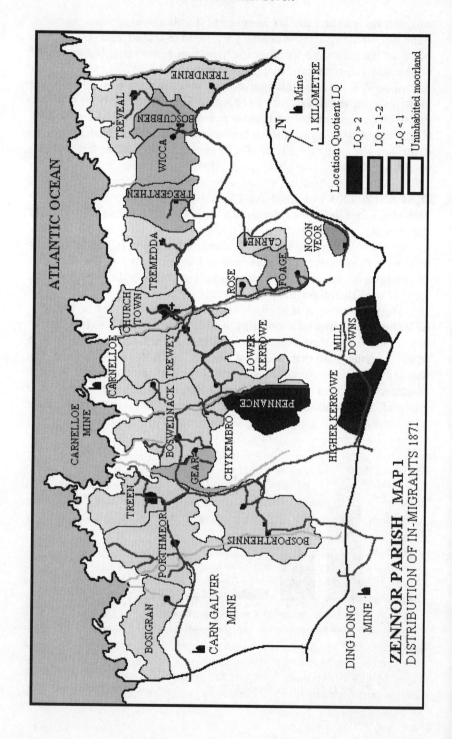

ZENNOR PARISH MAP 1
DISTRIBUTION OF IN-MIGRANTS 1871

27 per cent of the total, coming from Towednack: the neighbouring parish to the east.

The median distance moved by in-migrants was 4.75 kilometres, and none of them had migrated a greater distance than the 71 kilometre move by Caroline Bamfield from Wadebridge, the wife of Edwin Bamfield of Tregerthen.

All the in-migrants moving to reside in Zennor had been born in Cornwall. In fact every one of the permanent residents of the parish in 1871 was Cornish by birth.[8] Moreover, the population of the parish seems to have been quite stable over the previous years because 70 per cent of the residents bore the names of the twenty-six traditional Zennor families whose names had made up the entries in the church registers a hundred years before.[9] The situation is very different today.

In this study, the coastguards serving temporary terms of duty in their isolated community on the cliffs at Treen were not considered as permanent residents and were excluded, as was a group of temporary visitors staying at the Gurnard's Head Hotel.

THE SPATIAL PATTERN OF IN-MIGRANT SETTLEMENT

The fairly high value of 49 for the Index of Segregation[10] for the parish in 1871 indicates that in-migrants occupied segregated areas within it rather than being evenly distributed. From Map 1, which shows the distribution of in-migrants amongst Zennor parish townships in that year according to Location Quotient, it can be seen that the newcomers were indeed segregated and did not settle evenly throughout the parish. There was a certain amount of clustering. The newcomers settled mainly in the high moorland townships of Mill Downs, Higher Kerrowe, and in Pennance near the southern border of the parish. The pattern was very similar in 1881 with an additional cluster of newcomers at Noon Veor. The occupants of these townships were recognized locally as a distinct group and known as the 'Mountainy People'.[11]

Those settling in the high moorland townships, where the land was poor and where conditions were harsher than in the coastal plain, were almost exclusively engaged in mining, and many would have worked in Ding Dong Mine a couple of kilometres away. This area was not considered desirable by the local people and seems to have served as a staging area for in-migrants. Of the sixty-three in-migrants in these townships in 1871 only twenty-nine were still there ten years later and only twelve remained after twenty years. The others had moved on, either to less isolated, richer, parts of the parish, like John Pascoe, a stonemason formerly from Constantine who moved down to Trewey where he took over a 10-acre farm, or away from Zennor altogether, like Richard Uren, a tin miner formerly from Gulval, who moved overseas.

The total closure of mines in the Zennor area between 1874 and 1878 due to the discovery of rich deposits of tin in Australia[12] had a disastrous effect on Zennor as a whole and on the southern townships in particular. The number of Zennor workers engaged in mining fell steadily from ninety-seven in 1871 to twenty in 1881 to eight in 1891, these latter walking every day to Levant Mine in Pendeen to work and including Matthew Osborn and his sons,[13] the last nineteenth-century miners in Zennor. Between 1871 and 1881 52 per cent of the houses in Mill Downs, Higher Kerrowe, Noon Veor, and Pennance went out of use as their population fell by 35 per cent.

GENDER BIAS IN MIGRATION

The general finding in England and Wales was that females were more migratory than males within the country of their birth. This aspect did not show up in Zennor where the number of female in-migrants up to 1871 was eighty-six compared with eighty-four males. This ratio of 51 to 49 equals the ratio of females to males within the population of the parish as a whole.

The variation from the general finding may be due to two local factors. Firstly, the large number of male miners in-migrating to work in the tin mines of the Zennor area, particularly just before 1871 when tin production was booming due to anarchic conditions in the Malaysian tin-producing region,[14] boosted the proportion of in-coming males (45 per cent of all adult male in-migrants were miners). Secondly, there was a lack of work available at that time to females in the parish. By far the largest sector of female employment was domestic service, and here most positions (59 per cent) were filled by local girls, so reducing the opportunities for female in-migrants. Only a very small amount of work was available for dressmakers or milkmaids and all these were local girls. Rough work as a bal maiden at the tin stamps was not attractive and no local girls did this work: all were in-migrants. There was little, therefore, to attract a female worker to Zennor and almost half (45 per cent) of adult female in-migrants came in as wives.

OCCUPATIONAL BIAS IN MIGRATION

A further analysis was made to see if there was any correlation between migrant occupation and migration distance.

A breakdown of male in-migration by occupation and distance as shown in Figure 2 indicates that miners tended to be short-distance

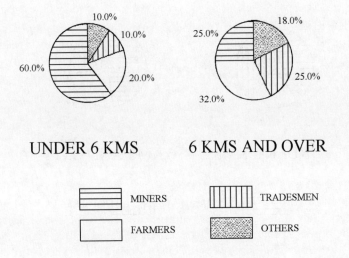

UNDER 6 KMS   6 KMS AND OVER

MINERS   TRADESMEN

FARMERS   OTHERS

Figure 2: Occupations of male in-migrants at Zennor in 1871, comparing shorter and longer distance migrants

migrants whilst tradesmen and craftsmen tended to be long-distance migrants.

It was noticeable that the group of people comprising crafts-people and tradespeople comprised many in-migrants, and this led to the question of whether this group was more mobile than the other residents of the parish. Such proved to be the case. Whilst 21 per cent of the residents of Zennor as a whole were in-migrants in 1871 no less than 36 per cent of the crafts and trades people were. Perhaps this is not surprising, as there has always been a well-known tradition of craftsmen moving, sometimes quite long distances, to find work as journeymen following their training by master craftsmen before settling down permanently as master craftsmen themselves.

An interesting cluster of in-migrants to Zennor were the stone-masons, three of whom had come from the same village of Constantine, some 29 kilometres away, and one of whom had come from Wendron, some 23 kilometres away. No local person followed this craft in 1871. There appears to be a pattern of chain-migration here following a John Pascoe from Constantine, the longest-established stonemason in the

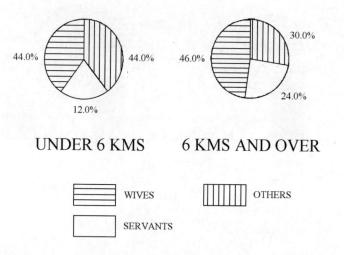

UNDER 6 KMS   6 KMS AND OVER

WIVES   OTHERS

SERVANTS

Figure 3: Occupations of female in-migrants at Zennor in 1871, comparing shorter and longer distance migrants

parish (since 1850), and another John Pascoe, related to the first perhaps, who came from Wendron (near Constantine) and stayed for a time in the 1850s. Between 1851 and 1871 no fewer than three stonemasons from Constantine and four stonemasons from Wendron operated at Zennor[15].

From Figure 3 it appears that female servants, like the tradesmen amongst male migrants, tended to be longer-distance migrants. The movement of wives appears to be generally independent of distance. Some 10 per cent of all wives in Zennor in 1871 had migrated there after marriage to live with a husband already established in the parish.

It is interesting to note in passing that women living in Zennor appear to have been more adventurous in choosing their spouses than men living in Zennor. No less than 26 per cent of resident females born in Zennor were married to a partner from another parish in 1871 whereas only 15 per cent of resident males born in Zennor were.

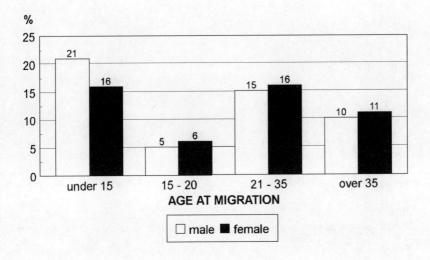

Figure 4: Zennor in-migrants according to their age at migration

AGE DISTRIBUTION OF IN-MIGRANTS

The ages of individual migrants at the date when they arrived in Zennor were calculated by longitudinal nominal record linkage using documents such as a range of census records and parish registers. The results are shown in Figure 4. This shows that most migrants to Zennor were adults, which fits in with the general pattern found by Ravenstein. In 1871 some 63 per cent of in-migrants to the parish were at or over the age of 14 at the time they moved, and 52 per cent were over the age of 21. However, the substantial presence of young children in their midst shows that quite a number of family units had migrated. Some 19 per cent of the total in-migrants were aged 5 years or under at migration. Figure 4 shows a breakdown of the in-migrants to Zennor by age at the time of their migration.

Modern studies have confirmed that migrants are predominantly adolescents and young adults between the ages of 15 and 35, both in Britain and elsewhere in the world.[16] This is also true of Zennor, where 42 per cent of all in-migrants had ages between these limits at the time they arrived in the parish, most being in the sub-group of ages from 21

Table 1: Counter-migration flow migrants to and from Zennor as recorded in the 1881 census

	TO Zennor Male	TO Zennor Female	FROM Zennor Male	FROM Zennor Female	Net Male	Net Female	Net Flow
(1) Penzance	0	0	10	24	-10	-24	-34
(2) St Ives	2	5	26	31	-24	-26	-50
(3) Gulval	9	12	16	8	-7	4	-3
(4) Maldron	9	6	8	9	1	-3	-2
(5) Morvah	9	3	3	3	6	0	6
(6) Towednack	12	10	14	11	-2	-1	-3
(7) Antony	0	0	0	1	0	-1	-1
(8) Bodmin	1	0	0	0	1	0	1
(9) Budock	0	0	1	1	-1	-1	-2
(10) Camborne	0	0	0	1	0	-1	-1
(11) Crowan	0	1	1	0	-1	1	0
(12) Constantine	3	0	3	1	0	-1	-1
(13) Falmouth	0	0	1	0	-1	0	-1
(14) Fowey	1	0	0	0	1	0	1
(15) Germoe	0	1	1	0	-1	1	0
(16) Gwennap	0	0	1	0	-1	0	-1
(17) Gwinear	0	1	0	0	0	1	1
(18) Gwithian	0	0	1	0	-1	0	-1
(19) Landrake	0	0	2	0	-2	0	-2
(20) Lanivet	0	0	1	0	-1	0	-1
(21) Lansallos	0	1	0	0	0	1	1
(22) Lelant	2	0	6	6	-4	-6	-10
(23) Liskeard	0	0	1	0	-1	0	-1
(24) Ludgvan	4	8	2	12	2	-4	-2
(25) Mawnan	0	0	4	1	-4	-1	-5
(26) Menhenoit	0	0	5	5	-5	-5	-10
(27) Mevagissey	1	0	0	0	1	0	1
(28) Paul	0	0	1	4	-1	-4	-5

Table 1 (continued):

	TO Zennor Male	TO Zennor Female	FROM Zennor Male	FROM Zennor Female	Net Male	Net Female	Net Flow
(29) Perranuthnoe	0	0	0	1	0	-1	-1
(30) Phillack	3	0	2	0	1	0	1
(31) Redruth	0	0	1	0	-1	0	-1
(32) St Austell	1	0	2	1	-1	-1	-2
(33) St Buryan	0	2	1	0	-1	2	1
(34) St Erme	0	0	1	0	-1	0	-1
(35) St Erth	0	0	1	1	-1	-1	-2
(36) St Hilary	0	0	3	5	-3	-5	-8
(37) St Just	4	1	11	10	-7	-9	-16
(38) St Keverne	0	0	1	0	-1	0	-1
(39) St Levan	4	3	0	3	4	0	4
(40) St Pinnock	0	0	1	0	-1	0	-1
(41) Sancreed	0	0	0	2	0	-2	-2
(42) Sennen	0	0	4	5	-4	-5	-9
(43) Sithney	1	0	0	1	1	-1	0
(44) Stithians	0	0	1	0	-1	0	-1
(45) Tywardreth	0	0	0	1	0	-1	-1
(46) Veryan	0	0	1	3	-1	-3	-4
(47) Wendron	3	2	0	0	3	2	5
(48) Agramont	0	2	0	0	0	2	2
(49) Minehead	0	1	0	0	0	1	1
(50) Portsea	0	1	0	0	0	1	1
(51) Selsea	1	0	0	0	1	0	1
(52) Southsea	3	2	0	0	3	2	5
(53) Sudbury	1	0	0	0	1	0	1
TOTAL	74	62	138	151	-64	-89	-153

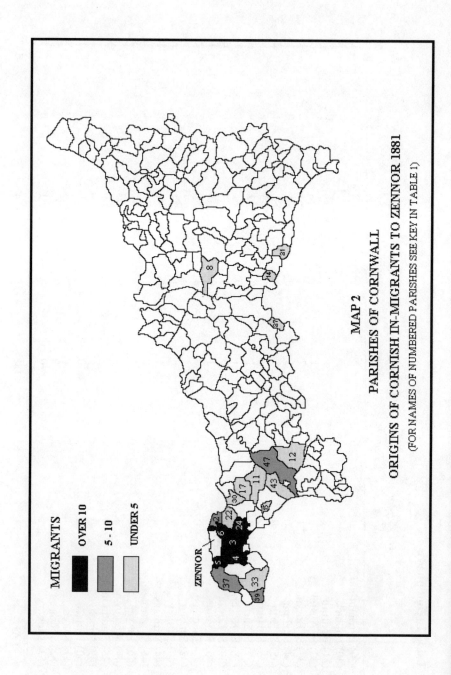

MIGRANTS

OVER 10

5 - 10

UNDER 5

MAP 2

PARISHES OF CORNWALL

ORIGINS OF CORNISH IN-MIGRANTS TO ZENNOR 1881

(FOR NAMES OF NUMBERED PARISHES SEE KEY IN TABLE 1)

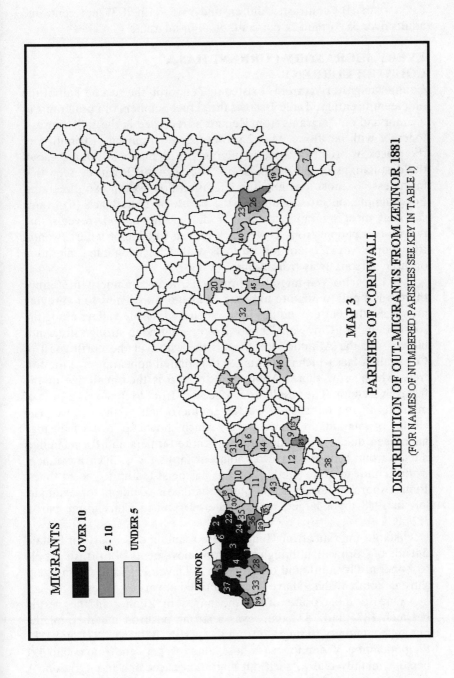

MIGRANTS

OVER 10

5 - 10

UNDER 5

ZENNOR

MAP 3

PARISHES OF CORNWALL

DISTRIBUTION OF OUT-MIGRANTS FROM ZENNOR 1881

(FOR NAMES OF NUMBERED PARISHES SEE KEY IN TABLE 1)

to 35 years. By contrast, children under 15 formed 37 per cent, and adults over 35 formed 21 per cent, of all in-migrants.

EVERY MIGRATORY CURRENT HAS A COUNTER-CURRENT

Counter-migratory currents existed in Zennor in the second half of the nineteenth century. Table 1 shows the actual numbers of in-migrants to Zennor and out-migrants from Zennor as recorded in the 1881 census[17] together with net flows. Map 2 shows the geographical distribution of the places of origin of these in-migrants to Zennor and Map 3 shows the destinations of the out-migrants from Zennor. It can be seen that in the case of most locations the migration flow was in two directions. For example, an investigation of the parish of Towednack (6), which supplied most migrants to Zennor during the period, reveals that twenty-two people from Towednack moved to Zennor whilst twenty-five people from Zennor moved to Towednack, giving a net migration of three persons away from Zennor by 1881.

In respect of out-migration, for the farming community in Zennor there was a pull to migrate to better farmland with a view to improving prospects; this better land lies in the sheltered, fertile valleys along the southern half of Cornwall. Zennor is very exposed to strong salty winds blowing off the Atlantic Ocean, as is the whole of the north coast of Cornwall, a fact which accounts for the stunted appearance of the few trees which grow there. Another factor too is the small size of the farms in Zennor. The result, as can be seen from Map 3, was a drift of migrants to the parishes along the southern half of the county. The cluster of migrants at Mawnan (25) which shows up in the map may have been due to chain migration, as three farmers and their families moved from Zennor to live on adjacent farms there. Such movement from Zennor to more southerly farms has persisted up to recent times. John Osborn, a farmer from Bosporthennis in Zennor, for example, left in 1958 for a larger, more sheltered farm in Constantine parish (12).[18]

No out-migrants from Zennor were found in other parts of Britain outside of Cornwall, although significant movements of Cornish people to London, Plymouth and other towns in Devon,[19] and to Glamorganshire in South Wales,[20] have been identified at various times.

Due to the closure of all the mines in Zennor in the period between 1874 and 1878 there was a strong push on members of the mining community to migrate from the parish. Between 1871 and 1881 the population of Zennor as a whole fell by 18 per cent from 600 to 491 persons, mainly due to such out-migration exceeding in-migration. A particular group of out-migrants from Zennor shows up in the parishes of Menheniot and Liskeard (23, 26). The lead mines of this district were still working in 1883[21] after all the tin and copper mines in Zennor had closed, and it is known that much of the mine labour force in Menheniot in the nineteenth century was drawn from West Cornwall.[22] The group comprising members of the Quick family, who had been tin miners in Zennor and who moved to Menheniot to find work after the closure of the Zennor mines, were thus following a well-established path. It has also been found that many miners in the Menheniot lead mines actually had to live in the town of Liskeard, three miles from Menheniot, because of the lack of accommodation in the village itself. Presumably this would have been the case for William Michell who moved from Zennor to Liskeard to work at the lead mines as a mine engine driver.

In the case of the old traditional Zennor families only out-migration occurred. Such was the case for the Osborn family for example, where there was no in-migration during the period in question. Robert Osborn, a working engineer, left Trewey in Zennor as a single man in the 1840s for Towednack, where he had married and founded a family by 1871. The family of another Robert Osborn, formerly a farmer at Wicca in Zennor, migrated a longer distance of 34 kilometres to Budock (9) in 1850 where his son Robert junior, born in Zennor, was working as a farm labourer and his daughter Jane, born in Zennor, was working as a dairy keeper in 1871. Both ends of the social scale were represented amongst the migrants: William Osborn left Zennor as a young man for Sancreed (41) and was working in 1871 as an agricultural labourer on a small 3-acre (1.25-hectare) farm there, and John Osborn left his farm at Boscobban in Zennor with his family in the 1860s to farm a 109-acre (44-hectare) farm at North Treveneague in St Hilary (36) and become a vestryman of that parish.

Some migrants left Britain completely, such as Matthew Osborn, a tin miner of Trewey, who left soon after his marriage in 1870 with his new bride for the United States of America, soon to be followed there by his unmarried brother John, also a tin miner. Another brother, Christopher, a farmer, left for Australia,[23] as did Arthur Chellew from Churchtown.[24]

None of the above returned to Zennor, but there were cases of people leaving Zennor eventually returning home. John Osborn, from Foage, lived during the 1850s in Gulval (3), but returned after a few years to live at Foage again. Thomas Quick of Wicca went to Australia but had returned by 1891.[25]

OUT-MIGRATION FROM COUNTRYSIDE TO TOWN

The drift from the countryside to the towns was well under way by the second half of the nineteenth century[26] and it is interesting to check the migration currents and counter-currents between Zennor and its two market towns. From Table 1 it can be seen that by far the largest net flows of migrants were from rural Zennor to these two towns.

Whilst people did migrate to Zennor from the nearest town of St Ives, which had a population in 1881 of 6,445, the number of St Ives people moving to Zennor by that year was only seven whilst the number of Zennor people moving to St Ives was fifty-seven, the largest single group of out-migrants leaving Zennor (20 per cent of the total). The result was a net movement of fifty people away from Zennor into this town.

The situation with regard to the other market town used by Zennor people, that is Penzance with a population in 1881 of 11,684, is not so clear because it was included in Madron, and people from Penzance at the time under consideration often gave their place of origin or destination as Madron rather than Penzance. However it appears that the number of Zennor people moving to Penzance was thirty-four, the second largest single group of out-migrants (17 per cent of the total), whilst none moved from Penzance to Zennor, giving a net movement away from Zennor to Penzance of thirty-four persons.

These figures show that many people from Zennor were choosing to migrate to the nearby towns, and this movement overwhelmed any in-migration from such towns to Zennor. This confirms that the drift from the countryside to the town existed in the case of Zennor just as it did elsewhere.

There is an interesting difference between the respective migrations from Zennor to its two market towns. The migration to Penzance by 1881 was predominantly female, some 71 per cent of all out-migrants, most being independent women. On arrival 41 per cent of these females took up positions as servants, as for example Charity Nicholls who became a servant to Charles Ross, a wealthy Penzance banker, and Elizabeth Eddy who became a servant of the doctor Leonard Williams. St Ives, a smaller and less important town than Penzance and a fishing port, was less prosperous than Penzance and the opportunities for servants were less. Although a larger number of out-migrants from Zennor are recorded in the census as having moved there by 1881 than to Penzance, only one of these became a servant. Most female migrants moving there were the dependent wives and daughters of men moving into town seeking work.

In respect of women migrating to become servants, several examples of linked migration from Zennor were found where sisters migrated to work as domestic servants for the same employer, such as Catherine and Ellen Trevorrow who both left the parish to work together for John Young at Veryan (46). Such linked migration has been noted as not uncommon and shows the importance of kinship links as a support mechanism.[27]

CONCLUSION

To conclude it can be seen that during the period considered here the patterns of in-migration and out-migration in respect of the parish of Zennor did not, in general, differ substantially from those of England and Wales as a whole. The general findings of Ravenstein and other researchers are reflected there. The isolated situation of the parish does not appear to have caused any substantial distortions, although in the earlier part of the period the presence of mines seems to have biased in-migration towards male migrants.

NOTES AND REFERENCES

1. Census of Great Britain Reports and Summary tables: Population Tables.
2. Contemporary Kelly's Directories of Cornwall.
3. A.K.H. Jenkin, *Mines and Miners of Cornwall*, Truro, 1961.
4. *Mining Journal*, 4 June 1870.
5. Public Record Office (PRO) RG10/2335.
6. E.G. Ravenstein, 'The Laws of Migration', *Journal of the Royal Statistical Society*, 48, 1885, pp. 167–235; E.G. Ravenstein, 'The Laws of Migration', *Journal of the Royal Statistical Society*, 52, 1889, pp. 48–82.
7. D. Mageean, and W.T.R. Pryce, 'Statistics of Migration' in M. Drake and R. Finnegan, (eds), *Sources and Methods for Family and Community Historians: A Handbook*, Cambridge, 1994.
8. PRO RG10/2335.
9. The traditional Zennor families were those bearing the family names Baragwanath, Berryman, Bone, Christopher, Curnow, Daniel, Eddy, Edwards, Grenfell, Hollow, Mann, Matthews, Michell, Nankervis, Newton, Nicholls, Osborn, Perry, Phillips, Polmear, Quick, Richards, Stevens, Thomas, Trembath and Wallis. The Zennor parish registers show that these families had been resident in the parish for over 100 years by 1871, but of course some of them were at one time migrants themselves. The Stevens, Quick and Michell families, for example, came to Zennor from Dungarvan in southern Ireland in about 1470, and the Osborns came to Zennor in a chain migration from Morvah in the middle of the seventeenth century.

10. R. Lewis, 'Measures of Residential Segregation' in Drake and Finnegan, (eds), 1994:

Index of Segregation for the parish $= \dfrac{\Sigma(\%T - \%M)\Sigma\%T}{2(\Sigma\%T - \Sigma\%M)}$ and

Location Quotient for a township $= \dfrac{\%M}{\%T}$ where

%M = % of total migrant population resident in a given township, and
%T = % of total population of the parish resident in that township.
11. C.B. Powell Noy, farmer of Bosporthennis, Zennor.
12. D.B. Barton.
13. Wilmot A. Hosken, of Bude, Cornwall.
14. Barton, 1967.
15. H. Rossler, 'Constantine Stonemasons in Search of Work Abroad', in Philip Payton (ed.), *Cornish Studies Two*, Exeter, 1994, pp. 48–82, deals with the particular subject of the migration of stonemasons from this area in search of work.
16. D.B. Grigg, 'E.G. Ravenstein and the Laws of Migration', *Journal of Historical Geography* 3, 1977, pp. 41–51.
17. PRO RG11/2342 and 1881 census birthplace index.
18. J. Osborn, of Constantine, Cornwall.
19. C.T. Smith, 'The Movement of Population in England and Wales in 1851 and 1861', *Geographical Journal*, Vol. 117, 1951, pp. 200–10.
20. D. Friedlander, and R.J. Roshier, 'A Study of Internal Migration in England and Wales: Part 1, *Population Studies*, Vol. 19, 1966, pp. 239–79.
21. For example Wheal Trelawny Lead Mine: *Kelly's Directory of Cornwall* 1883 and J.H. Collins, *Observations on the West of England Mining Region*, 1912.
22. B. Deacon, 'Migration and the Mining Industry in East Cornwall in the Mid-nineteenth Century', *Journal of the Royal Institution of Cornwall*, New Series, Vol. 10, Part 1, 1986, pp. 84–104.
23. Wilmot A. Lory, of Penzance, Cornwall.
24. Rev. D. Chellew, of Melbourne, Australia; Philip Payton, *The Cornish Overseas*, Fowey, 1994, p. 237.
25. PRO RG12/1854.
26. R. Lawton, 'Population Changes in England and Wales in the Later Nineteenth Century: An Analysis of Trends by Registration Districts', *Transactions, Institute of British Geographers* 44, 1967, pp. 55–74.
27. C.G. Pooley, and I.D. White, (eds), *Migrants, Emigrants and Immigrants, A Social History of Migration*, London, 1991.

THE LEMON FAMILY INTEREST IN CORNISH POLITICS

Brian Elvins

The story of the Lemon family is a classic example of 'rags to riches', of how an obscure Cornish family rose in a few generations to respectability and the highest ranks of 'county society'; a rise which climaxed in representing Cornwall in Parliament as Knights of the Shire. Both Sir William Lemon 1st BT. (1748–1824) and his eldest surviving son, Sir Charles Lemon (1784–1868) served long periods as members for the 'county'. The family influence even extended to include Sir William's son-in-law, J.H. Tremayne (1780–1851), who was also a 'county' member fo 20 years. What has to be assessed, however, is whether the Lemon family interest, operating separately from the main political parties and putting the ties of kinship first, played as pivotal a role in Cornish parties as has been claimed.

Norman Gash, for example, in his famous study of the post-1832 electoral system, *Politics in the Age of Peel*, published some years ago, claimed that it illustrated the fact that the Cornish gentry preferred 'the claims of family connexion, personal popularity, and good neighbourliness to those of party loyalty and political principle'.[1] More recently too, in 1993, Edwin Jaggard, a specialist writer on nineteenth-century Cornish party politics, has argued that among the reasons for the failure of the Conservatives to make headway in the West Cornwall division after 1832, the so-called 'Lemon connection' was 'at times the most decisive factor working against the Conservatives'.[2]

'THE GREAT MR LEMON'

The rise of the family began with 'the Great Mr Lemon', as he was known. William Lemon was born in humble circumstances in

November 1696 in the parish of Breage, west of Helston. He began work as a labourer but had gained sufficient education at the village school to become an office clerk and later, manager of a tin-smelting house near Penzance. The turning point in his career was 22 April 1724, when he married Isabella Vibert of Gulval, for through her, he received enough money to enable him to start speculations in Cornish mines, which turned out to be extremely successful.

With two associates, he began working a mine, north of Marazion, which he called Wheal Fortune. It is said that Lemon realized £10,000 out of Wheal Fortune, which enabled him to extend his operations. He moved to Truro, where he was twice mayor in 1737 and 1750, and began working the great Gwennap mines, south of Redruth, on a scale unprecedented in Cornwall, so becoming the leading Cornish mine proprietor, besides being one of its principal merchants and tin smeltors. Sheriff of Cornwall in 1742, he subsequently, in the words of the *Gentleman's Magazine* 'wisely laid out the product of the bowels of the earth in the purchase of many fair acres on its surface'. In 1749 he moved into the ranks of the country gentry by purchasing Carclew, in the parish of Mylor, from the Bonython family. Here he built, according to the magazine, 'one of the most beautiful mansions in Cornwall'. He died in March 1760, being buried in the parish church in Truro, where his name is perpetuated in Lemon Street and Lemon Quay. He thus outlived his only son, William junior, who died three years earlier at the age of 33.[3]

The third generation completed the family's rise to gentility. William Lemon III, born 6 October 1748, succeeded his grandfather at the age of eleven. He received the education common to the sons of the gentry, attending Christ Church, Oxford where he matriculated in January 1765, shortly after his sixteenth birthday. He completed this phase of his upbringing with the Grand Tour of Europe in 1768 and soon after, in January 1770, entered politics as MP for the nearby borough of Penryn. At the end of 1772 he briefly resigned his seat in an attempt to become a 'county' member but following his defeat, resumed his place at Penryn for two more years. The year 1774 saw the culmination of his success story. In May, at the age of 26, he was created a baronet and, in the general election in October, was returned for the 'county'. This was a seat he was to retain for the next half-century until his death.

The family's rise in Cornish society was cemented by marriage into established 'county families'. William Lemon junior had begun the trend by his marriage to Anne, the daughter of John Willyams of Carnanton near St Columb, a marriage which produced two sons, William and John, and a daughter Ann. Then followed a double marriage into the Bullers, an established 'county family' near Looe. In 1770, Ann Lemon married John Buller, the son of James Buller of Morval, while on 3 April the following year, William married Jane, James Buller's eldest daughter. Lemon and John Buller were, at this time, partners together in the banking firm of Lemon, Buller, Lubbock, Farley and Co. Lemon retired from the firm in 1785.[4]

William Lemon and his wife, Jane, subsequently had twelve children; she died in 1823 at the age of 76. Several of their marriages widened the Lemon connection with other Cornish landed families. Two, in particular, were important. In January 1813, Caroline, Sir William's 24-year-old youngest daughter, married John Hearle Tremayne of Heligan, near St Ewe. Tremayne, who was some nine years older than his wife, had, in fact, been Lemon's fellow 'county member' since 1806.[5] The second marriage, which took place in July 1824, was equally significant for its impact on Cornish politics. The influential Francis Basset, Lord De Dunstanville, (1757–1835) of Tehidy, having lost his first wife in June 1823, married Lemon's fourth daughter, Harriet. She was almost 50 years of age while De Dunstanville himself was 67. It was concerning this marriage that Thomas Creevy, the diarist, wrote rather maliciously:

> It is an old passion on his part. He is as rich as a jew and will endow her, I take for granted, accordingly. His only issue at present is one Daughter of Miss Lemon's age, ugly as sin, cross as the devil and a Baroness that is to be in her own right. Another barony, however, is still reserved for Miss Lemon's Son, so the Lord send her a safe delivery.[6]

In view of Harriet Lemon's age, the last eventuality was un-likely, although she did live for another forty years until her death in December 1864.

Lemon's eldest son, William killed himself in 1799 when he was only 25, but the second son and eventual heir, Charles made an even more impressive marriage. In December 1810, he married Lady Charlotte Strangways, the fourth daughter of the 2nd Earl of Ilchester, one of the country's leading aristocratic Whig families. This meant that Charles Lemon was also a brother-in-law of another prominent Whig; the 3rd Marquess of Lansdowne, who was married to Ilchester's fifth daughter, Louise.

These relationships clearly marked how far the Lemon family had risen since the humble labourer at Breage in the 1720s. The Lemons had thus become, in Jaggard's phrase 'powerful, grudgingly respected gentry' but their lowly origins were not forgotten. For

example, in the 1820s, the Tory friends of Sir Richard Vyvyan questioned the suitability of Edward Pendarves as a candidate for a 'county
seat', because of his supposed lack of background. A relative, Mrs J.
Stackhouse exclaimed in his defence, 'I would venture to show family
with him (Vyvyan) at any time. If that was a necessary qualification for
a county member, how came Sir William Lemon to be chosen?'[7]

William Lemon's rise in Cornish politics was rapid. Cornwall's
Parliamentary representation had been dominated since 1750 by long-
established families such as the Molesworths, St Aubyns and Bullers.
In 1772, when a by-election was needed, following the death of Sir
John Aubyn 4th Bt., Lemon came within sixteen votes of victory
against H.M. Praed of Trevethoe, who polled 1,081 votes against 1,065
for Lemon.[8] However, two years later, in the general election, he came
top of the poll in a fierce four-cornered contest. Lemon increased his
vote to 1,099 but his brother-in-law, John Buller, with whom he was
allied came only third with 960. The sitting MP Sir John Molesworth
5th Bt. was returned with 1,050 votes and Praed in last place on 890.[9]

Lemon was returned unopposed in 1780 and 1784 and by the time
of the next contest in 1790, he was considered to be above the conflict.
Francis Gregor of Trewarthenick standing as a supporter of Pitt, and
Sir John St Aubyn 5th Bt. fought each other for the other seat.[10]
Indeed, he came undisputed head of the poll with 2,254 votes, almost
double that of either of the other two candidates. Gregor polled 1,270
votes and St Aubyn 1,137.[11] This was the last contest that Lemon
had to face. He was returned unopposed in the next seven general
elections; 1796, 1802, 1806, 1807, 1812, 1818 and 1820.

AN 'INDEPENDENT' WHIG
The virtue which Lemon, in common with other 'county members',
emphasized throughout his career, was his 'Independence'. In 1774, for
example, he criticized his opponent as being 'a mere Tool . . . who
without the least spark of independence or freedom of spirit has
belonged to all Ministers in their turn'. By contrast, Lemon claimed, as
he did in 1818, 'to be guided by that feeling of Independence which
he had always preserved and which had uniformly been his guide'.[12]
Yet although Lemon laid claim to be 'Independent', in practice he
invariably supported the Whigs. This was especially true in the 1790s,
after the impact of the French Revolution on the British political scene.
In the words of Richard Polwhele (the Cornish historian):

> Whilst many, fearful of incurring the suspicion of
> republicanism, abandoned the cause of Liberty, Sir William
> stood firm in the ranks of independence and even had the

resolution to express his dissent from the Minister at that unheard of moment when opposition to the Administration was considered as synonimous [sic] with disaffection from government.[13]

He was not a frequent speaker in the Commons but he voted often enough to reveal his general political position. He opposed Pitt's government before 1800 and again between 1804 and 1806. By contrast he supported the short Addington ministry and the equally brief Grenville government of 1806–7.

Lemon also opposed the subsequent ministries of Portland, Perceval and Liverpool, supporting, for example, the censure motion against the government in May 1819. He was invariably to be found voting against the government motions which threatened the freedom of the individual. In April 1810, he voted against the imprisonment in the Tower of London of the Radical, Sir Francis Burdett. In early 1817, he opposed the Suspension of Habeas Corpus and a Seditious Meetings Bill and the following year, supported a motion for an enquiry into allegations of oppression as a result of the Suspension. At the end of 1819, he opposed the repressive legislation which came to be known as the Six Acts and in 1821 was in the minority supporting an enquiry into the 'Peterloo Massacre'.[14]

Votes like these annoyed some fellow Cornish landowners. The Rev. John Rogers of Penrose, a Canon of Exeter Cathedral, complained in January 1820:

> I have long ceased to be surprised at any opposition vote of Sir William Lemon—he is just as systematic an opposer of the measures of government whether right or wrong as the most devoted tool of administration is in favour of them. He is an upright and amiable man but I have no respect for his politics.[15]

Lemon was rather less consistent on the claims of Roman Catholics. In March 1813 he supported the motion for a committee on Ireland but on 24 May voted against the first clause of the Catholic Relief Bill. In 1817 he voted in the majority against another motion for a committee and again, in 1821, was to be found in the minority opposed to the successful motion in favour of the Catholics.[16] On the issue of Parliamentary Reform, however, his position was consistent throughout his career. He told the Commons in January 1817, that 'he should support the principle of Reform as he had done throughout his life from the time that important measure was brought forward by Sir

George Saville', (i.e. 1779–80). He had voted in favour of it in 1783 and again in 1793.[17] Lemon maintained this position even when the subject became unpopular because of the French Revolution, voting in 1797 in favour of the proposals of the Whig leader, Grey. In May 1810, he voted for Brand's motion, in 1817 and 1819 for Burdett's motions, and supported Lord John Russell in his proposals in May 1821 and April 1822.[18]

From the few speeches he made on the subject, Lemon does not appear to have had any specific scheme in mind, though it is clear that he favoured only moderate proposals. At the meeting for his election in 1812, he stated that 'he was pledged to no plan. He depended on the wisdom of the legislature for a remedy'; a sentiment he reiterated five years later in the Commons.[19] His association with and commitment to the cause continued to the end of his life. He gave his final vote for another of Russell's motions in April 1823, the year before his death.[20]

The hold which the Lemon family interest had over the two 'county seats' might have been expected to arouse resentment among the Tories in Cornwall. However, this was avoided because Tremayne showed no inclination to follow his father-in-law's politics. Tremayne certainly agreed on the virtue of 'Independence' in a 'county member', stating as late as 1826 that 'a member for a great county should watch all parties without being entangled with any'. He thus earned the reputation, at the time, of being 'a thoroughly independent person and wholly unconnected with any party'.[21] Tremayne did agree with the line that Lemon took on Catholic Relief, motions in favour of Retrenchment by governments and the special interests of Cornwall. However, he consistently opposed Parliamentary Reform and supported the Tory government of Lord Liverpool on crucial issues such as the Suspension of Habeas Corpus (1817), the Six Acts (1819), and the measures against Queen Caroline in 1821.[22]

Therefore, the two men were not perceived in Cornwall as representing a single family interest. Indeed, the *West Briton*, the Reform newspaper, commented in 1818 on the 'county' representation in the following terms:

> The two parties that divide the county each have a representative of whose independence they can justly boast. The high independence and undeviating integrity of Sir W. Lemon will ever secure (him) the grateful attachment of a county which he has long and so faithfully served. As to general policy we do indeed differ from Mr Tremayne but his independence is above suspicion, nor can there be any doubt that his opinions and conduct result from honest conviction.[23]

PENDARVES VERSUS VYVYAN

The connections which Sir William had built up came actively into play after his death on 11 December 1824. Ironically, it was Tremayne, having faced no contest since his original election in 1806, who now found his place under threat as a result of his father-in-law's death. This was the first serious test for the Lemon family interest since it had emerged on the Cornish political scene. The by-election to find a successor to Sir William, in fact, initiated a political struggle which lasted 18 months and ended with Tremayne no longer a 'county member'. The struggle had actually begun before Lemon's death for, as early as October, canvassing by two opposing sides had commenced, in the expectation that Lemon might resign his seat.[24]

On the one side, the 50-year-old E.W.W. Pendarves, a prominent figure in the Cornish Reform movement, had decided to stand with the support of fellow reformers in the Western half of the 'county'[25]; friends such as Humphrey Willyams of Carnanton and John Scobell of Nancealverne[26] and finally, leading figures in the Cornish mining interest such as Michael Williams and the three Davey brothers, Stephen, William, and Richard.[27] Pendarves, although not standing specifically on a Reform 'ticket', was regarded by all as a Reformer and he re-affirmed his support for the cause during the campaign.[28]

On the other side, Cornwall's leading Tories such as R. Pole Carew of Antony had decided to back a 25-year-old landed baronet, Sir Richard Vyvyan of Trelowarren. His address, issued only two days after Lemon's death, referred to differences with Pendarves 'on several momentous points of public policy'. A Tory peer—the 2nd Earl of Mt. Edgcumbe—likewise explained his opposition to Pendarves thus: 'I can only regret that a man of such pleasing manners and otherwise so respectable, should have taken such an unfortunate line in politics as to oblige us to oppose him. In fact, we had no alternative.'[29]

In the event, Vyvyan was returned unopposed at the by-election, in January 1825, because of Pendarve's withdrawal, though the latter committed himself to fighting in the general election which was expected in the near future. Such a conflict had clear implications for Tremayne's position as the other MP and he had, therefore, issued an address before 24 December 'thus early to declare that it is not my intention readily to abandon hope of your support on that occasion'.[30]

Tremayne's failure to retain his seat was, in the end, due to a combination of factors. It was partly because of the position he adopted from the start and the conditions he laid down. It was also due to the increasingly clear-cut party political rivalry between Vyvyan, standing as an avowedly Tory candidate, strongly against both Catholic Emancipation and Parliamentary Reform, and Pendarves as a

Reformer. Both sides publicly proclaimed that their candidate did not pose a threat to Tremayne.[31] However, the determination of both camps that their man should win led to an increasing squeeze on his position.

The main thrust of Pendarve's campaign, indeed, was against Vyvyan and his political principles. He was accused of being 'in the fullest sense of the term an Ultra Tory' and part of an attempt by the aristocracy to impose two Tory members on Cornwall. The 'Independence' of the Yeomanry against such domination, which Pendarves came to symbolize, was a potent cry and more effective in attracting support from the voters than Tremayne's claim to be an 'Independent' Cornish MP.[32]

The concern of Vyvyan for Tremayne's position was, at the outset, quite evident. However, it gradually changed to exasperation and even hostility. Vyvyan complained to Carew:

Tremayne will not spend, he will not accept a subscription, his friends expect the County to return him, yet advise him not to let himself be supplanted by the party which first brought him in—all must be sacrificed to Mr Tremayne and after all is sacrificed, he is under no obligation![33]

Likewise, Carew, although wanting Tremayne to succeed, increasingly saw Vyvyan's success as his main priority. He replied to a Tremayne supporter that 'I cannot allow private feelings to interfere with a public duty and it is therefore that I endeavour to support the present representatives against one—whose politics I conceive to be fraught with danger to our Church and State'.[34] It was clear that if a choice had to be made, political principles would cause such Tories to support Vyvyan, instead of Tremayne.

Tremayne made his position clear in a public address on 7 February 1825: 'I presumed on the consciousness of 18 years faithful service as to hope that I might have been only nominally engaged in the impending contest.' He felt that his position should be the same as Lemon's in 1790, when he was above the electoral contest. He had also resolved privately, that 'it must be without an expense on the part of myself or of my friends' and that he would observe 'a strict neutrality' between the two other candidates.[35] As the campaign proceeded, he became, as he admitted to Carew, 'wholly indifferent to the election' for 'I discovered that by far the greater part of my Constituents were more anxious to keep Sir R. Vyvyan or Mr Pendarves (as the case might be) out, than to keep me in'.[36]

All this made it difficult for Tremayne's relatives to act successfully on his behalf, though they certainly tried. De Dunstanville, who first took the initiative in September 1825, was quite open about his motives: 'My great object is Tremayne's security, . . . being nearly connected with him by marriage'.[37] Later Sir Charles Lemon and the Bullers also involved themselves. These efforts resulted in the circulation and subsequent publication of an address on 2 June 1826, signed by 1238 freeholders, who declared: 'admiring your genuine Independence, we think you ought not to be involved in the expense of a contest and we do pledge ourselves individually to give you one of our votes at the election'.[38]

The list was headed by Sir Charles, Rev. William Molesworth, seven different members of the Buller family, followed by supporters of both the other candidates. Given an estimated size of the electorate at around 2,700,[39] this impressive total seemed to augur well for Tremayne's chances. However, his relatives had failed to face up to the practical difficulty, for ordinary voters, of 'performing a journey of 50 miles and be at the expense of their own conveyance and nourishment'. The *West Briton* for once, agreed with its Tory rival, the *Royal Cornwall Gazette*, remarking that 'Tremayne's private fortune renders such an expense comparatively a matter of no great moment to him'.[40]

As a result, although Tremayne and Pendarves won the traditional show of hands at the nomination at Bodmin on 15 June, he withdrew prior to the poll at Lostwithiel on the 20th. The Lemon family interest had thus failed its first major challenge. Alfred Jenkin, steward to Mrs Agar of Lanhydrock and a neutral observer, acknowledged that the party battle had been important with his comment 'the public feeling in favour of E.W.W. Pendarves has been intense'. However, he was also convinced that 'if J.H. Tremayne and his friends had used but moderate endeavours to obtain his return, Sir R.R. Vyvyan would have been thrown out' for 'he does not seem to be at all a favourite. J.H. Tremayne, however, evinced such indifference respecting it as deprived him of every prospect of success'.[41]

The loss of Tremayne as a county MP, even if self-inflicted, clearly hurt his relatives. De Dunstanville reacted to what he called 'the degraded state of the county' by proposing to leading Tories such as Carew and the Earl of Falmouth that a secret election fund should be built up by the investment of an annual sum of money in Exchequer Bills. 'If the measure takes effect Tremayne should be sounded as to whether he means to come forward. For my part I must distinctly and unequivocally state that if ever he offers himself, he is entitled to the best support I can give.'[42] However, after discussion, the scheme was not proceeded with. The resentment of the Rev. W. Molesworth, who had married into the Buller family, took the form of a public attack on

Pendarves and Vyvyan at their unopposed re-election in August 1830. He declared 'there was a large body of Freeholders of no contemptible strength who disapprove of ultra principles of any description. Neither of the Honourable Gentlemen were after the hearts of this middle but important body of their constituents'.[43]

CHARLES LEMON

After 1830, the family interest centred upon Charles Lemon. His early career was a mirror image of his father's. After attending Christ Church, Oxford, he too had become MP for the borough of Penryn in 1807, at the age of 23, through the influence of De Dunstanville. For the five years he was in the House until 1812, his voting pattern was, like his father's, directed to supporting the Whigs on key issues. He opposed Burdett's commitment in 1810, supported the motion for Parliamentary Reform in May, and voted in favour of a motion for retrenchment. Unlike his father, however, he was favourable to the claims of the Catholics, voting in the minority in April 1812, for a committee on Ireland. He was, therefore, listed by the Whigs as a 'present supporter'.[44]

He was not returned again for Penryn until 1830, when he was 46, having succeeded to the title and the Carclew estate in 1824. It seems likely that he resumed a public career, at least in part, because of a series of personal tragedies in the mid 1820s. His parents having died in successive years (1823 and 1824), he suffered the loss of his nine-year-old daughter, Charlotte, in May 1825; the death of his 12-year-old son, Charles, from drowning at Harrow School on 18 April 1826, and finally the death of his wife just over a month later, on 27 May, at the age of 42. 'His deep attachment to Lady Charlotte's memory . . . kept him unmarried' for the next 42 years.[45] In May of the following year, his sister, Caroline Tremayne, gave birth to her second son, Arthur, and he eventually became Lemon's heir.

Lemon missed the crucial vote which brought down Wellington's Tory government in the November. However, he supported the Whig Reform Bill both in the vital Second Reading on 22 March 1831, and again on 19 April, voting against the successful amendment which opposed a reduction in the number of MPs, a vote which precipitated a dissolution.[46] Lemon had been approached by the strong Reform group in Cornwall before the end of March 1831 to partner Pendarves in the election against Vyvyan. His immediate reaction had been to consult 'my own friends and connections . . . My wish is not to commit myself with them unless I can obtain the support of a party in the county sufficiently strong to give me personal weight without reference to any present or accidental principle of excitement'. Given that the recipient of this letter was Carew—one of Vyvyan's main backers— it is evident how extensive the Lemon connections were, spreading beyond the immediate family and how trusting Lemon was!

His initial inclination was to decline the invitation: 'I yielded for a moment to a suggestion which I have again abandoned from a consideration of some circumstances in the County politics in which I do no wish deeply to engage.'[47] He soon changed his mind, however, agreeing to stand with Pendarves, but stressing that he stood 'as a candidate zealously interested in the cause of Reform but a man of no party'. His relative, Edward Buller of Morval, likewise recommended him at the nomination meeting by saying that 'the political career of Sir Charles Lemon had not been long but he had shown the same independence as his father'.[48]

The family connections figured prominently in the election speeches of the Tory candidates. Vyvyan exclaimed 'They find Sir Charles supported by the Bullers and the Radicals; the boroughholders and the Reformers' and that he supposed was what was meant by Sir Charles being of no party! His fellow candidate, Lord Valletort, even blamed his defeat on the family interest:

With those who opposed him on political grounds, he felt no cause for quarrel . . . but there were some who were his opponents on other grounds; who approved of his principles, whilst for personal and family reasons, they supported his opponent. To them he chiefly owed his failure and he regarded them with very different feelings.[49]

However, this was to exaggerate the influence of the Lemon connection. The campaign had been fought by a joint committee for both candidates and the final result revealed that support for Pendarves and Lemon was even throughout all the Hundreds in Cornwall, with no discernable extra votes for Lemon for family reasons. Pendarves topped the poll with 1819 votes and Lemon was close behind on 1804, twice as many as their opponents. Lemon denied that he owed his victory 'to the assistance of two or three friends. I am not insensible to the exertions of my private friends . . . but I owe my situation to the uninfluenced suffrages of the Freeholders and their approval of the principles on which I stood'.[50]

On the hustings, Lemon had pledged himself only to the principle of Reform and not to the specific detail of the Bill. In fact, his support for the subsequent proposals of the government was very consistent. He voted for the Second and Third Readings of the second version of the Bill in July and September and for clauses concerning Cornish boroughs such as St Germans, Helston, and the union of Penryn with Falmouth. Likewise he supported the third version of the Bill in the autumn of 1831 and spring of 1832, and voted for the motion on 10 May opposing the possible formation of a Wellington ministry. His 'Independence' was revealed on only two specific occasions: when he opposed the proposal to give eight new members to the Metropolitan districts and substitution of Methyr Tydfil for Gateshead.[51]

In the new Parliament after 1833, Lemon continued to give general support to the Whig government and only asserted his 'Independence' on two key topics. First, on religious issues, especially those affecting the many Nonconformists in Cornwall, he supported the motion for the admission of dissenters into universities. He even voted for the Second Reading but changed his vote on the Final Reading in July 1834. He later explained this change because of 'the omission of clauses preserving to the members of the Established Church, the Governing of the universities and the property of its endowment'. Secondly, in June 1833, he voted to omit from the Irish Church Temporalities Bill the critical clause (No. 147) concerning appropriation of the surplus revenue of the Irish Church, to which the Lords had objected.[52]

It is clear that Lemon felt strongly on this matter, thus sympathizing with ministers such as Graham and Lord Stanley, who resigned when the same issue came up again in May 1834. It was in this connection that Lemon received a 'friendly warning' from the leader of the Cornish Yeomanry, J. Penhallow Peters:

> Your friends will be mightily disappointed if you turn out of the straight line to please any man or party whatever . . . It is a difficult thing to divide from friends (Lord Stanley) but you have a precedent. Your father was wedded to the people and never committed adultery.[53]

However there is no evidence that Lemon considered defecting with the Stanleyites and this is not surprising, given his connections with the Whig families of Ilchester and Lansdowne.

The family's Cornish connections, meanwhile, continued to be prominent in Cornish elections. In December 1832, when returned unopposed for the new West Cornwall division, Lemon's nomination was proposed by Tremayne, who contended that it was not 'inconsistent' for him, an opponent of the Reform Bill, to support 'one who has always been a resolute Reformer', because it was vital that 'the best men of all parties' be returned.[54] It was in the election two years later, however, that the family interest was accused of playing a particularly controversial role.

THE 1835 ELECTION

The 1st Earl of Falmouth of Tregothnan, a leading Tory peer in West Cornwall, brought forward his son, Lord Boscawen Rose, as a candidate. The latter, who had only taken his degree (a first in classics) at Oxford in 1833, issued his election address on 29 December 1834. On the following day, Falmouth wrote to Peel, then the Prime Minister, seeking government help against 'the Radical candidate, Pendarves against whom and not Lemon, Boscawen's canvass must be directed'. Within two days, however, he was complaining about Tremayne's conduct:

> We could not have conceived that Mr Tremayne should have drawn Sir T. Acland and other men of property and influence here, into a league having for its object, to stifle at once any conservative attempt upon the plea of wishing to secure the sitting Whig—Sir Charles Lemon . . . and indicating a total indifference to any other object than that of seating his Whig brother-in-law. This league of Mr Tremayne's comprises some of the largest estates in this division.

One further complaint was that Lemon's 'other connection, Ld De Dunstanville who would have counteracted it, is unfortunately in a dying state and entirely under the control of his Lady, Sir C's sister'. Peel, who had at once taken steps to enlist the help of the Duchy of Cornwall for Boscawen, replied that in this instance any interference by him 'would not be of the least avail for in Public Life they have never had any connection with me and my private intercourse with them has been limited in the extreme. I hardly know Mr Tremaine [sic] to speak to'.[55]

By 12 January 1835, Boscawen had withdrawn from the election, leaving Lemon and Pendarves to be returned unopposed.[56] Falmouth, in his final letter to Peel, had no doubt where the blame lay: 'Owing to the continued refusal of Tremayne to look to any other object than that of securing Sir Charles Lemon, . . . or to give us the slightest assistance, our efforts for the Cause in this Division of Cornwall have for the moment failed.'

It would appear from Lord Falmouth's complaints that the Lemon interest had been crucial to the outcome of the election, hence the prominence which Gash gave to the episode and the conclusion he drew from it.[57] Such a judgement must be questioned, largely because many of Falmouth's assertions cannot be accepted without reservation. His labelling of Pendarves, for example, as a Radical is an inaccurate description of his political position. The truth is that Falmouth attributed too much influence to Tremayne. That the latter did refuse to aid Boscawen since it might endanger Lemon's seat is undoubtedly true, and equally that De Dunstanville's influence was thrown behind Lemon.[58]

It must be emphasized, though, that Tremayne could not bring much direct influence to bear on the Western division since most of his estates lay in East Cornwall. Equally, Falmouth's assertion that De Dunstanville would have curbed the influence of his wife, and 'counteracted' Tremayne, but for his illness, was wishful thinking. After all, De Dunstanville had taken the lead in mobilizing support for Tremayne in 1826, and likewise backed Lemon in his elections in 1830 and 1831, so was hardly likely to desert the latter at this point.

Finally, the extent of the influence in West Cornwall of Sir Thomas Acland, who had sat in Parliament between 1812 and 1826 with Tremayne, may be questioned. The Acland land in Cornwall consisted of some 5,249 acres worth £5,648 a year, alongside much more extensive estates in Devon and Somerset. Acland's manor of Trerice, near Newlyn East, was in the West division, but the bulk of the estate was in East Cornwall. Acland was lord of the manor of Bude on the north coast and when his son, Charles, entered politics, he sat for consituencies in that part of Cornwall: East Cornwall 1882–5, and North-East division 1885–92.[59]

The outcome of the 1835 election, in fact, had been brought about by an entirely different factor. The influential Redruth Reform Committee, acting for Pendarves, and knowing that Boscawen's campaign was aimed mainly at Pendarves, planned its own campaign on the basis of exhorting the electors to vote for both sitting members. As the *West Briton* put it:

> We hope that no reformer will give plumpers to either of the Reform candidates but vote for both. It is true that a set is made against Mr Pendarves but the best and only effective way of securing him is to vote for him and Sir C. Lemon.[60]

Since the two had been linked together in the public's mind as Reformers, this was an effective and successful tactic.

In addition, influential Liberal supporters such as the young T.J. Agar-Robartes (1808–82) of Lanhydrock, who seconded Lemon's nomination, extended equal assistance to both candidates. His steward, Alfred Jenkin, was instructed to canvass the tenants on that basis. He worked closely with the Redruth committee on this joint campaign, also agreeing that:

> should cases occur in which only one vote will be given on the Liberal side, it is desirable that such votes should be placed at my disposal to be given for the benefit of either Sir C. Lemon or Mr Pendarves as the case seems to require.

He was able to report to Robartes:

> the tenants, with few exceptions, (were) disposed to vote on the Liberal side, some preferring Lemon to Pendarves and others to the contrary, evident that the current of feeling reigns strongly in favour of the Liberal candidates . . . From the union which now seems to prevail between the supporters of the Liberal candidates, Lord Boscawen will be signally defeated.[61]

It was this 'union' and the determination to support both Reform candidates, irrespective of any slight political differences between them, which had as much influence in causing Boscawen to withdraw, as Tremayne's exclusive concern for his relative. Therefore, Gash's view that 'the relics of a genuine county sentiment still remained to cut across and occasionally stultify the conventional lines of party' was not a totally accurate reflection of the political scene in Cornwall, which in the previous decade, had seen the development of genuine party political divisions.[62]

WITHDRAWAL FROM PUBLIC LIFE?

Lemon's conduct in the Commons over the next six years showed the same pattern as before. He supported the Whig choice of Abercromby, as Speaker, in February 1835, against the Conservative choice, Sir C. Sutton. He missed the vote on the Address a week later, when Peel's ministry was defeated, because of his attendence at the funeral, in Cornwall, of De Dunstanville.[63] However, he did support a similar motion, twelve months later, when Melbourne was once more Prime Minister. As before, he opposed the moves on appropriation, voting against Russell's motions, in April 1835, which brought down Peel's ministry and in July 1836 voted with the minority against the Whig government on the appropriation clause of the Irish Church Bill.[64]

The pattern continued after Lemon was returned unopposed in 1837. In 1838, when a motion to re-insert the appropriation clause in the Irish Tithe Bill was debated, he naturally voted against it.[65] Yet he supported the Whig government on other important votes. He voted against an amendment to the Address in February 1839, voted for the Whig choice of Speaker in May, and supported Melbourne on a no confidence motion in June 1840. When the Whigs were finally defeated by a single vote, on a no confidence motion, on 4 June 1841, Lemon was to be found in the minority.[66]

Some of these votes led to a degree of opposition in Cornwall to his place. A Radical opponent—Carteret Ellis—a Cornish-born London barrister, threatened to stand against him in 1837. However, Ellis received no encouragement from the recently formed official Liberal organizations. The Redruth Reform Association, chaired by Michael Williams, and the West Cornwall Reform Association, with its chairman, Humphrey Williams, both pledged support to the existing members. The *West Briton*, too, commented, 'We regret some of the votes of Sir Charles . . . yet he has violated no pledges and his principles are the same as those he professed when he came forward'. Lemon used the occasion of the election, on 5 August, to explain his votes. He denied that any of them had endangered the ministry and accused the Radicals of doing so. 'They pitch the note of contempt . . . till it has become almost a fashion to despise the Whigs.'[67]

The family interest was not called into play in 1837. In fact, Tremayne took no further part on the West Cornwall hustings after 1835. Lemon's proposers in 1837 were not family, but John Hawkins of Trewithen, at 78 the oldest freeholder in the division, and Agar-Robartes. Tremayne actually took part in the East Cornwall election, proposing the Conservative candidate, Lord Eliot. A year later, Lemon's conduct was also the subject of a strong attack in the *Royal Cornwall Gazette*, provoking him to reply: 'my conduct indicates a train of thought perfectly intelligible to every honest mind but of course not assented to by those who differ from me in the opinion that the present government ought to be supported.'[68]

There were signs that Lemon's electoral prospects were declining and that the family interest was not the force it might have been. In the spring of 1838, Lemon informed Tremayne, in confidence, that Lansdowne had proposed him for a peerage, and that John Basset —nephew and successor to part of the late De Dunstanville's estates— might come forward for the vacancy, standing on much the same political ground as Lemon. Tremayne replied: 'I cannot embark in any requisition to your successor . . . I hope never again to take much Interest in Western affairs, where I have not £400 a year, exclusive of property . . . and therefore I am not called upon to interfere.'[69] A year later, too, Falmouth, when writing to Peel about West Cornwall, 'perhaps the most radical in the kingdom', referred optimistically to the 'prospect of soon redeeming it from its present representation'.[70] Strenuous efforts were made by the Conservatives in the registration courts in 1839 and 1840, when substantial gains were claimed. A final straw in the wind was a report, in July 1840, in a London paper friendly to the Whigs, that Lemon would not stand again: a report which he, at once, denounced as 'unauthorised and untrue'.[71]

Lemon's announcement that he was standing down came on 8 June 1841, four days after the defeat of the Whig government. This was in spite of the fact that the West Cornwall Reform Association had declared its support for both sitting members and started canvassing on that basis. However, a hint about Lemon's intentions had already been given, on 31 May, by Jenkin that 'Ld Boscawen and E.W.W. Pendarves' agents are canvassing very actively, but I am not aware that anything is doing in that way on behalf of Sir Charles Lemon'. In spite of Gash's belief, there does not appear to have been any negotiation behind the scenes with Falmouth.[72]

Lemon's address did not actually give a reason for his retirement, though twelve months later, in explanation, he referred to lack of support among farmers in the division because of scare stories that protection would be withdrawn by the Whigs: 'While the panic was at its height, he felt he but little chance of success in a contest. Coupled with the sense of his impaired health, this made him resolve to withdraw from public life'.[73]

It would appear, too, that there was a loss of support from relatives and friends, which also influenced his decision. Jenkin had initially reported that 'Lady Basset, J.H. Tremayne and Canon Rogers intend to divide their influence between Ld Boscawen and Sir Charles Lemon provided that the latter does not coalesce with E.W.W. Pendarves'. Later he amended this to state 'Lady Basset, Canon Rogers and the Duke of Leeds have thrown their full weight in Ld Boscawen's scale'.[74] The support of figures like Lady Basset (De Dunstanville's daughter Frances) for the Conservative cause meant that the independent Lemon interest was breaking down in the face of the conflict between the two parties in the division.[75]

'THE LOWEST RANKS OF WHIG-RADICALISM'
Lemon's 'firm intention to withdraw from public life' only lasted six months. Lord Falmouth's death, on 29 December 1841, meant Boscawen's elevation to the title. Conservative attempts to find a candidate for the vacancy collapsed: supporters even tried writing to Peel, the Prime Minister, seeking 'pecuniary assistance' for the extra expense of living in London otherwise 'Sir C. Lemon who has thrown himself into the arms of the Radical Party has every chance of walking

over the course'. Indeed, in early January, after approaches from local Liberals, Lemon had, 'intimated his willingness to be put in nomination if a requisition to that effect, numerously and respectably signed, be presented'.[76]

The requisition was organized by the local Reform Association under Willyams. It totalled some 1,900 signatures, including Pendarves loyalists such as Scobell, Williams and the Davey brothers, as well as personal Lemon supporters like the Bullers, Rev. W. Molesworth, and members of the Fox family of Falmouth. It stressed Lemon's 'independent conduct through four successive parliaments as the best guarantee for the future'. The local paper praised him as 'one of the most independent and unwavering supporters of liberal legisation'. Lemon was at pains to deny that 'he had acted in these circumstances under the advice and influence of some of his connections of opposite politics . . . His opinions and conduct were his own and he alone was responsible for them'.[77]

There had evidently been a renewal of ties with the official Liberal bodies in the division. Willyams, Chairman of the Reform Association, seconded Agar-Robartes's nomination of Lemon at his formal return, while his election agent had been the Secretary of the Association, William Ferris. It seems both needed the other. The Liberals needed Lemon if they were to retain their monopoly of the two seats. Lemon could not do without their support, if he was to be re-elected, since the family connections were no longer sufficient, and despite his apparent reluctance, he appears to have wanted to return to the Commons. The Tory *Royal Cornwall Gazette*, in a hostile editorial, referred to loss of support from 'four, at least, of the principal landowners in the division, who are now dead against him' and that he was no part of the 'lowest ranks of Whig-Radicalism'.[78]

Once back in Parliament, Lemon's support for Russell, the Whig leader, was evident. In 1844, for example, he voted for his motion on the state of Ireland and followed the rest of the party in giving Peel total support over the various stages in the repeal of the Corn Laws, between February and May 1846. When, however, the Whigs voted, on 25 June, against the Irish Coercion Bill, in order to bring down Peel, Lemon voted in the minority in favour of the bill.[79]

In the general election of 1847, when he was again returned unopposed with Pendarves, he nevertheless pledged himself 'to support the present government' of Russell and the Whigs.[80] No opposition manifested itself, either, in 1852 when Lemon and Pendarves, now linked inextricably together, were returned again. To all intents and purposes, they were returned by the same body of opinion and the same organization, the West Cornwall Reform Association, as indicated by the considerable overlap between the proposers and seconders of the two MPs. Willyams, who had seconded Lemon's nomination in 1842, proposed Pendarves in both 1847 and 1852, while Michael Williams, having seconded Lemon in 1847, performed the same function for Pendarves in 1852. Likewise, J.S. Enys, who seconded Pendarves in 1847, nominated Lemon in 1852, while Col. Scobell, who seconded Lemon on the latter occasion, had been, with Willyams, one of Pendarves' original backers in 1826.[81] It is worth emphasizing, too, that Willyams and Lemon were related, for Sir Charles's grandmother was Anne Willyams, daughter of John Willyams of Carnanton.

On the death of Pendarves in 1853, Lemon was joined in Parliament by Michael Williams, remaining there till his own retirement in 1857. Edwin Jaggard is convinced that the Lemon connection continued to influence events even after this date, being used by Sir Charles on behalf of his two nephews. As he stated in another of his articles, 'the Liberal, Sir Charles Lemon retired but threw his support behind his nephew', John Tremayne Jnr (1825–1901) who was a Conservative candidate for West Cornwall. For reasons, which Jaggard has explained in detail elsewhere, this candidacy failed. Subsequently, the name of the younger nephew, Arthur Tremayne (1827–1905) was also mentioned as a possible Conservative candidate for the division. Jaggard believes that Sir Charles may even have used his influence in a negative fashion for: 'In the 1850s and 60s he possibly stopped John and Arthur Tremayne from standing as Conservative candidates or leading the Cornish party.'[82]

CONCLUSION

When Lemon died in February 1868, at the age of 83, his title died with him but by his will the Carclew estate passed to Arthur Tremayne, the second son of his sister Caroline, who had died in 1864. The Carclew estate which Sir William had greatly enlarged in his lifetime, consisted, according to the official Return of Owners of Land in 1874, of 8,823 acres with an annual value of £16,776. In 1865 when Arthur Tremayne was being mooted as a possible Conservative candidate for West Cornwall, the view was expressed that 'it would be unkind . . . to invite him to be a candidate . . . as he could scarcely be expected to announce a course in direct opposition to Carclew'.[83] This was certainly the last trace of the family interest.

It was Professor Gash who first drew attention to the Lemon family interest, as indicating the Cornish gentry's 'relative indifference to the feuds of reformers and anti-reformers that agitated the distant metropolis'.[84] Without doubt, the family did play a distinct role in

Cornish politics for a long time. However, the party battle in Cornwall between Reformer/Liberal and Tory/Conservative was a fierce one and gradually the family interest had to operate within that struggle, whether it wanted to or not. Eventually the Liberal elements in it were subsumed into the mainstream West Cornwall Reform Association.

If, as has been contended in this article, the Lemon connection was in decline, it may be doubted whether it was so important a factor in the Conservative failure in West Cornwall after 1832. It is certainly true that 'the ramifications of the ubiquitous Lemon connection'[85] confused the political situation. However, its actual impact upon elections, even the supposed critical one involving Boscawen's candidacy in 1835, was not that decisive. Indeed, it might be suggested that its decline was, actually, of some help to the Conservatives. It enabled the Basset/De Dunstanville influence, for example, to be thrown separately behind their efforts. In West Cornwall this was far more potent than any that might have been exerted by Tremayne, who, as we have seen earlier, acknowledged his limited influence there, playing no further part after 1835. There were, as Jaggard has himself well explained, other more valid reasons for the Conservative failure in the division than the Lemon connection. Without doubt, among the most important was the effectiveness of the local Liberal organization, a factor which still perhaps merits further investigation.

NOTES AND REFERENCES

1. Norman Gash, *Politics in the Age of Peel*, London, 1953, p. 190.
2. Edwin Jaggard's interesting article, 'Liberals and Conservatives in West Cornwall, 1832–68', in Philip Payton (ed.), *Cornish Studies: One*, Exeter, 1993, p. 21.
3. *Gentleman's Magazine*, 1824, XI, p. 641; S. Baring-Gould, *Cornish Characters and Strange Events*, 1st Series pp. 343–5; P. Payton, *Cornwall*, Fowey, 1996, p. 208. The main source for biographical detail on all Cornish figures is G.C. Boase, *Collectanea Cornubiensis*, 1890; and G.C. Boase and W.P. Courtney, *Bibliotheca Cornubiensis*, 1844–82.
4. John Lemon (1754–1814) Lieut-Col Guards, MP died unm. For his and William's parliamentary careers, see R. Thorne (ed.), *The House of Commons 1790–1820*, London, 1986, IV, pp. 412–14. Also W.T. Larence, *Parliamentary Representation of Cornwall*, 1824, p. 95. There is a portrait of Sir William, which used to hang at Carclew, facing p. 95.
5. Thorne, 1986, V, pp. 412–13 for his parliamentary career, and W.B. Elvins, 'The Reform Movement and County Politics in Cornwall 1809–52', unpub. M.A. thesis, University of Birmingham, 1959, for background of Cornish politics at the time.
6. John Gore (ed.), *Creevy's Life and Times*, London, 1934, p. 195. For Basset's career as an MP till 1796, see Lewis Namier and John Brooke

(eds), *The House of Commons 1754–1790*, London, 1964, II, pp. 62–4. Frances, daughter of his first marriage, born May 1781, was only six years younger than her step-mother (b. 1775). On her father's death, she became Baroness Basset of Stratton, dying unm. January 1855.

7. [C]ornwall [R]ecord [O]ffice Rashleigh Mss, DD(R), Mrs J. Stackhouse to W. Rashleigh, 2 February 1826.

8. C.R.O. Carew Mss vol. II, BO/23/67, Buller Papers; Copy of Poll Book December 1772. Of a total of 2,177 electors on the roll, only one did not vote, while thirty others were rejected.

9. Elvins, 1959, Chap. 1; W.P. Courtney, *Parliamentary History of Cornwall*, 1889, p. 405; H.S. Smith, *Parliaments of England* 1714–1852, (ed. F.W. Craig, London, 1973); Namier and Brooke (eds), 1964, I, p. 222, II, pp. 133–4, III, pp. 34–5.

10. C.R.O. Carlyon Mss 5M/FC/10/8, Gregor to Thos. Warren, 27 August 1789, 'the intentions of his supporters are perfectly friendly to Sir W. Lemon'.

11. Thorne, 1986, II, p. 40. His figures are slightly different from those given here, which have been derived from a copy of Poll Book. C.R.O. Paynter and Whitford Mss CP/5. Total Electorate 2,574; rejected, unpolled and dead 177; only 143 voted exclusively for St Aubyn and Gregor.

12. C.R.O. Buller Papers BO/23/63 and 69, Printed Paper 27 Sept. 1774; *West Briton*, 3 July 1818.

13. R. Polwhele, *History of Cornwall*, 1816, IV, quoted in *Gentleman's Magazine*, 1824; Thorne, 1986, IV, p. 413.

14. *Hansard* 16 (1810), 35 (1817), 37 (1818), 41 (1819), New Series 5 (1821).

15. C.R.O. Rashleigh Mss, DD(R) 5313, Rogers to W. Rashleigh 24 June 1820. In a previous letter (24 November 1919) Rogers indicated his political sympathies, 'The vigorous proceedings of the Ministers against Infidels and Incendaries . . . Do them much credit and will be attended with good effects.'

16. Thorne, 1986, IV, p. 413; *Hansard* 24 25 (1813), 34 (1816), 36 (1817), N.S. 4 (1821).

17. *Hansard* 35 (1817); Thorne, 1986, p. 413; John Cannon, *Parliamentary Reform 1640–1832*, London, 1981, Chap. 4 for the activities of Sir George Saville, Yorkshire County MP.

18. Thorne, 1986, IV, p. 413; *Hansard* 17(1810), 36 (1817), 40 (1819), N.S. 5 (1821), 7 (1822); Cannon, 1981, pp. 159–61, 170–4, 184, for details of some of these proposals.

19. *West Briton*, 16 October 1812; *Hansard* 35 (1817) p. 143, 'The petitioners left the subject of reform to be considered by the superior wisdom and sound discretion of the House. With these views he cordially concurred.'

20. *Hansard* N.S. 8 (1823).

21. *West Briton*, 16 June 1826, speech at nomination; Thorne, 1986, V. p. 413, a remark by Joseph Phillimore in 1818.

22. *Hansard* 25 (1813), 33 (1816), 36 (1817), 41 (1819) N.S. 4 (1821); Thorne, 1986, V, p. 413. He referred to 'Catholic Emancipation and Parliamentary Reform, both of which I abhor' in letter to his father 30 May 1818, but in

18 April 1821 letter, said 'I own I cannot say I wish it (Emancipation) longer withheld'. C.R.O. Tremayne Mss 119.

23. *West Briton*, 15 May 1818.

24. *West Briton*, 17 December 1824; *Royal Cornwall Gazette* 3 October 1824, 20 November 1824, 4 and 18 December 1824; [R]oyal [I]nstitution [C]orn-wall, Jenkin Letterbooks, A. Jenkin to Mrs A.M. Agar. 29 November 1824, enclosing letter from W. Davey Jnr of Redruth 10 Novemer, 'In consequence of the canvass of Sir R. Vyvyan . . . the Friends of Mr Pendarves have serious thoughts of putting him in nomination as a person more eligible'.

25. William Peter of Chiverton, Chairman of the election committee, William Davey Jnr his election agent, and Rev. William Hockin, Rector of Phillack were all active in the Reform party with Pendarves.

26. Humphrey Willyams (1792–1872), partner in the Miners Bank and copper-smelting firm of Sims, Willyams and Co., MP Truro 1848–52. John Scobell (1779–1866), Lieut-Col. Mounts Bay Militia, Chairman Board of Guardians 1847–66.

27. Michael Williams (1785–1858) developed Gwennap mines, MP West Cornwall 1853–58. The Davey family [Steph (1785–1864), Will (1789–1849), Rich (1799–1864), MP West Cornwall 1857–68] were solicitors in Redruth and managers of the mines of the Williams family. See John Rowe, *Cornwall in the Age of the Industrial Revolution*, Liverpool, 1953.

28. *West Briton*, 17 December 1824, 17 January 1825: 'If sent to Parliament he would certainly support any motion that might be made for an enquiry into the state of the representation, but he was pledged to no particular plan.'

29. *Royal Cornall Gazette*, 18 December 1824; C.R.O. Carew Mss CC/N/58 Mt Edgcumbe to Carew 20 December 1824. The Earl of St Germans replied, likewise, to Pendarves: 'I should not have gone about to have dug you out an opponent but . . . I feel it too repugnant to my ideas of what is the true balance of the three estates of the country to be able to wish you success in this matter . . . I regret that my political principles lead me to decide against personal regard.' C.R.O. Pendarves Mss 16 December 1824.

30. *West Briton*, 24 December 1824.

31. On first meeting Vyvyan in 1820 Tremayne commented to his father (8 March): 'I have seldom seen a young man whom I liked better on a short acquaintance . . . I am much mistaken if he does not one day become a Customer for the Representation of this country and I really think it is a great thing for the County.' Tremayne Mss.

32. *West Briton*, 7 January 1825.

33. Carew Mss CC/N/58, Vyvyan to Carew, January 1825, ('It would be a source of considerable mortification to me if my succeeding Sir W. Lemon should be the cause of weakening Mr Tremayne's influence'.) and Vyvyan's note to Carew 31 October 1825.

34. Carew CC/N/59, Carew to Rev. W. Molesworth 1 June 1826.

35. *Royal Cornwall Gazette*, 12 February 1825, *West Briton*, 9 and 16 June 1826.

36. Carew CC/N/59, Tremayne to Carew 4 March 1826.
37. Carew CC/N/58, De Dunstanville to Carew 13 September 1825.
38. *West Briton*, 2 June; *Royal Cornwall Gazette*, 3 June 1826. Sir Charles's family tragedies—dealt with later—would have hindered his efforts to help Tremayne before this time.
39. Thorne, 1986, II, p. 40.
40. *Royal Cornwall Gazette*, 10 June, *West Briton*, 2 June 1826. Tremayne succeeded to the family estates in Cornwall and Devon on his father's death, 10 February 1829. In 1874 they totalled 9,539 acres worth £11,929 a year. Financial considerations may not, therefore, have been so crucial to his decision as Thorne suggests (1986, II, p. 41). It was more a feeling that his past services merited an unopposed return.
41. R.I.C. Jenkin Letterbooks, 22 June 1826. For Vyvyan's later political career, See Brian Bradfield, 'Sir R. Vyvyan and Tory Politics 1825–46', unpub. Ph.D. thesis, University of London, and articles in *English Historical Review*, October 1968, and *University of Birmingham Historical Journal*, 1968.
42. Carew CC/N/59, De Dunstanville to Carew, 23, 31 October, 13 November, 5 December 1826.
43. *West Briton*, 13 August 1830; Rev. W. Molesworth to Pendarves 17 August 1830, Pendarves Mss. Molesworth had, also, on 17 June 1826, appealled, in vain, to Carew to persuade Vyvyan to withdraw in favour of Tremayne. Carew CC/N/59.
44. Thorne, 1986, IV, p. 411; *Hansard* 16, 17 (1810), 21 (1812).
45. C.R.O. Memoirs of Loveday Sarah Gregor (1792–1864), p. 299. The memoirs were started in 1851.
46. *Hansard* 3rd Ser., 1 (1830), 3 (1831).
47. Carew CC/N/64, Lemon to Carew, 30 March, 5 April 1830, Carew's reply 2 April. On 31 March, Vyvyan was consulting with Carew about his election tactics!
48. *West Briton*, 6 May 1931. Another relative, J.W. Buller, replaced him at the election on 10 May.
49. *West Briton*, 13 May 1831, 20 May 1831, *Royal Cornwall Gazette*, 14 May 1831, 21 May 1831.
50. *West Briton*, 20 May 1831, 3 June 1831. Elvins, 1959, Appendix 6.
51. *Hansard* 3rd Ser. 4–7 (1831), 10, 12 (1832); W.B. 9 March 1832.
52. *Hansard* 3rd Ser. 18 (1833), 22–5 (1834); W.B. 16 January 1835.
53. J.P. Peters to Lemon 22 March 1834, quoted in report of 1837 election, *West Briton*, 11 August 1837. For the Derby Dilly see R. Stewart, *The Foundation of the Conservative Party 1830–1867*, London, 1978, pp. 108–18, 376, and D.W.J. Johnson 'Sir James Graham and "the Derby Dilly" ', *University of Birmingham Historical Journal*, IV, 1953.
54. *West Briton*, 21 December 1832.
55. B.L. Add Mss 40408 ff88–90, 40409 ff17–23, 40302 f144, f156, 40410 f32.
56. *West Briton*, 16 January 1835. Tremayne emphasized that Lemon 'asks for your suffrages for himself, not connected with any other candidate'.
57. Gash, 1953, pp. 189–92.

58. Lemon missed an important vote on the Pensions List in February 1834, because of De Dunstanville's illness. R.C.G. 1 March 1834 and Peters to Lemon, 22 March 1834 (see note 53).

59. A.H.D. Acland (ed.), *Memoirs and Letters of Sir Thomas Dyke Acland*, London, 1902, Chap. 2; John Betjeman, *Cornwall*, London, 1964, p. 25; Return of Owners of Land (1874): Somerset 20,300 acres, Devon 19,225 acres.

60. *West Briton*, 26 December 1834, 9 January 1835. Chairman was Thomas Teague. William and Stephen Davey were Committee members.

61. R.I.C. Jenkin Letterbooks, A. Jenkin to W. Johns and T.J. Agar-Robartes, 5 January 1835. Thomas James Agar had taken the additional surname of Robartes in 1822, on inheriting the extensive Lanhydrock estate from his mother, A.M. Agar, the wife of the Hon. C.B. Agar. She and her son returned to Lanhydrock to live, in July 1826, after an 18-year absence. (*Royal Cornwall Gazette*, 22 July 1826). In the 1874 Return, the size of the estate was given as 22,234 acres worth £30,730 a year.

62. Gash, 1953, p. 190.

63. De Dunstanville died 5 February 1835. See Payton, 1996, p. 207 for account of the funeral.

64. *Hansard* 3rd Ser. 26–29 (1835), 31, 34 (1836). See Derek Beales, 'Parliamentary Parties and the "Independent" member, 1810–1860', in R. Robson (ed.), *Ideas and Institutions of Victorian Britain*, London, 1967, for a perceptive analysis of voting patterns on crucial motions, and also T.A. Jenkins, *Parliamentary, Party and Politics in Victorian Britain*, London, 1996.

65. *Hansard* 3rd Ser. 44 (1838).

66. *Hansard* 3rd Ser. 45 47 (1839), 51 (1840), 58 (1841).

67. *West Briton*, 18 November 1836, 19 May 1837, 11 August 1837. The Redruth Committee had become the Redruth Reform Association, and likewise the Reform Committee of the West division had become the West Cornwall Reform Association in June 1835. William Davey was its Treasurer and William Ferris of Truro, its Secretary. (*West Briton*, 6 February 1835, 12 June 1835, 26 June 1835.)

68. *West Briton*, 11 August 1837, *Royal Cornwall Gazette*, 15 June 1838.

69. C.R.O. Tremayne Mss, Bundle 114, Lemon to Tremayne, 18 May and Tremayne's reply, 20 May 1838.

70. B.L. Add. Mss 40426 ff283–7; Falmouth to Peel 9, 19 May and Peel's reply 12 May 1939.

71. *Royal Cornwall Gazette*, 18 October 1839, 9 October 1840; *Royal Cornwall Gazette*, 24 July 1840 and *West Briton*, 31 July 1840.

72. *West Briton*, 28 May 1841; Jenkin Letterbooks, Jenkin to Agar-Robartes, 31 May 1841; Gash, 1953, p. 191.

73. *West Briton*, 4 February 1842, report of meeting at Penzance.

74. Jenkin Letterbooks, Jenkin to Agar-Robartes, 22 May. C.R.O. Robartes Mss, Jenkin to Mrs Agar 1 June 1841. Tremayne would still appear to have been loyal to Lemon. For Lady Basset, see note 6.

75. *West Briton*, 30 July 1841 and 6 August 1841 indicate that Lemon's

relations with Pendarves were not all that cordial with Lemon denying a Pendarves claim that Lemon's friends had forced him to break up his coalition with Pendarves.

76. B.L. Add. Mss 40501 ff130–36; G.W.F. Gregor to Peel, 29 January, 3 February and Peel's reply 31 January 1842; Jenkin Letterbooks, Jenkin to Agar-Robartes, 10 January 1842.

77. *West Briton*, 14 January 1842, 21 January 1842, 4 February 1842. For Lemon's close relations with the Fox family, see Horace Pym (ed.), *Caroline Fox's Memories of Old Friends*, 1883.

78. *Royal Cornwall Gazette*, 4 February 1842. Information about Ferris in Jenkin's letter Agar-Robartes, 24 January 1842.

79. *Hansard* 3rd Ser. 73 (1844), 84–7 (1846).

80. *West Briton*, 23 July 1847.

81. *West Briton*, 12 August 1847, 23 July 1852.

82. Edwin Jaggard, '"The Age Derby" outside Parliament: New Orthodoxy for Old?' pp. 62–83, especially pp. 67 and 73, in *Journal of the Royal Institution of Cornwall* [JRIC], Vol. 10, 1986–7, and Jaggard, 1993, pp. 25–7.

83. C.R.O. Vyvyan Mss, 22/M/BO/36/46, J.J. Rogers to Sir R. Vyvyan, 5 June 1865. John Tremayne Jnr was Conservative MP for East Cornwall, 1874–80, and Arthur Tremayne was Conservative MP for Truro 1878–80. Carclew was destroyed by fire in 1934, and no Lemon manuscripts appear to have survived.

84. Gash, 1953, p. 190.

85. Jaggard, 1993, pp. 17–28.

SOCIALISM AND THE OLD LEFT: THE LABOUR PARTY IN CORNWALL DURING THE INTER-WAR PERIOD

Garry Tregidga

INTRODUCTION

A consistent feature of Cornish politics in the twentieth century has been the failure of the Labour Party to establish itself as one of the two main parties in the region. Even in 1945, when Labour swept to a landslide majority in the House of Commons, the party was still in third place in Cornwall with only a quarter of the vote. This electoral marginalization, demonstrated more recently in the 1997 election with just a solitary victory in Falmouth and Camborne, reflects the party's wider problem in identifying with the political and social culture of the region. While the Liberals, and even some Conservatives, have been able to exploit regional discontent and develop a distinctly Cornish image, Labour candidates since the Second World War have found it difficult, as Payton put it, to 'present themselves in a "Cornish" light'.[1] Despite the notable exception of Harold Hayman, MP for Falmouth and Camborne (1950–66), Labour has been portrayed as not just the third party but also the metropolitan party: an irrelevance to the local Liberal versus Conservative alignment.

In order to understand this failure we must analyse the party's regional experience during the crucial period between the two world wars. The formative decades of the 1920s and 1930s created a new class-based political system that relegated the Liberal Party to third place. Although the old political order effectively survived in Cornwall, I will suggest that the socialist challenge was more significant than is usually recognized. West Cornwall was actually regarded as a potential

Labour stronghold in the immediate post-war years, while by the 1930s the party was trying to create a local image based on its concern for regional economic problems and the area's cultural identity. The aim of this article, therefore, is to explain the failure of the socialist incursion into Cornwall, noting the party's early potential and suggesting some reasons for its failure to sustain this breakthrough after the early 1920s. It concludes with a study of the second socialist challenge in the 1930s that also provides fresh insight into both the political career of the late A.L. Rowse and the changing nature of the Celto-Cornish movement.

ON THE ROAD TO SOCIALISM

The dramatic rise of the Labour Party in the first quarter of the twentieth century has been well documented. This is particularly the case at the regional level with a growing number of studies on the party's industrial or urban strongholds, places such as Yorkshire, Nottingham and Clydeside, where the breakthrough of socialism seemed almost inevitable.[2] Yet Labour historians rarely look at those areas like Cornwall where the party failed to make a breakthrough during this period. On a superficial basis the region certainly appears to be a political backwater. The first socialist intervention at the parliamentary level was by a SDF (Social Democratic Front) candidate at Camborne in 1906 who polled a derisory vote of just 1.5 per cent. Labour failed to undermine the supremacy of Cornish Liberialism during the so-called 'Age of Alignment' in the 1920s, and it was not until 1945 that the party won a seat in Cornwall. It is no wonder that Claude Berry, president of Bodmin Divisional Labour Party, concluded in 1929 that it was in 'areas like Cornwall, where the population is so scattered, where individuality is . . . so ingrained, and where our creed and our programme are . . . imperfectly understood and appreciated, that we have our hardest task'.[3]

However, at the beginning of the inter-war period Cornwall was actually at the forefront in the rise of socialism. A remarkable feature of the local contests in the 1918 election was the respectable showing of Labour. Although the party lacked a pre-war parliamentary tradition in Cornwall, its two candidates, George Nicholls at Camborne and A.E. Dunn at St Ives, both achieved good results with 48.0 and 38.4 per cent of the vote respectively (see Table 1). This was particularly the case in Camborne where it was commonly accepted that if the prospective Conservative candidate had returned from India in time for the election, Nicholls would probably have won the seat. What is even more surprising is the fact that the party was more successful in Cornwall than in some other parts of Britain more usually considered as socialist strongholds. Both Sheffield and Stepney had

Table 1: A comparative study of election results in selected constituencies in 1918 and 1929

Area	Seat	Election	Labour	Liberal	Co Liberal	Conservative	Other
West Cornwall	Camborne	1918	48.0%	52.0%	–	–	–
		1929	25.3%	35.8%	–	32.6%	6.3%
	St Ives	1918	38.4%	–	58.6%	–	3.0%
		1929	17.1%	43.2%	–	39.7%	–
Sheffield	Attercliffe	1918	34.7%	–	65.3%	–	–
		1929	60.3%	14.7%	–	19.5%	1.0%
	Hillsborough	1918	26.6%	–	73.4%	–	–
		1929	57.3%	13.9%	–	28.8%	–
Stepney	Limehouse	1918	25.2%	–	59.9%	14.9%	–
		1929	55.9%	16.6%	–	26.5%	1.0%
	Mile End	1918	25.1%	11.7%	–	63.2%	–
		1929	47.1%	22.6%	–	30.3%	–
Bermondsey	Rotherhithe	1918	15.5%	34.5%	–	50.0%	–
		1929	61.6%	19.1%	–	19.3%	–
	West	1918	18.6%	40.6%	28.5%	–	12.3%
		1929	60.2%	22.2%	–	17.6%	–
Methyr Tydfil	Aberdare	1918	21.4%	–	–	–	78.6%
		1929	64.6%	23.3%	–	12.2%	–
	Merthyr	1918	47.3%	–	52.7%	–	–
		1929	59.6%	22.8%	–	17.6%	–

emerged as key Labour areas by the late 1920s, but in the first post-war election relatively low shares of the vote, roughly only a fifth to a third, were normal. Labour's share of the vote was actually greater in Camborne and St Ives than it was in future strongholds like Bermondsey, Doncaster, Aberavon and Motherwell, while the result in Camborne was even fractionally better than in that great socialist citadel of Merthyr.[4]

The early success of the Labour party in West Cornwall was undoubtedly linked to the local expansion of the trade union movement. During the First World War the Workers Union had established a 'strong and effective membership' in the area as wartime conditions enabled union activists to build up support amongst two key groups: tin miners and munitions workers.[5] This was particularly the case in the Camborne or Mining Division where as early as 1917 Francis Acland, the sitting Liberal MP, was seriously considering the idea of withdrawing in favour of a Labour candidate because of the growing significance of the left-wing threat in his constituency. Socialist activists were able to build on a radical tradition established by C.A.V. Conybeare's victory over the local Liberal establishment back in 1885 when the Mining Division was, as Deacon put it, 'at the leading edge of British politics'. On that occasion it was a 'self-confident and egalitarian community' of working men and small tradesmen that guaranteed victory for the Radical cause.[6] By 1918 that same spirit was providing the motivation for a left-wing challenge. Towards the end of the previous year Acland was already informing his wife that the power of the Labour movement was at least equal to counties more usually regarded as Labour strongholds:

> We only got 30 at the meeting in Redruth yesterday out of 200 [invitations] sent out. I think the Labour party have sent word round to the working men that they're not to come, and they feel proud of staying away. At nine meetings I've had under 300 people & I doubt if one could pick out nine villages in Yorks or Lancs where I should have had such a poor attendence.[7]

The development of the Labour movement in the central mining district was echoed in other parts of Cornwall. In 1914 the Workers Union had only 400 members in Cornwall, but by 1918 membership had apparently risen to over 15,000 and the union was now targeting agricultural labourers, especially in the area around Truro. Apart from the general environment of the war years, local factors had also contributed to this process in areas like St Austell where the defeat of the 1913 clay strike had led to a considerable increase in union membership. These developments were obviously going to increase the political significance of the trade unions in Cornwall. As S.C. Behenna, Cornwall organizer for the Workers Union, remarked in 1918, 'when he commenced his work in the county he was snubbed by the leaders of the two political parties; today those leaders were saying to him, "Behenna, shall we come on the platform with you?" ' But the Labour movement was determined that its interests would not be represented after the war by the old parties. In February 1918 twenty trade unions and local co-operative associations held a meeting in Truro which called on Labour to contest every seat in Cornwall since 'they had no concern for either Liberal or Tory'.[8]

This early period also showed signs of a weakening of the special relationship between Liberalism and Methodism. It was symbolic that Nicholls preached at Pool Wesley Chapel during the 1918 election campaign, while the Rev. Booth Coventry, one of the leaders of the 1913 clay strike, was an active campaigner for the local Labour movement after the war. Even the Rev. J.H. Rider, chairman of the Cornish District of the Wesleyan Methodists, declared that Methodism would be a strong ally of the Labour Party in its 'fight for the underdog'.[9] Many new converts from Liberalism still retained the old belief that one of the principal objectives of a progressive party was to campaign against the vested interest of the 'drink trade'. For example, W.G. Uglow, the president of the Cornwall Division of the Sons of Temperance Friendly Society, was also a leading member of the executive committee of the Camborne Divisional Labour Party, and in October 1920 he persuaded his local party to adopt a virtually 'prohibitionist' scheme for the closure of 90 per cent of public houses in Cornwall.[10] By courting support from the Free Churches, Labour was further consolidating the party's claim to be the natural heir of pre-war Cornish Radicalism.

In addition, the socialist challenge was gaining respectability in local government. In Britain as a whole the municipal elections of 1919 witnessed a massive breakthrough for the party in urban centres like Liverpool, Bradford and Nottingham. Although there is a tendency to focus on the independent tradition in local government in Cornwall, this advance was also reflected in the region at this time. Indeed, recent research by Crago suggests that even back in 1904 SDF or Labour candidates were polling an average vote of about 25 per cent in local elections in Truro, and W.A. Philips, one of the party's candidates, won a seat on the city council in a by-election during that year. When Philips became the Mayor of Truro in 1919, he also became the first Labour member to hold that office in the entire South West of

Britain.[11] The party won a number of local victories in the Redruth/ Camborne and St Austell areas in the immediate post-war period, but what was perhaps even more surprising was Labour's success outside of the main centres of population at places like Tregony and Indian Queens. A good example occurred in 1920 when Labour won a notable victory in a County Council by-election for the essentially agricultural ward of Grampound with their candidate winning over 60 per cent of the vote in a straight fight with the Liberals.[12]

This ability to advance into other areas was significant since the rural hinterland of Cornwall, particularly in the eastern half of the county, was hardly ideal territory for the new party. The absence of any large-scale industry ensured that the majority of businesses employed only a small workforce, while landscape and climate encouraged a pastoral form of agriculture based on small family farms of 50 acres or under. It was basically only four groups, railwaymen, quarrymen, dockers and lorry drivers, who tended to join a trade union in the 1920s, and this naturally limited the potential Labour vote. The party therefore required a secure base, such as West Cornwall, from which it could expand into the east of the region. A model for this process can be seen in Wales where the Labour Party first established a core area in the southern mining seats during the years immediately before and after the First World War. Having obtained credibility and electoral strength it was natural to expand into the more remote parts of the Principality. Although this proved to be a slow process, by the early 1950s Labour was finally replacing the Liberals as the premier party in rural North Wales.[13]

This form of realignment obviously did not happen in Cornwall since there was no permanent Labour base until Hayman's victory at Falmouth and Camborne in 1950. Even the possibility of expansion from Plymouth did not occur because the strength of the dockyard and Royal Navy interests ensured that many working-class voters were unwilling to commit themselves to Labour until after the Second World War.[14] Yet in the short term the signs were promising, as the early socialist advance in Camborne was echoed elsewhere. The unlikely rural constituency of North Cornwall adopted a prospective Labour candidate in 1920, while a divisional party was formed in the following year.[15] The party was even more active in the mid-Cornwall constituency of Penryn and Falmouth, a seat that also covered Truro and the china-clay area around St Austell. Joe Harris, a trade-union organizer in Cornwall, was selected as prospective candidate in 1920, and with financial support from the trade unions the party was able to appoint C.A. Millman, the former secretary of the Bodmin Liberal Association, as its full-time agent. By 1922 the local party, with over

800 members, was organized in twenty-five polling districts, and had established active branches in the villages of Roche, Trewoon and Foxhole: the heartland of the old mid-Cornwall Liberalism. In contrast, the demoralized Liberal Association had failed to select a candidate, while local propaganda work in the area was negligible. Political observers predicted that the next election would see a straight fight between Labour and the Conservatives.[16]

The evidence, then, for the immediate post-war years suggests that the process of transition from Liberal to Labour was taking place in Cornwall, perhaps even more rapidly than in many other regions of Britain. There was widespread apathy amongst the Liberals following their disappointing result in the 1918 election when Camborne was the only seat in Cornwall to elect an Asquithian candidate. Following Acland's decision in 1920 to stand down at the next election, local newspapers were talking of the 'Swan Song' of Cornish Liberalism. The Labour Party was not slow to recognize that it now had a unique opportunity to exploit the vacuum in centre-left politics in Cornwall. Indeed, the party's national leadership regarded Camborne 'as a seat that must be won at any cost', and this outside interest was demonstrated in 1920 when W.J. Abrahams, the president of the National Union of Railwaymen and a leading figure in the party, was adopted as prospective parliamentary candidate.[17] With the party gradually strengthening its position throughout the rest of the peninsula, an electoral breakthrough for the Cornish Labour movement seemed almost inevitable by the early 1920s.

THE LIBERAL RESURGENCE

By 1923, however, the political situation in Cornwall had changed completely. In the general election of that year the Liberals, regarded even locally as a spent force just a year or two previously, swept to a landslide victory in all five constituencies. Labour, in contrast, barely saved its deposit in St Ives, which was the only seat that the party contested. Even the electoral disaster of the following year confirmed that the Liberals were still the main alternative to the Conservatives, and in 1929 the party once again completely monopolized Cornwall's parliamentary representation. Not surprisingly, the socialists came third in all five constituencies at this election. Tactical voting in the predominantly rural divisions of Bodmin and North Cornwall ensured that the Labour candidates polled less than a tenth of the vote, while even in the industrial heartland of West Cornwall the party's share of the vote was well down on 1918 (see Table 1). It was a result which naturally frustrated local Labour supporters. Within less than a decade the political image of Cornwall had been transformed from a likely future as a Labour stronghold to the popular view that it was now the 'last refuge of Liberalism'.[18]

Although further research is required in order to really explain the failure of the Labour challenge in the early 1920s, we can at least identify some possible explanations. In the first place Isaac Foot's sensational victory at the Bodmin by-election in February 1922 gave a psychological advantage to the Liberals since his revivalist campaign restored the party as the true heir to the old Radical tradition. Party activists in neighbouring constituencies were suddenly talking of a 'great revival' of Liberalism in the region, while new candidates were selected for Penryn and Falmouth and Camborne.[19] This revival totally undermined Labour's strategy of acting as a surrogate Liberal party. Leading activists like Dunn and Millman had deliberately concentrated on traditional radical issues like temperance and the cost of living which had proved popular when the Liberals had been demoralized at the end of the war. Although this strategy was now redundant, the party's position was not helped by well-publicized calls from some activists, such as Harris, for a more left-wing stance.[20] An analysis of local election results in 1922 suggests a considerable decline in support and morale throughout the region. For example, in the St Austell district there was only a limited and unsuccessful challenge by the party, while three of its five candidates came bottom of the poll at Redruth.[21]

Perhaps the main problem, however, was the collapse of the Labour vote in the Camborne seat, the powerhouse of socialist politics in Cornwall. In the 1922 election there was a dramatic decline in Labour fortunes in the Mining Division with the party polling just over a fifth of the vote in a three-cornered contest. Local observers questioned the party's ability to recover from such a 'staggering blow', and this proved to be an accurate prediction, since the Labour vote barely increased above the 20–25 per cent level until 1945. Internal problems had certainly contributed to this defeat. Abrahams had resigned as candidate before the election because of inter-union rivalry in the area, while it is surprising that in 1922 the Camborne branch of the Workers Union, which had 2,000 members, was not affiliated to the local Labour Party.[22] But the underlying reason for this decline was undoubtedly the collapse of the tin industry after the war. Although the party's rise was possibily assisted by the anger generated by the first wave of mine closures, the prospect of long-term employment after 1920 was disastrous. The terrible social consequences of unemployment and poverty totally undermined the old confidence of the movement. It was also reported in the local press that emigration had 'considerably weakened' the party in the area as key activists left in search of employment, while many voters supported Algernon Moreing, the Lloyd George Liberal candidate, in the desperate hope that he could restore the industry's 'old prosperity' because of his financial interests in mining. Labour could thereafter make little progress in a climate of apathy and despair, and by the 1930s the constituency organization had virtually ceased to exist.[23]

Economic problems also affected other sources of support. Howard suggests that unions representing agricultural labourers 'suffered more than most' from the onset of depression in 1921. Falling membership, due to rural poverty and indifference from the national Labour movement, ensured that local union branches were in 'no position to lead a Labour assault on the countryside', and in rural areas like East Anglia the party actually lost electoral support throughout the 1920s.[24] In Cornwall there was the added problem that the union movement had just started to target agricultural labourers after the war, and it was significant that it was not until 1929 that Labour finally put forward candidates in the rural seats of East Cornwall. The china-clay industry also found it difficult to recover its pre-war share of the market. The production figure for the early 1920s was actually lower than the 1880s, and this resulted in the closure of a large number of clay pits in the St Austell area. By 1922 it was said that the 'tramping business was becoming a profession' due to the large number of unemployed clay workers wandering around the district in search of work. In the general election of that year the Labour candidate for Penryn and Falmouth polled less than a fifth of the vote. This disappointing result undermined the morale of the party just as it was becoming a serious force, and leading figures in the local party like Harris and Millman retired from active politics after the election.[25]

This loss of momentum, particularly in the tin and china clay areas, came at a crucial moment for the party since its social and electoral foundations in Cornwall were still fragile. Payton claims that the Cornish Liberals were able to survive as the 'fossilized' alternative to the Conservatives after the First World War since Cornwall's dismal economic position had created a 'Politics of Paralysis'. The process of de-industrialization, which followed the collapse of the mining industry in the late nineteenth century, had prevented the emergence of a confident and secular trade-union movement, and it was left to religious nonconformity, still entrenched as the dominant and conser-vative force in Cornish society, to provide the focus for centre-left politics.[26] The existence of such a negative environment obviously raises the question as to why the post-war Labour advance even took place. A possible explanation comes from Perry's ongoing research into Cornwall's economic history which suggests that there was a 'remission in the Great Paralysis' during the years leading up to the First World War. By this time the working population had basically recovered to the level of the 1860s, while large productivity increases had occurred for important sectors of the local economy like mining and agriculture.[27] This brief recovery, combined with the development of trade unionism as a result of wartime conditions, presumably stimulated the surprising breakthrough of the Labour Party in 1918. Developing this theme, we can perhaps conclude that the immediate post-war years hint at an alternative political future for Cornwall, perhaps more similar to the Welsh experience, but because of weak foundations the socialist challenge was then swept aside by the long-term reality of paralysis and economic depression.

Indeed, the old order rapidly re-established itself. This was particularly the case with the Liberal Party's links with the Free Churches since Foot's victory in the Bodmin by-election provided the Cornish Methodists with a charismatic spokesman at Westminster. In the following year Foot was joined by Leif Jones, Liberal MP for Camborne, who was well known to Cornish voters as the president of a leading temperance organization and son of a famous poet-preacher from Wales. Labour, in contrast, failed to select any Nonconformist candidates with a similar reputation since Cornwall was no longer regarded as a potential stronghold. There were other problems for Labour. The dominance of Wesleyan Methodism in the Camborne division made it difficult for the party to consolidate its position. Labour tended to fare better in the urban centres like Derby where, as Thorpe put it, free church membership was 'spread among the various denominations' or in those areas, as in Durham, where Primitive Methodism was the main nonconformist denomination.[28] Labour had some hopes of attracting support from the United Methodists, the old Bible Christians, but apart from some of the eastern villages in the china-clay district the party was unsuccessful. In the rural Bible Christian belt of North Cornwall and Bodmin, the Liberal–Free Church alliance was even more intact. Weinbren stresses the importance of the social and communal activities of the British Labour movement at this time, but in the rural villages of Cornwall the chapel survived as the social centre of the community. This environment naturally preserved the old social system, and the rural Methodists, in particular, tended to follow the lead of their lay preachers, their local heroes, who remained loyal to the Liberal cause.[29]

It is interesting that the eventual survival of the tradional alignment in Cornish politics reflects Rokkan's model of centre–periphery politics. Rokkan's work was based on the political history of Scandinavia where socialist parties, the New Left, had established an early supremacy at the state level because of support in urban and industrial areas. In the remote Nordic countryside, however, the pre-dominance of small farms, the relative strength of religious nonconformity and an essentially 'egalitarian class structure' preserved a traditional culture which provided a more secure environment for the Old Left, the Liberal and Agrarian parties. In practical terms this regional political culture, according to Rokkan, was based on three core factors: (1) the anti-metropolitan hostility of a subject province; (2) a belief that the economic needs of rural communities were ignored by urban-based parties; and (3) the survival of religious Non-conformity.[30] Voters at the local level were, therefore, subject to conflicting influences by the 1920s, and this created a complex and interactive process with the dominant cleavage, class politics or a combination of local factors, shifting from election to election.

In a Cornish context this process was quite evident after the First World War. Once the threat from the Labour Party had been removed, the Liberals were able to dominate the local political debate by focusing on Old Left issues like temperance and free trade. The appeal of temperance to Cornish voters is not surprising given the strength of religious Nonconformity, but the region's free-trade tradition was equally important. This was demonstrated in 1923 when the Liberals, with the support of local Labour activists, were able to sweep to a landslide victory by exploiting the fear that the first signs of recovery in virtually all of Cornwall's staple industries, such as china clay, agriculture, mining, shipping and fishing, would be undermined if a tariff system was imposed for the benefit of other regions. Although class politics emerged as the dominant cleavage in the subsequent election of 1924, it was significant that it was the Conservatives, and not Labour, who really benefited from the class issue as many middle-class Liberals apparently moved to the right in order to prevent the return of a socialist government. By the end of the decade the focus had moved back to a local agenda. Religious issues like temperance and anti-Catholicism dominated the 1929 election campaign, and the Liberals regained their traditional supremacy throughout Cornwall.[31] Once again the Labour Party had been marginalized. Unable to establish a smooth transition from Liberal to Labour in the early part of the decade, it was now relegated to the sidelines in a contest based on traditional issues.

BACK TO RADICALISM

Yet the 1930s were to witness another bid by the Labour Party to undermine the supremacy of Cornish Liberalism. Economic paralysis in the west of Cornwall meant that the main focus in socialist activity now moved to mid-Cornwall where a new generation of Labour activists recognized that a breakthrough would only succeed if the party stressed its continuity with pre-war Radicalism. In one sense this was a return to the strategy of the immediate post-war period when Labour was able to benefit from the problems confronting the Liberal party. But under the effective leadership of A.L. Rowse, the parliamentary candidate for Penryn and Falmouth in the 1930s, a more sophisticated approach to strategy was developed. Labour was now presented as the party which could champion local interests, ranging from Nonconformity to Tyr ha Tavas (Land and Language), while it was claimed that the next Labour government would finally address the deep-seated problems confronting the Cornish economy. Although this anti-metropolitan stance was short-lived, partly on the grounds that there were few natural champions of such a strategy once Rowse dropped out of active politics in the early 1940s, it marked an important stage in the emergence of a distinctive political agenda for Cornwall.

The early part of the decade was not a very positive time for either Labour or the Liberals. The formation of the National government in 1931 divided the Liberals into three factions and led to a dramatic reduction in the number of Labour MPs in the House of Commons, falling from 288 to 52 at the subsequent election. But it soon became obvious after 1931 that it was the Liberal Party that was the real loser. Against the background of poor by-election results, local government defeats and further defections, the Liberals soon gave the impression that they were fighting for their very existence. Even in Cornwall, where the Liberal tradition was more deeply entrenched than in many other parts of Britain, this sense of hopelessness was clearly evident. In 1934 Sir Ronald Wilberforce Allen, the party's candidate for Penryn and Falmouth, declared that party activists must 'not apologise for our existence as Liberals. There is a tendency to feel ashamed to call ourselves Liberals, we must not go on talking as if we are just the remnants of a defunct party'.[32]

However, the Labour Party was actually doing quite well at this time. At the national level it was winning parliamentary by-elections and municipal elections, mainly at the expense of the Liberals, and this favourable environment provided an opportunity for the Cornish Labour movement. The local party was certainly not slow to take advantage of this new situation. Prospective parliamentary candidates were selected for Camborne and Bodmin, while by 1934 the party was once again winning seats in local government in towns like Falmouth, Truro, Liskeard and Lostwithiel.[33] In 1932 the party even launched its own monthly newspaper, the *Cornish Labour News*, which was an idea

proposed by Rowse and Claude Berry, a journalist and author. This
newspaper, under Berry's editorial leadership, made a conscious
attempt to appeal to regional sentiment. Articles on local economic
problems, such as unemployment and the plight of the Cornish fishing
industry, went alongside items of historical or cultural interest. For
example, the early editions of the paper focused on ideas for an
economic plan for Cornwall that could be implemented by the next
Labour government.[34] The existence of the *Cornish Labour News* was
significant in the sense that it finally provided a focus for the party to
present a distinctly local image.

Rowse emerged as the main advocate of this strategy. In 1931 his
election campaign had been undermined by accusations that he was an
atheist and a dangerous revolutionary preaching an alien gospel. This
experience confirmed his belief that in order to win Cornish seats like
Penryn and Falmouth it was essential that Labour should adapt its
message to local conditions. In short, the party needed to stress
its continuity with the old Radical cause and a wider commitment to
the Cornish way of life, both economically and socially. Religion was
an obvious area. Although Rowse was later to write of the 'humbug' of
Cornish Methodism, he presented himself in the mid 1930s as the
political champion of Nonconformist issues like temperance. This was
made quite obvious in the general election of 1935 when he inserted a
message of support from a local Methodist preacher in his election
address. In the previous year he had even described himself as a
'Political Wesley', preaching in the Cornish countryside.[35]

His political message is also interesting since it was more akin to
pre-war Cornish radicalism than the conventional Labour Party stance
of the 1930s. Instead of just appealing to the party's trade-union
supporters, notes that Rowse prepared for his political meetings clearly
indicate that he was trying to recreate the old broadly based Radical
alliance of pre-war years by appealing for the support of fishermen,
small farmers and shopkeepers: groups that had tended to remain loyal
to Cornish Liberalism. His concerns were therefore with the power
of absentee landlords and local vested interests. Rowse argued that
money obtained from Cornwall in the form of royalties and ground
rents was being squandered in London, and he raised the old idea of
land reform with the Cornish estates being divided up into independent
small holdings. His stance on tithes, a traditional cause of nonconformist farmers, was actually more orthodox than Isaac Foot. While
Foot in 1935 proposed a compromise agreement on this issue, Rowse
advocated the total abolition of tithes since the system was providing a
'fat living' for the parson and squire.[36] Finally, Rowse enthusiastically
championed the traditional Liberal doctrine of free trade, which had

been discarded by the National government. It is significant that his defence of free trade was based on its regional benefits for Cornwall, and he argued that tariffs were being used by the government to help other regions such as East Anglia and the Midlands:

> Tariffs . . . maybe all right for the motor car industry or glove making, but we don't make gloves or hosiery or motor-cars in Cornwall. What about china clay? That is what concerns us. What earthly use can tariffs be to the china-clay trade? We have looked after the motor car and artificial silk trades long enough: it is time that Cornish industry was considered as well as Morris's Motor Cars. What I have said about china applies also to tin mining, slate quarrying and Cornish agriculture which doesn't want to be strangled with a wheat quota but needs cheap feeding stuffs for cattle.[37]

The anti-metropolitan tone of this extract points to the strong theme of 'Cornishness' in his political campaign strategy. In the first place this was clearly shown by his articles in *Cornish Labour News* which often mentioned his joy at coming home for political campaigns in the land of his birth. For example, in August 1934 he wrote of his attachment to 'every lane and field and village of home . . . out in the country lanes all smelling of honey suckle, or up in the china-clay district with the fresh breeze blowing off the downs and glorious views across the country or to the sea.'[38] At a deeper level newspaper cuttings in the Rowse collection indicate that he was taking a keen interest in the development of Tyr ha Tavas, the new youth branch of the Cornish movement. In 1937 he declared that 'all that I want to be is a spokesman for the Cornish people'. He added that if Tyr ha Tavas was serious in its talk about 'Cornwall for the Cornish [and] the particular character of the Cornish people', they should give him their support because he represented their only chance of there being a Cornish Prime Minister.[39]

Rowse's comments came at an appropriate time. Although ostensibly a language organization, Tyr ha Tavas represented the transition phase from the antiquarian concerns of the early Revivalists to the political nationalism of Mebyon Kernow. Members were encouraged to take an interest in the social and economic problems facing Cornwall, while Edmund Hambly, the group's leader, developed links with Cornish MPs. Moreover, it is interesting that the main advocates of a political agenda for the group, Francis Cargeeg and E.G. Retallack Hooper, were associated with the Labour movement. Cargeeg was an active trade unionist at Plymouth dockyard during the 1930s, and was

increasingly concerned with the social problems of Cornwall. Retallack
Hooper, more commonly known by his bardic name 'Talek', eventually
became president of Mebyon Kernow and played a prominent role in
that organization's early local election campaigns in the 1960s.[40] A
Labour supporter in the 1930s, he provided the link between Tyr ha
Tavas and the *Cornish Labour News*. He was naturally an enthusiastic
supporter of the attempt to give the local Labour party a distinctly
Cornish image, and in the *Cornish Labour News* in December 1932 he
put forward the idea of a humane and small-scale socialism based on a
blend of social justice and cultural identity:

> Cornish socialism must be definitely Cornish—by which I
> mean that we work for the new economic system to be
> applied in Cornwall in a Cornish way. Our industries—
> notably mining and china-clay, fishing and farming—demand
> treatment that cannot be dictated by ready-made up-country
> methods . . . That we have a Celtic history, language and
> mentality is not to be despised but rather to be worked for. It
> is humanity itself that must come first and good causes must
> be built on *economic* freedom of the people themselves . . . so
> many of our best Cornishmen being deprived of a right to live
> by a system which piles up armaments on one hand and
> preaches to Bible societies on the other. Omseveagh why
> gonesugy Kernow! [Arise—workers of Cornwall!][41]

This new 'Cornish Socialism' started to pay electoral dividends
in 1935 when Rowse was able to push his Liberal opponent in Penryn
and Falmouth into third place and was only 3,000 votes behind the
Conservatives. The mid-Cornwall area now became the main focus for
Labour activity in the region, and Rowse's success provided the crucial
breakthrough for the election of the first Labour MP in Cornwall when
Evelyn King won the seat in 1945. But just as this new approach was
starting to make an impact on a wider level, its fragile foundations
were undermined. In the first place Berry's resignation as editor of
Cornish Labour News in the late 1930s meant that the paper lost
its distinctly Cornish stance. The focus now shifted, with more articles
on the party's activities in other parts of Britain and, perhaps not
surprisingly, to international issues and the growing threat of war in
Europe. Rowse was apparently disenchanted with this new editorial
policy, and by the late 1930s he was writing fewer articles for the
paper.[42]

Furthermore, Rowse was gradually moving away from
independent Labour politics. His old emphasis on the need for Labour

to stress the party's continuity with pre-war Cornish radicalism was now moulded into a platform for an alliance with the Liberals. By the end of the decade he had emerged as one of the main advocates at the national level for a centre-based Popular Front to challenge the National government. For example, in a leading article in the *Political Quarterly* in 1938 he rejected the idea of a United Front with the Communists and other left-wing groups, and argued instead that Labour had to 'extend its appeal to the centre' by forming an alliance with the Liberals.[43] This strategy was quite successful in Cornwall with Rowse persuading Labour activists to support Isaac Foot in the St Ives by-election in 1937 on the grounds that Foot was the 'inheritor of the tradition of Cornish Radicalism, the devoted servant of the twin causes of peace and progress'.[44] By 1939 a regional Liberal–Labour alliance seemed quite likely with Labour candidates withdrawing in Bodmin and North Cornwall. But the logic of this new electoral strategy meant that the Cornish Labour movement was forced to accept the survival of the Liberals as the main centre-left party. If an election had taken place as expected in 1939 Rowse would probably have been the only Labour candidate in Cornwall, since the Liberals, even in Camborne, were still the main alternative to the National government. Rowse, who was apparently the key figure in arranging the withdrawal of the other Labour candidates, saw no problem with this strategy since he realized that the party's position in seats like Bodmin was 'hopeless'. This view is certainly confirmed by a study of Labour's local membership figures for 1937 which suggests that 1,356 of the party's 2,288 members in Cornwall were concentrated in the single constituency of Penryn and Falmouth.[45]

By the end of the decade, then, the strategic position of 'Cornish Socialism' was already being undermined. Indeed, it was the Liberal Party, briefly revitalized by new candidates and the prospect of straight fights with the Conservatives, which was able to consolidate its position in Cornwall. Even in 1945 some Labour and Communist activists publicly campaigned for the Liberals on the grounds that Cornwall had a radical Liberal tradition.[46] Moreover, with Rowse's resignation as a prospective Labour candidate in the early 1940s the party also lost one of the few individuals who could carve out a distinctly Cornish agenda for the socialists. Although Hayman effectively took over Rowse's role after the war, he was very much an exception. The main emphasis was now on state socialism rather than the community socialism of Rowse and Retallack Hooper. This was demonstrated in 1952 when the local representatives of the three political parties were asked their views on the question of home rule for Cornwall. The Liberal and Conservative members of the panel came out in favour of devolution, but the Labour member, the party's candidate for Bodmin, dismissed the idea as unnecessary and a 'backward step'.[47]

The electoral performance of Labour was similarly disappointing after the war. While the party briefly became the second force in 1950, it remained in third place in the Bodmin and North Cornwall constituencies. A Liberal revival in the mid-1950s was based on a rising tide of anti-metropolitanism, which reflected the discontent of the local farming community and growing concern over employment and low wages. With the exception of Hayman, who consolidated his grip on the Camborne constituency, Labour candidates failed to exploit this discontent, and by 1959 the Liberals were once more the second party in the region in terms of the overall share of the vote.[48] Above all, Labour failed to win over the groups targeted by Rowse in the 1930s. The small farmers, fishermen and shopkeepers provided the mainstay of rural life in Cornwall, but Labour attracted only limited support from these groups after the Second World War. Even in the early 1950s the 'hard core' of Nonconformist farmers still voted Liberal in the old Bible Christian heartland of Bodmin and North Cornwall. This was in contrast to the situation in rural Wales where Labour was steadily gaining ground at the expense of the Liberals during the 1950s. Although the Liberals retained their former strongholds at Montgomery and Cardigan, the rural Radical vote was generally moving over to Labour and Plaid Cymru, a factor that prevented a Liberal recovery in the Principality during the subsequent decade of the 1960s.[49] The Cornish Liberals, however, were able to consolidate their grip on the rural seats. In the absence of an effective challenge from Labour, the survival of rural Liberalism at this time was to provide the basis for the parliamentary victories of Peter Bessell and John Pardoe in the 1960s.

CONCLUSION

The events of the inter-war period are crucial for understanding the nature of Cornish politics in the twentieth century. Although Labour made good progress in the aftermath of the First World War, the failure to achieve a regional breakthrough when Liberalism was in decline effectively ensured that the socialists would remain the third party. The early advance of the party certainly suggests that there was some potential for Cornish socialism, and given alternative circumstances Labour might well have emerged as the dominant party in the region. Yet the socialist revolution lacked roots since the collapse of the mining industry in the nineteenth century had prevented the creation of a secure environment for the Labour movement. Once Cornwall was faced, yet again, with poverty and unemployment in the early 1920s, the Cornish turned back to a political system based upon traditional lines. The attempt by Rowse and his supporters to integrate socialism into the political culture of Cornwall in the 1930s was an acceptance of this fact. In order for Labour to make a breakthrough it needed to recognize the continuing appeal of the religious and community agenda of the Old Left. With the Liberal Party, the conventional champion of this agenda, apparently on the road to extinction by the early 1930s, Cornish Labour now had another opportunity to build on its limited working-class support by taking on the mantle of tradional radicalism. By the end of the decade, however, this strategy was already giving way to a campaign for an electoral alliance between Labour and the Liberals. Since the concept behind the Popular Front was based on an acceptance of Liberal supremacy on the centre-left, one might add that this development provides the final confirmation of the failure of the socialist incursion into Cornwall.

NOTES AND REFERENCES

1. P. Payton, *The Making of Modern Cornwall: Historical Experience and the Persistence of Difference*, Redruth, 1992, p. 231.
2. For example, D. Clark, *Colne Valley: Radicalism to Socialism*, London, 1981; I. Mclean, *The Legend of Red Clydeside*, Edinburgh, 1983; P. Wyncoll, *The Nottingham Labour Movement 1880–1940*, London, 1985; K. Laybourn, *The Rise of Labour; The British Labour Party, 1890–1979*, London, 1988.
3. *Cornish Guardian*, 6 June 1929.
4. Statistics based on F.W.S. Craig (ed.), *British Parliamentary Election Results, 1918–1949*, Glasgow, 1969. Table 1 only lists selected constituencies in Sheffield and Stepney, but the Labour vote was quite low in the other seats. Thus, in 1918 the party's vote in the other three seats contested in Sheffield (Park, Brightside and Central) was 20.4, 35.8 and 37.3 per cent respectively, while in Stepney (Whitechapel and St Georges) it was 29.2 per cent. In 1929 all four constituencies elected Labour candidates. Similarly, the Labour percentage vote in Motherwell, Doncaster and Aberavon in 1918 was only 23.2, 25.0 and 35.7 per cent; by 1929 the party's share of the vote had risen to 58.0, 56.0 and 55.9 per cent respectively.
5. *Western Morning News*, 2, 5, 12 and 16 December 1918.
6. B. Deacon, 'Conybeare for Ever!', in T. Knight (ed.), *Old Redruth: Original Studies of the Town's History*, Redruth, 1992, pp. 37–43.
7. Acland papers, Devon Record Office, 1148 M 14/667, Francis Acland to Eleanor Acland, late 1917.
8. *Cornish Guardian*, 21 February 1918; A.L. Rowse, *St Austell Church; Town; Parish*, St Austell, 1960, p. 82.
9. *Cornish Guardian*, 8 May 1919 and 27 February 1920; *Western Morning News*, 2 December 1918.

10. *Royal Cornwall Gazette*, 20 October 1920.
11. T. Crago, 'From S.D.F. to Workers Union: C.R. Vincent, A Cornish Socialist', B.A. dissertation, University College of St Mark and St John, 1998, pp. 21–4; *Royal Cornwall Gazette*, 18 February 1920.
12. *Cornish Guardian*, 14 March 1919 and 27 February 1920.
13. E.W. Martin, *Shearers and the Shorn: A Study of Life in a Devon Community*, London, 1965, p. 76; M. Kinnear, *The British Voter: An Atlas and Survey since 1885*, New York, 1968, pp. 134–7.
14. An interview with David Morrish, Exeter, 16 September 1994.
15. *Royal Cornwall Gazette*, 1 June 1921; Kinnear, *British Voter*, pp. 108–11.
16. *Cornish Guardian*, 16 August 1921, 6 January 1922 and 24 February 1922.
17. *Royal Cornwall Gazette*, 3 November 1920.
18. *Cornish Guardian*, 6 June 1929.
19. *Cornish Guardian*, 14 April 1922 and 11 December 1923.
20. *Royal Cornwall Gazette*, 12 and 19 May 1920, 8 November 1922.
21. *Royal Cornwall Gazette*, 5 April and 8 November 1922; *Cornish Guardian*, 21 March 1922.
22. *Royal Cornwall Gazette*, 22 November 1922; *West Briton*, 2 November 1922.
23. J. Rowe, 'The Declining Years of Cornish Tin Mining' in J. Porter (ed.), *Education and Labour in the South West*, Exeter, 1975, pp. 66 and 73; *West Briton*, 24 October 1935; *Cornish Guardian*, 23 March 1939.
24. C. Howard, 'Expectations Born to Death: Local Labour Party Expansion in the 1920s', in J. Winter (ed.), *The Working Class in Modern British History: Essays in Honour of Henry Pelling*, Cambridge, 1983, pp. 69–72.
25. R. M. Barton, *A History of the Cornish China–Clay Industry*, Truro, 1966, p. 172; interview with John Tonkin, 14 October 1990; *Cornish Guardian*, 26 January 1923.
26. Payton, 1992, pp. 139–60; see also P. Payton, 'Labour Failure and Liberal Tenacity: Radical Politics and Cornish Political Culture, 1880–1939' in P. Payton (ed.), *Cornish Studies: Two*, Exeter, 1994, pp. 83–96.
27. For further information on this subject see R. Perry 'A Remission in the Great Paralysis?' in *Cornish History Network Newsletter*, Issue 3, December 1998, pp. 2–3 and R. Perry 'Seminar Report—A Remission in the Great Paralysis' in *Cornish History Network Newsletter*, Issue 4, March 1999, pp. 2–3; see also R. Perry, 'Celtic Revival and Economic Development in Edwardian Cornwall', in P. Payton (ed.) *Cornish Studies: Five*, Exeter, 1997, pp. 112–24.
28. A. Thorpe, 'J.H. Thomas and the Rise of Labour in Derby, 1880–1945', *Midland History*, Vol. 15, 1990, p. 118.
29. D. Weinbren, *Generating Socialism: Recollections of Life in the Labour Party*, Stroud, 1997, pp. 30–56; K. Beswetherick, 'Then and Now' in *The Journal of the Cornish Methodist Historical Association*, Vol. 9, 1997, pp. 14–15; interview with F.L. Harris, 10 June 1990.
30. S. Rokkan, *Citizens: Elections: Parties: Approaches to the Comparative Study of the Processes of Development*, Oslo, 1970, pp. 72–144.

31. *Western Morning News*, 31 October and 3 November 1924; *Cornish Guardian*, 6 June 1929.
32. *Cornish Guardian*, 22 November 1934.
33. This part of the article is based on material in the private collection of A.L. Rowse consisting of letters, newspaper cuttings and the *Cornish Labour News*. I am grateful to Mrs Valerie Brokenshire for allowing me to examine this collection which has been recently moved to the University of Exeter.
34. *Cornish Labour News*, issues 1–6 (1932–33).
36. *Cornish Labour News*, January 1934; notes for a political speech, *c. early 1930s*.
37. *Cornish Labour News*, December 1932, No. 3.
38. *Cornish Labour News*, August 1934.
39. *Cornish Labour News*, May 1937, No. 56; newspaper cuttings from the *West Briton*, 20 August 1936 and 7 October 1937, Rowse papers.
40. For a more detailed discussion of Tyr ha Tavas see G. Tregidga, 'Politics of the Celto-Cornish Revival, 1886–1939', in P. Payton (ed.) *Cornish Studies: Five*, Exeter, 1997; *Cornish Nation*, Issue 10, Summer 1998, p. 9.
41. *Cornish Labour News*, December 1932, No. 3.
42. Undated letter concerning the *Cornish Labour News*, late 1930s, Rowse papers.
43. A.L. Rowse, 'The Present and Immediate Future of the Labour Party', *Political Quarterly*, Vol. IX, 1938, p. 28.
44. *Cornish Guardian*, 24 June 1937.
45. A.L. Rowse, *A Man of the Thirties*, London, 1979, p. 56; *Labour Annual Conference Report*, 1937, p. 109.
46. *Cornish Guardian*, 15 March 1945; *Western Morning News*, 25 April 1945.
47. *Cornish Guardian*, 8 May 1952.
48. *Western Morning News*, 17 May 1955.
49. Kinnear, *British Voter*, pp. 134–7; P.J. Madgwick, *The Politics of Rural Wales: a Study of Cardiganshire*, London, 1973, pp. 63–4.

THE CHANGING FACE OF CELTIC TOURISM IN CORNWALL, 1875–1975

Ronald Perry

INTRODUCTION

In earlier issues of *Cornish Studies*, Philip Payton, Bernard Deacon and others have plotted the different historical pathway that Cornwall has followed compared with other regions.[1] This article explores one facet of this difference: the use of the so-called 'Celtic heritage' for the promotion of tourism. Payton and Deacon identified, in Cornish society, a kind of three-way, ideological tug-of-war between pre-industrialists, seeking to revive a lost Celtic civilization; industrialists, dreaming of a return to former mining glories; and post-industrialists, building a leisure-oriented economy. They contrasted the early Celto-Cornish Revivalists who, in Deacon's words, 'positively wallowed in the un-reason of Romanticism' with industrial enthusiasts who, in Payton's phrase, were trying to 'revive the mining corpse'. The existence of both a pre-industrial and an industrial past, Deacon and Payton argue, differentiates Cornwall from some other Celtic communities, and, in their analysis of the tensions created by this dual heritage, they encompass a range of political, cultural and social, as well as economic factors. This present study focuses upon the impact of economic and demographic processes which tend to be muffled by post-modernist discourses on the cultural construction of place.

'PAINTING THROUGH THE MISTS OF LEGEND'

To late Victorian Cornwall, traumatized by the collapse of mining, tourism offered one possible solution to its dilemma. The idea of using the Celtic heritage as a way of attracting visitors was, however, little discussed. Antiquarians and philologists had, for decades, come in search of Celtic remains, and some guide-writers had elaborated on Celtic themes and upon the brooding Celtic emotionalism which they detected in the native people. But, for most visitors, the tourist identity of Cornwall was not unlike that of other resorts: a watering-place with a mild winter climate and picturesque seascapes suitable for the elderly, the infirm and the leisured.

Internally, the reigning culture, despite the decline of mining, remained industrial. If people dreamt of restoring past glories, their vision was a return to a role as a world-class centre of deep-lode mining, not a Celtic kingdom. Underlying this was a general reaction—not confined to Cornish miners, farmers and fisherman, of course—that work that was not tough, dirty and sometimes dangerous was not 'real work' at all. Interlaced with this antagonism, in a land where Methodism and teetotalism dominated, was an association of the holiday trade with drunkenness and frivolity. For example, Edward (later Sir Edward) Hain, St Ives shipowner, Mayor and MP, was not opposed to tourist development: indeed, he was Chairman of a group that built the Porthminster Hotel there. Yet, as he pointed out, while guide-writers might call it 'the Naples of the North', the puritanical attitudes of local fisher-folk effectively stifled any Neapolitan exuberance.[2]

These fishermen, however, were the focus of writers and artists who flocked to Cornwall in the later decades of the nineteenth century to construct a powerful pre-industrial identity that had nothing to do with Cornwall's Celtic roots or industrial heritage. They painted, according to Stanhope Forbes, doyen of the Newlyn School, with 'unflinching realism', but their particular construction of reality excluded any references to industrial Cornwall. Conspicuous by their absence were the mine chimneys and engine houses that ringed the coast, the dynamite factories that spread along the dunes of Hayle or Perranporth, the shipbuilding yards of Falmouth or Hayle. Their only allusion to the works of industry, apart from the farmer, the fisherman, the quarryman and the village blacksmith, was the currently fashionable arts-and-crafts dream world. The 'Industrial Class', painted by Stanhope Forbes, portrayed diligent youths embossing copper plates, not miners, clay-workers or engineers.[3] This was what the market dictated, and the painters had little choice in their subject matter, as Newlyn artist Walter Langley discovered. Having made a good living depicting the picturesque lives of poor fishermen, he went back to his native Birmingham to paint the industrial poor, only for a lack of clients to make him return to Newlyn again. To succeed, artists had to paint, as the Newlyn pioneer, Norman Garstin recognized, 'through the mist of legend'.[4] It was these anti-industrial visions that 'wallowed in the un-reason of Romanticism' and dominated outsiders' perceptions of Cornwall, not the imaginings of Celtic Revivalists.

There were always, it is true, a few travellers who wanted to see industrial Cornwall. The mines of West Cornwall attracted a number of distinguished visitors, including members of the Royal Family, while a guide-writer of 1859 advised that Fowey Consolidated Mines, one of the most important copper mines of the day, 'might well be selected for examination', particularly the 'celebrated Austen's engine, a veritable Cornish giant'. In 1880, Walter Tregellas, a Cornish amateur archaeologist and historian, recommended a visit to the china-clay works around St Austell, and gave a detailed account of clay-working methods, as did other guide-writers of the period.[5] In general, though, the authors of guidebooks warned their readers to avoid the 'Black Country' of Cornwall, as they called its industrial towns. The sole difference between Redruth and Camborne, one writer explained, was that Camborne was big and ugly with trams, whereas Redruth was big and ugly without trams.

'ONE OF THE FINEST WATERING PLACES IN EUROPE'
Even those rare residents who combined an interest in Celtic heritage with a willingness to promote tourism made no connection between the two. E. Whitfield Crofts and the Reverend Wladislaw Lach-Szyrma are cases in point. Crofts, who later, as 'Peter Penn', ran a 'Cornish Notes and Queries' column in the *Cornish Telegraph*, produced a *Tourists' Companion to West Cornwall* in 1877. His aim was to make the region 'as much resorted to as the Lake District, the Welsh mountains and the more remote Highlands', an aim that was thwarted by industrialism: 'it is a fact that to many thousands of Englishmen, Cornwall is practically synonymous with all that is dull, barren, ugly and horrible.' He quoted from Lach-Szyrma, of Polish extraction, who had scoured the Cornish countryside with Henry Jenner, father of the Cornish Revivalist movement, for Celtic artefacts and language, and who had written on an astonishing range of topics, including *Two Hundred and Twenty-Two Antiquities in or near Penzance*. At the same time, Lach-Szyrma's concern for the distress of his parishioners at Newlyn led him to seek ways of improving their economic lot, and he was one of the prime movers in modernizing the harbour and setting it on its path to becoming the premier fish-landing port in the west. However, he was realistic enough to realize that fishing alone would not support the area. 'More depends upon a reputation as a watering place,' he wrote in 1876, 'than as a seaport or a mart for fishing and mining.' Better rail access and modern accommodation, he maintained, could make its 'wonderfully equable climate' and a seascape 'rivalling the Bay of

Naples', into 'one of the finest watering places in Europe'.[6] Although steeped in the Celtic past, neither Crofts nor Lach-Szyrma used it to attract visitors.

By the turn of the century, Lach-Szyrma's conditions had been met. A modern railway network was largely in place. Hotels, villas and terraced lodgings had been built. Nevertheless, it was becoming clear to the more perceptive tourism-promoter that these were necessary, but not sufficient, conditions to bring visitors to Cornwall in substantial numbers. For all around Britain and on the Continent, holiday resorts were mushrooming, some with easier access to big cities, as well as superior social and entertainment infrastructures. Tourism was more than ever a cut-throat business, and tourist operators elsewhere were meeting the challenge by creating their own distinct regional identities to give them a competitive edge over their rivals.

Cornwall's run-of-the-mill holiday promoters stuck to the well-tried formula of the Victorian watering-place, until they were stirred out of their complacency when, right on their doorstep, hoteliers formed a United Devon Association, and flooded the offices of railway and shipping companies with promotions, including 'Pilgrim Fathers' tours for the American public. In response to this challenge, the Mayor of Truro called a conference in 1900 which was attended by representatives of most Cornish resorts. A working party was formed, and Quiller-Couch, Cornwall's leading man of letters at the time, agreed to act as Chairman. Prophetically, they did not follow their neighbour's example by calling themselves a 'United Cornwall Association', for unity was never achieved. They could not agree on what Cornwall's collective tourist identity was, or, indeed, whether it had one at all. The Mayors of Truro and Penzance favoured marching alongside Devonians under a 'West of England' banner, a suggestion which drew loud applause at the conference. Quiller-Couch, of course, had his own popular concept, 'The Delectable Duchy'. Sir Edward Durning-Lawrence, MP for Truro, son of a Cornish carpenter, and a power in the City of London, proposed 'Cornwall is a Pleasant Place to Spend a Month In'. The Cornish Association's title was 'Cornwall as a Health and Pleasure Resort'.[7]

None of these identities seemed likely to set the Tamar alight, but only the merest handful of opinion-formers saw any potential in playing Cornwall's trumpcard, its Celticity, to offset its neighbour's advantages in accessibility: Silvanus Trevail, Cornish architect and hotel developer; Thomas Hodgkin, a Quaker banker from north-east England, who married into the important Cornish Quaker family of the Foxes of Falmouth and became President of the Royal Cornwall Polytechnic Society of Falmouth; and the Reverend Sabine Baring-

Gould, who lived just over the border in Devon and was famous as a prolific novelist, pioneer of folk-lore, and author of some of the best-loved Victorian hymns, and who was elected President of the Royal Institution of Cornwall.

Silvanus Trevail was the prime mover in building that great chain of hotels, mansions and apartments that dominate the coast of Cornwall to this day, accommodation which, he claimed, was

> equal to probable demands . . . our next business is to fill them . . . some will say "continentalise" them . . . with casinos, theatres, winter-gardens . . . all the other costly paraphernalia that goes to make one watering-place so much like the other . . . nothing is more tiring to the educated tourist than this sameness.

Instead, Trevail urged his fellow-hoteliers to make it plain to their guests that, once they crossed the Tamar, they were in a land apart. 'Never tire of placing, in hotels and lodging houses', he advised, 'local histories, guidebooks and maps.' And since he was a man who practised what he preached, he used his skills in Celtic design to decorate his King Arthur's Castle Hotel at Tintagel with medieval motifs and furnishings, including a gigantic Round Table with place names for Arthurian knights, and advertised it as standing on 'the most romantic spot in England', the very place where Tennyson had composed his Arthurian *Idylls*.[8]

Dr Hodgkin, a writer on pre-Norman England, also believed that 'the great recommendation of Cornwall is its unlikeness to the rest of England'. It offered, he said, 'the stimulus of foreign travel with the comfort of home', with its 'churches dedicated to the Celtic saints'.[9] The principal chronicler of the saints, however, was Baring-Gould, who had produced a series of imaginative reconstructions of the lives of early Celtic missionaries to Cornwall, as well as tales of smugglers and wreckers. To him, tourism was an entirely welcome and preferred alternative to mining. Instead of labouring underground to prise copper out of the rocks, he argued, Cornishmen could now, with little effort, receive it, ready minted, from the hands of 'trainloads of tourists . . . coveys of bicyclists', and if Celtic myths and legends could help to bring visitors, then so much the better.[10]

Trevail, Hodgkin and Baring-Gould had concocted a powerful, if ambiguous, formula for tourist promotion involving the concept of Celtic Cornwall: familiar but exotic, remote yet accessible, ancient and modern at the same time. But they were lone voices. The Cornish Association came to nothing. Persuading Cornwall's leaders to unite in a common tourist image was, the *West Briton* concluded, 'like flogging a dead horse'. 'City-state' rivalries led each resort seek to build its own reputation, and Cornishmen left it to the Great Western Railway to define Cornwall's collective tourist identity for them. In 1904, the company launched its 'Cornish Riviera' campaign, with a guidebook that became an Edwardian best-seller, posters on all the principal stations, heavy advertising in the English press, and an express train that became one of the legends of the age of steam.

CORNISH RIVIERA AND CELTIC REVIVAL: COINCIDENCE OR COLLUSION?

The launch of the Cornish Riviera occurred in the same year that Cowethas Kelto-Kernuak, a pioneer Celto-Cornish society, succeeded in gaining admission for Cornwall to a Pan-Celtic association at a Congress in Caernarfon. Was this coincidence or collusion? Philip Payton and Paul Thornton have argued that the Cornish Riviera campaign involved a 'high degree of collusion' between railway publicists and Cornish Revivalists,[11] but in the years before the 1914 War, at least, there is little evidence of this. It is true that the Cornish Riviera guide quoted from the writings of Baring-Gould, and awarded him the accolade of the 'historian *par excellence* of the Cornish Saint'. In general, though, the Celtic voice was muted in Edwardian editions of the guide, and readers had to wait until nearly the end before the word 'Celtic' appeared.[12] Indeed, outsiders must have wondered at the origins of the Cornish when a famous GWR poster turned a map of Italy on its side and compared it with a map of Cornwall, flanked by a strangely clad Cornish maiden and an Italian peasant girl.

As for those members of Cowethas Kelto-Kernuak who, as writers about Cornwall, had an interest in both Celticity and tourism, they kept the two in separate mental compartments. Louis Duncombe-Jewell, secretary and prime mover of the group in its earliest days, wrote a guide to Fowey, but he went to great pains to dissociate himself from the romanticism of some travel-writers of the day. His references to Celtic remains and Cornish language were both sparse and matter-of-fact, in complete contrast to the passion of his articles and papers in *Celtia*, the journal of the Pan-Celtic movement.[13] Quiller-Couch, a founder member of Cowethas Kelto-Kernuak, brought fame to Fowey with his *Troytown* tales. 'He is to this part of the Riviera what Thomas Hardy is to Wessex', concluded the Cornish Riviera guide. Yet he detested the Riviera association, and there was no trace of Celticity in his *Troytown* saga. As for Baring-Gould, as author of a guide to the French Riviera, he felt obliged to warn readers of his books on Cornwall that it did not enjoy a Mediterranean climate.[14] Only

Lach-Szyrma was whole-hearted in his enthusiasm for both the climatic
and the Celtic aspects of the Cornish Riviera concept. He suggested
opening a Cornish Restaurant in London, decorated by some of
the famous Cornish-based artists of the day, and serving traditional
Cornish recipes, and growing grapes in Cornwall to produce a Cornish
Riviera Champagne.[15]

At this point, a misconception about the Cornish Riviera campaign
of the Great Western Railway needs to be cleared up. Now acclaimed
by historians as a brilliant stroke of marketing,[16] it was, in terms of its
original stated objectives, a failure. The title of the first guide spells out
its objective quite clearly: *The Cornish Riviera as an Ideal Winter
Health and Leisure Resort.* Acting 'in the best interests of British
householders', the GWR set out to dispel 'the once prevalent idea that
Cornwall was to be visited only in summer and autumn', and aimed to
make it just as popular in winter. To this end, its pages were crammed
with meteorological statistics comparing Cornwall's winter temper-
atures with those of Montpellier, Pau and the French-Italian Riviera.
Already, two years later, the up-dated *Cornish Riviera* guide was
claiming that the objective had been achieved, and that Cornwall was
now Britain's winter watering-place, *par excellence.* But the dividing
line between fantasy and reality in GWR guides was always blurred.
Cornwall remained primarily a summer holiday resort.[17]

A MAGICAL LAND WHERE THE SUN ALWAYS SHINES

'The history of Cornwall as a foreign or semi-foreign Celtic province',
concluded F.E. Halliday in 1959, 'ended with the invasion of the motor
car, mine among them, in the 1920s'. Of course, the 'motorist hordes',
as Quiller-Couch called them, were the merest trickle compared with
the deluge that was beginning when Professor Halliday was writing his
history. Nevertheless, they were one of the forces that stirred Old
Cornwall Societies into action to gather up the fragments of traditional
Cornish life before they were lost for ever. Resentment of tourism was
seldom articulated, however, for during a world depression, nearly all
of Cornwall's staple industries—farming, fishing, mining, clay—were in
deep distress. The holiday trade seemed almost the only hope; tourist
incomes came like manna from heaven, and, as Payton and Thornton
have shown, Revivalists colluded with railway publicists, who spread
awareness of Cornwall in a way which local organizations could not
match.

There was a price to pay for this collusion, however, for the
railway companies had been forced, by changing tourist tastes, into a
radical transformation of their message. Edwardian summer visitors,
swathed from head to toe, even when they ventured into the sea,

seemed to accept the notion that Cornwall had a Mediterranean aspect. The 1920s, however, ushered in the age of the sun-worshipper, and travel-writers had to strain every nerve to convince scantily clad sun-bathers that Cornwall was the place for Mediterranean luxuriance, in summer as well as winter.

The GWR propaganda machine responded with its customary bravura. 'Everyone has dreamt of a land where the sun always shines', wrote the new author of the *Cornish Riviera* guide, S.P.B. Mais. 'We had to have a name for this Elysium, so we called it the Cornish Riviera . . . Penzance is proving a formidable rival to Madeira, the Scillies to the Azores, and Mullion to Monte Carlo.'[18] If any doubts remained about the Cornish Riviera, the title of another GWR guide rammed the message home: *Sunny Cornwall in England's Mediterranean Region.* Local writers confirmed this message. 'Tan without torture', promised a Falmouth guide. 'Clad only in the minimum of decency, one can sprawl in the sun after one's bathe', affirmed a guide to Penzance.

This railway-inspired campaign succeeded brilliantly in opening Cornwall to a wider public, but at the cost of romanticizing Cornwall in a way that masked the poverty and distress of the Cornish people. For the Celtic theme also had to be revamped, to attract a new and wider clientele. Scholarly and antiquarian references were scrapped in favour of full-blown fantasy. 'You may go to Cornwall with the idea that you are in for a normal holiday', warned S.P.B. Mais, 'and find yourself in an atmosphere of warlocks, miracle-working saints and woe-working witches.' When, later, Mais wrote guides for Southern Railway trains to what it called 'King Arthur's Land', he repeated the formula. 'At one moment you are in comfortable Devon . . . the next you are on strange soil, suddenly thrown back five thousand years.'[19] The best-known guide-writers of the day echoed his whimsical humbug. H.V. Morton, in *The Magic of Cornwall*, reported that, when he spotted a cow with a crumpled horn, 'I said to myself I was in fairyland'.

To spread the message through southern England, the GWR ran locomotives with such names as *Tre-Pol-and-Pen*, *Chough* and *Tregeagle*, and the Southern Railway responded with *King Arthur Class* engines, including *Merlin*, *Lyonesse* and *Pendragon*.[20] These powerful locomotives embodied the ambivalence of the Cornish Riviera message: lost in the mists of time, yet equipped with the latest technology. Such flights of fancy, however, were not incompatible with the Celtic Revivalism of the day, which, with its emphasis on ceremony, ritual and language, also distanced itself from reality, and failed to win the hearts and minds of the ordinary Cornishman and woman. And so it was this Celto-Mediterranean concept of a land of mystery and magic, where the sun always shone, that became a powerful marker of Cornwall's territory and language, and even, Payton and Thornton have argued, 'a major influence on the cultural constructions of Cornwall that emerged in the intervening period'.[21]

THE TOURIST EXPLOSION FROM THE FIFTIES

Given the success of the Cornish Riviera identity before the war, it was hardly surprising that tourist promoters, including British Railways, which had swallowed up the Great Western and Southern Railways, repeated the well-tried formula when they rebuilt the tourist trade after the war. 'Out of England and into Cornwall . . . the slightly foreign atmosphere, the Celtic air of remoteness, are irresistible to the prosaic city dweller', was how E.M. Trembath, Newquay's Publicity Officer, defined Cornish tourist identity in Cornwall's first *Development Plan* of 1952.[22] Well into the 1960s, the popular *Blue Guide* echoed this Edwardian message. 'Cornwall contains all the climatic advantages of Continental residence without the drawback of long fatiguing travel, foreign language, unusual habits and strange attendance'.[23] Some Cornish mariners co-operated to the full: a guide-writer related how as he drove off the Saltash ferry, the man working it said, 'Well, you're in a foreign country now', and old men in knitted jerseys and sailors' caps offered to explain the difference between piskies, knockers and spriggans.[24] Arthur Mee, another leading guide-writer, carried on where he had left off in the 1930s: 'It is magic that leaps to mind when we think of Cornwall.'[25]

The dominating presence and the promotional flair of the GWR had gone, however, and railway customers was set to fade away as well. While guidebooks and promoters were recycling this trusty old Celto-Mediterranean message, the whole nature of Cornish tourism was changing. Mass car-borne tourism had arrived. Trembath had hazarded a guess that the annual total of visitors could not be far short of half a million, of whom a half came by train. A generation later, it was estimated at nearly three and a half million a year, nine out of ten of whom arrived by road. At peak periods, Cornwall contained two visitors for every three residents, and, in popular resorts, tourists greatly outnumbered locals.

What is more, the resident population itself was radically altering. For, where tourists went, others followed—second-homers, retirees, working-age in-migrants and their families—polarizing the distribution of population. Incomers and tourist operators dominated coastal locations, while the Cornish concentrated in less picturesque inland areas.

Tourism was not the only propellant force in the economy,

however, for Cornwall, in the period from the end of the war to the mid 1970s, found itself in an unaccustomed state of relative prosperity. Farming was doing well. Manufacturing employment, aided by a massive reinforcement of regional funding, rose by over 50 per cent. Mining was experiencing one of its periodic remissions, oil was being prospected in the Celtic Sea. Meetings were held to discuss the future of Falmouth as a container port, and Newlyn, Fowey and Falmouth as offshore-oil bases. Such was the euphoria that one visiting regional analyst felt able to assert that this 'rural periphery' was transforming itself into 'a part of the prosperous south-east'.[26] The holiday trade no longer appeared, as it had in the twenties and thirties, the saviour of the Cornish economy, or even a necessity. Tourism now seemed expendable.

A new Cornish movement had also emerged, Mebyon Kernow (MK) or Sons of Cornwall, with stated objectives of greater economic independence and political autonomy. For almost the first time ideas of nationhood and cultural identity were openly connected with a Celto-Cornish culture. And these three factors—mass tourism and its associated in-migration, resurgence of traditional industries, and a robust Cornish movement—produced a reversal in relationships between Cornish Revivalists and tourist promoters. Co-operation between Revivalists and holiday promoters gave way to antagonism. The holiday trade was linked to the erosion of Cornish culture and the marginalization of the Cornish people. Professor Charles Thomas, then Director of the newly formed Institute of Cornish Studies, itself a symbol of an increased Cornish awareness, spoke of a 'beleaguered Cornwall' under 'erosive attack by social and economic factors too powerful to vanquish'. There were few Cornishmen left, he believed, and precious little left of old Cornwall.[27] As visitor numbers overstepped the threshold of social tolerance, schemes were proposed at MK meetings to curb tourist growth by physical controls or taxation.

Even before the full impact of people-led growth had been felt, measures were proposed to reduce the dependence of Cornwall on tourism. 'A good many Cornish people hate this mass invasion each year', stated the organ of the Cornish movement in 1958. 'Is tourism so vital?' Accompanying this question was a map showing the new firms in textiles, food and drink processing, and engineering that had been created since the war.[28] Two years later, however, 'A Business Man's Plan for Cornwall' in the same journal argued for an increase in Celtic tourism, citing the success of the Edinburgh Festival and the Welsh Eisteddfod. 'The Irish have fostered the impression of belonging to a land shrouded in Celtic mystery and folklore which is fascinating to visitors', and Cornwall, it was suggested, could do more in this direction, including the 'full-scale development' of the Cornish Riviera. 'I wish there was a really bold sign,' wrote the author of the plan, Peter Bessell, 'to tell all that they are now in the Royal Duchy of Cornwall ... Why not frankly "sell" the Cornish cream, pasty and saffron cakes, piskies, King Arthur, the countless and often incredible saints and Celtic ancestry'.[29] His, however, was a minority voice in a predominantly anti-tourist Cornish movement which resented the way that holiday promoters were now relegating Cornwall's mining past, along with its Celtic heritage, into a theme-park attraction.

FROM DEPOPULATION TO REPOPULATION

This survey began with a Cornwall traumatized by depopulation through massive outward migration. It ends with a Cornwall pressurized by repopulation due to large-scale inward migration. In between, Cornwall experienced a slight remission in Edwardian times, the grinding poverty of the inter-war years and a recovery in the post-war era. Throughout these turbulent decades, demographic and economic forces, largely beyond local control, helped to shape shifting coalitions of pre-industrial, industrial and post-industrial interests.

The late Victorian and Edwardian era was, for Cornwall, a time of de-industrialization. Growth in agricultural output, for instance, was higher in Cornwall than in any English county, and the farm workforce was actually increasing, against the trend elsewhere in Britain. An image of rustic simplicity, offered to outsiders, largely by outsiders, was therefore not inappropriate. There was little hint of a pre-industrial Celtic heritage, however, for very few both venerated the Celtic past and exploited it for a tourist future. It took a world slump in the 1920s and 1930s to see the flowering of a Celtic theme in holiday publicity, propagated once more by outsiders, but with the help of Celto-Cornish Revivalists. For all its whimsy, this message played a defining role in constructing a powerful Cornish identity, at a time when global forces had reduced the local economy to a state perhaps even more desperate than what had gone before.

Only after the war, when economic and demographic pressures threatened to swamp the Cornish identity, did an endogenous Celto-Cornish movement assert itself in a significant way. Association of tourism with counter-urbanization and cultural erosion, however, led industrial and pre-industrial Revivalists to combine in opposing growth in the holiday trade, a stance which was encouraged by a temporary remission in the Cornish economy. For a time, tourism seemed expendable, while, for holiday promoters, Celtic themes appeared only of minor importance, an optional extra in a mainstream sun-sea-sand identity. Not until the 1970s, when economic resurgence proved, once again, to be a false dawn, did Celtic tourism find favour among politicians, planners and tourist promoters.

NOTES AND REFERENCES

1. Bernard Deacon and Philip Payton, 'Re-inventing Cornwall', in Philip Payton (ed.). *Cornish Studies: One*, Exeter, 1993; Philip Payton, 'Reforming Thirties and Hungry Forties', in Philip Payton (ed.), *Cornish Studies: Four*, Exeter, 1996; Bernard Deacon, 'Proto-industrialization and Potatoes', in Philip Payton (ed.), *Cornish Studies: Five*, Exeter, 1997.
2. Edward Hain, in Arthur Quiller-Couch, *Cornish Magazine*, 1898, pp. 72–4; for similar comment, see also *West Briton*, 13 April 1893, and *Royal Cornwall Gazette*, 21 June 1894.
3. See, for example, Hazel Berriman, *Arts and Crafts in Newlyn 1890–1930*, Newlyn, 1986, and the painting of J.D. Mackenzie instructing an apprentice in the art of repoussé copperwork' by Stanhope Forbes, in Brisbane Art Gallery.
4. Roger Langley, *Walter Langley*, Penzance, 1997; Austin Wormleighton, *A Painter Laureate: Lamorna Birch and his Circle*, Bristol, 1995; Tom Cross, *The Shining Sands: Artists in Newlyn and St Ives*, Tiverton, 1994; Caroline Fox, *Stanhope Forbes and the Newlyn School*, Newton Abbot, 1993.
5. Murray's *Handbook for Devon and Cornwall*, second edition, London, 1859; Walter Tregellas, *The Tourist's Guide to Cornwall*, London, 1880; see also Charles G. Harper, *From Paddington to Penzance*, London, 1893, and Ward Lock, *Guide to Falmouth and the South Coast of Cornwall*, London, 1898.
6. Reverend W.S. Lach-Syyrma, *A Short History of Penzance*, Truro, 1878; these views echo those in *The Official Guide to Penzance*, Penzance, 1876, where it is advertised as 'the Mentone of England'.
7. *West Briton*, 27 April 1899, 4 May 1899, 18 May 1899, 15 June 1899, 8 March 1900, 21 March 1901, 29 August 1901, 9 January 1902, 6 February 1902, 13 March 1902, 31 July 1902.
8. For further discussion of Trevail as tourist promoter, see Ronald Perry, 'A Crowded Year in the 1890s', in James Whetter (ed.), *An Baner Kernewek*, 1996.
9. Thomas Hodgkin in Quiller-Couch, 1898, pp. 157–8; for further discussion of Dr Hodgkin, D.C.L., Litt. D. (1831–1913), see *Journal of the Royal Cornwall Polytechnic Society*, Vol. 81, pp. 30 and 82–100.
10. S. Baring-Gould, *A Book of the West*, 1899, reprinted 1981, p. 66.
11. Philip Payton and Paul Thornton, 'The Great Western Railway and the Cornish-Celtic Revival', in Philip Payton (ed.), *Cornish Studies: Three*, Exeter, 1995, pp. 83–103.
12. Great Western Railway, *The Cornish Riviera as an Ideal Winter Health and Pleasure Resort*, London, 1904; shortened to *The Cornish Riviera*, from 1905 until 1913.
13. Compare, for example, his Celtic references in *A Guide to Fowey and its*

Neighbourhood, Fowey, 1901, with his articles in *Celtia* (October 1901 and June 1902).

14. Baring-Gould wrote his *Guide to the French Riviera* in 1886; for his comments on the Cornish climate, see Baring-Gould, *Cornwall*, Cambridge, 1910.

15. See Lach-Szyrma's numerous contributions to 'Cornish Notes and Queries', in *Cornish Telegraph* 1903–6; see *Cornish Telegraph*, 7 October 1909.

16. See, for example, Alan Bennett, *Images of Cornwall*, Cheltenham, 1992; Gareth Shaw and Allan Williams, 'From Bathing Hut to Theme Park', *Regional Studies*, Vol. 11, 1991, pp. 16–32; Payton and Thornton, 1995.

17. F.E. Halliday, *A History of Cornwall*, London, 1959, p. xi.

18. S.P.B. Mais, *The Cornish Riviera*, London, 1928.

19. Mais, *The Cornish Riviera*, second edition, 1929, p. 3.

20. For more details of the railway campaign, see Payton and Thornton, 1995, pp. 94–8.

21. Payton and Thornton, 1995; on the reification of old Cornwall, see James Vernon, 'Border Crossings', in Geoffrey Cubit, (ed.), *Imagining Nations*, Manchester, 1998, pp. 165–67.

22. Cornwall County Council, *Development Plan Survey*, Truro, 1952.

23. Complete Guide to the English Riviera, Newquay, 1968.

24. Ronald W. Clark, *We Go to the West Country*, London, 1962.

25. Arthur Mee, *Cornwall*, London, 1967.

26. Derek Spooner, 'Industrial Movement, Rural Areas and Regional Policy', in *Regional Development and Planning*, Budapest, 1973, p. 147.

27. Charles Thomas, *The Importance of Being Cornish in Cornwall*, Redruth, 1973.

28. *New Cornwall*, Vol. 7, No. 6, 1959.

29. *New Cornwall*, Vol. 7, No. 9, 1960.

AN ICONOGRAPHY OF LANDSCAPE IMAGES IN CORNISH ART AND PROSE

Patrick Laviolette

PLUNGING and labouring on in a tide of visions,
Dolorous and dear,
Forward I pushed my way as amid waste waters
Stretching around,
Through whose eddies there glimmered the customed
   landscape
Yonder and near

                    —Thomas Hardy[1]

INTRODUCTION

In Britain at least, many people still imagine landscapes from a distant and elevated point of view—as if one stood in front of a motionless screen. Such a perspective parallels the artistic origins of the English word landscape, which initially alluded to raised pictorial representations of the world. Panoramic illustrations of towns and the countryside, however, harbour a vast measure of cultural information. For instance, they can inform us on the ways that both past and present societies perceive their environs and generate various senses of place. Further, they can give us insight into a culture's aesthetic, moral and ontological value systems. To some, the value systems that landscapes conceal are contradictory and therefore generate a nexus of contesting paradoxes. To others, they form a synthesis of consistent real and imagined views. Either way, as a distinctively British icon of history, the landscape concept opens a Pandora's box of paradigms. Nowhere else is this notion so filled with legacy. Nowhere else does the very term suggest more than scenery and *genres de vie* but also relates to quintessential national virtues. Indeed, rural Britain endlessly assumes the characteristics of both a wonder and wounder of the world, the fount of British resolve but also the source of British colonialisn. In this sense, we are dealing with a conglomerate of settings and scenes that impinge on every aspect of our lives.

Lowenthal notes how, throughout much of its history, relatively few large and medium-sized landowners and farmers have owned and managed Britain's southern countryside.[2] Generally, they have seen it as the proper place where proper people live. We are thus confronted with a socially segregated landscape, one that we presume to be white, English and middle-class. For its part, Cornwall is not a typical southern region. Hence, it has partially dodged the metaphor of spatial segregation. Conversely, it has developed its own particular metaphors as a land of myth and legend, as a coastal tourist trap, as an artistic oasis and as an economically impoverished rural region. To a certain extent, many Cornish villages and countryside tracts have become consummate artefacts, vast museum-like ruins.

More recently, a complex transformation of this rather exotic and intimidating territory has emerged. This has allowed the area to turn itself into a safe place for being viewed in and for certain kinds of activities such as climbing, walking, cycling, archaeology and of course various seaside pastimes. As a tourist venture, we can summarize Cornwall's current hyper-marginality by the thousands of looks that seasonally gaze over the land and sea from the summits of high-minded and privileged leisure or from the valleys of downmarket escapism. In some sense then, this peripheral rural countryside acts as a national playground that symbolizes both the insightful and the kitsch. Equally, however, as Thomas Hardy suggests above, the Cornish landscape illustrates a working environment, both past and present. In it we find an embodiment of post-industrial consciousness, a kaleidescope of perceptions and identities.

Given that significant variations exist in the perceptions of local residents versus those of visitors, Relph has devised a typology for the various types of insider and outsider views of place.[3] In this distinction he highlights how artists and authors generally fit the role ascribed to outsiders. This is so because they are either literally from another place or because their training has figuratively distanced them from the local populace's traditional attitudes and ways of seeing. Yet artists and writers are also principal agents in shaping and changing fashions for places. They communicate enduring regional images, the impact of which reaches out to tourists and the outside world. Examining a region's art and literature can, therefore give us an insight into the range of influence that creative forces have beyond the local. This essay attempts to gauge the level of this range of influence by providing both a semiotic analysis of Cornish landscape art and a deconstruction of Cornwall's literary landscape as depicted by Thomas Hardy, Daphne du Maurier and Virginia Woolf. In essence, the aim is to unearth certain of the key Cornish landscape portrayals that have emerged from the artistic and literary worlds in the past century and a half.

HISTORICAL ACCOUNT OF CORNISH LANDSCAPE ART AND PROSE

Prior to 1860, most Cornish artistic references illustrated scenes of St Michael's Mount or the country house at Mount Edgcumbe. Portraying the rest of Cornwall became popular largely after the opening of the Tamar bridge in 1859. Generally, the preferred subject matter in these early days of Cornish art was the coast. These representations, however, do not show coves of boats or fishermen. Instead, they portray moderately accessible sections of the wild coast, deliberately representing the haunts of nature. Between the time that artists started arriving in large numbers around 1860 and that period when the Newlyn art school got under way in 1880, the principal scenes of this district were of depopulated stormy headlands.[4]

Cornwall, which was to become a major focus of interest in the heroic period of landscape art (1870–1910), became fashionable for the first time during the romantic revival (1830–70). According to the observations of one art historian some time ago, the painter at Land's End could discover:

> Miles of grey and purple cliffs, cushioned with sea-pink, and bordered with golden furze and crimson heath—stretches of yellow sands lining the 'emerald crescent bays'—the silver sheen of the Atlantic—and a changeful sky, everywhere await his pencil.[5]

This author further reveals how the sea took the form of a powerful natural symbol as well as a metaphysical icon of human energy and futility. Consequently, shipwrecks and other tragedies at sea became favoured subject matter. Newlyn and St Ives were the most important coastal colonies during this period, with Falmouth, Fowey, Looe, Marazion, Mevagissey, Mullion, Penzance and Polperro acting as other significant seaside targets.

Having been in vogue since 1860, Cornwall attained its greatest popularity during the vernacular period of 1910–50. Indeed, during the world-war interim Cornwall was the most favoured area outside London for artists with a predelection for illustrating the panoramic.

As the mainstay of landscape art during the inter-war period, Cornwall maintained its reputation as a stronghold for coastal imagery. Especially noteworthy here is that this peninsula acted as the British archetype for picturing fishing coves and seaside villages.

The decline of this clichéd representation since 1940 exhibits the growing interest in displaying Cornwall's *terra firma*. Prominent in this genre are illustrations of the post-industrial scenes found either in abandoned tin mines or china-clay pits. The illustration of Cornwall's inland working environment has now become quite common. Many authors argue that the stereotyped inland image of Cornwall, usually contains some reference to mines or clay pits. This artistic revival in industrial landscapes may derive from the recent American interest in scenes of outstanding shapes and unusual forms such as cranes, kilns, scaffolding and winding gear. In Cornwall, this has manifested itself in an attraction for disused engine houses which exist for example in spectacular romantic views such as the one of Botallack; a scene that has become a Cornish logo. Ironically perhaps, the historical conservationist attitude has meant that industries have had to await the patina of age before acquiring aesthetic qualities.

Despite the interest in the Cornish interior, the coast has remained the most important feature during the recent formal period of landscape art (1950–80). Two types of coastal scenes add themselves to the portfolio of seascape illustrations during this time. The first type consists of remote lines of jagged cliffs. These usually depict an above bird's eye view of the water crashing against sombre coastal edges. The second reveals, in a semi-abstract style, long sweeping sandy bays. Although these scenes were of noted repute in the inter-war period, they have recently become popular due to their formal quality which emphasizes the central line of the shore with its hanging cliffs and clear reflecting sea.[6]

For their part, verse and prose in Cornwall have also been creations of the modern world. Two predominant literary views of the countryside have emerged since the 1870s. The first is Thomas Hardy's perspective in which the description of nature is paramount. Change and conflict are at the heart of his writings. The characters in his stories move about the physical environment—they are people of the land and it deeply affects them. Hardy includes a broad spectrum of characters in his works, and he focuses on the making of their livelihood. In such scenarios he insists on including peripheral perspectives. As such, farmers and labourers, the landed and the landless, the gentry and the destitute all figure as narrative voices. Generally then, his writings contain the discourses of both the privileged upper-middle class and that of the rural peasantry.

Contrarily, the second is the view from the big house. An important writer in this tradition is Virginia Woolf. Her countrysides have the quality of translucence, tranquillity and harmony. In her depiction of a world safe from change she provides us with an escape from modernity. In effect, she was amongst the last important English pastoral writers whose role it was to uncover the divine organization behind natural forms. The goal of the pastoral tradition was not particularization but poetry. Not reality but rhymes and rhythms. Not description but harmony. It is a tradition of repetition rather than representation. The countryside ideal that sprang from it was a mix between myth and reality. It encompassed at one end of the spectrum profound philosophical questions about the modernization of society and at the other, simple desires of escapism. In Cornwall, some of the philosophical questions revolved around the preservation of the *status quo*. Politically, Cornwall appeared as a timeless landscape in which social and economic realities had been painted out with picturesque brushes.[7]

By the 1920s, the country life movement had run its course and it would take forty years for any sign of resurgence. Enter Daphne du Maurier—who would continue the Cornish legacy of the rural narrative. She uses pastoral remnants that bespeak the existence of a tradition to which authors and readers alike are implicitly bound. She champions the idea that the countryside is a relic of ourselves, a kind of material manifestation of our identities and creative forces. In her eyes then, the landscape is a living and sensible commentary on our lives, actions and thoughts—a stifled exposé of a part of our souls.

Hardy, Woolf and du Maurier were amongst the major forebears of the pastoral literary movement which helped shape a nationwide countryside ideal at the turn of the century.[8] The use of the pastoral lexicon is one way in which ties with the past are indirectly established and promoted in their texts. For instance, the pleasant place or *locus amoenus* is an important stylistic tool of the pastoral tradition that these three authors have employed. It produces imagery in literature and a reaffirmation of tradition. It also functions to announce a pause in the novel's narrative diachrony, that is its unfolding in time. If the pastoralist is concerned with the past then the present concerns the hedonist and the future is the utopian's affair. Anthropology has a concept that parallels the *locus amoenus* of literary criticism in the form of the *imago mundi*. These images of sacred places constitute divine microcosms—little worlds of stones, water and trees—which are sacred for many cultures. Such miniature environments are locations of 'absolute reality' that embrace the timelessness of stones, the endless cycle of vegetative life and the inert process of water purification. In the images that they generate, such locales signify a fair view of the countryside as gliding from obscurity into clarity.[9]

SEMIOTIC ANALYSIS

The socio-semiotic process examines how signs and symbols capture articulated systems of meaning in their material settings. This technique bases itself on the premise that cultural objects are objects of use in particular historical contexts as well as constituents in systems of signification. As a conceptual tool, socio-semiotics relies on 'polysemy and the need to analyse the articulation of several sign systems for any given cultural object'.[10] Analysis in this instance builds a model for the sign, one that encompasses the viewpoints of both the producers and consumers of culture.

Studying landscape art socio-semiotically requires that we locate the processes of sign production and consumption within the context of iconographical image projection. This in turn ensures that we examine the mutually reinforcing matrix of social relations for the operation of interpretative codes. Such considerations put forth the full range of relationships between objects and individuals. From this, we begin to see sign functions as sign vehicles for the interpretation of spatiality since the production of meaning and its consumption by users rely on spatial codes of connotations.[11] A socio-semiotics approach exposes how these codes embed the meaning of new communities, subcultures, imagined communities and invented identities. These communities, cultures and identities themselves embody the diversity of landscapes and locales. In this sense, landscape diversity remains balanced between the fragmentation of symbolic meaning and the search for authenticity. The former derives in large part from pop-culture, the media and cultural dilution. Contrarily, the latter is as dependent on genuine artefacts, institutions and localized space as on cognitive processes of self-integration.

In providing a semiotic analysis of forty-five Cornish landscape paintings that are contemporary within the last 120 years or so, I hope to demonstrate how artists have communicated an iconography of images for the region which binds symbols and meaning to place.[12] According to Weiner this is an activity analogous to that of textual or discursive semantic analysis given that place and language unite. 'The manner in which human action and purposive appropriation inscribes itself upon the earth is an iconography of human intentions.'[13] Bearing this observation in mind, this section underlines the communicative potential of landscape art by appropriating the term language in its broadest possible sense and using it to read certain pictorial representations of Cornwall.

By associating the dates of the sampled works to their appropriate periods, we see that the thirty-nine dated pieces distribute themselves as follows: sixteen are of the heroic period (1870–1910), thirteen are of the vernacular epoch (1910–50), six are from the age of formalism and modernism (1950–80), and four are from the current post-modern era (1980–now). The majority of these views are of a panoramic, distant genre. Indeed, the forte of the landscape artists sampled here is that they use atmospheric sweeps of captivating light and dramatic coast-lines shrouded in mist and fog to generate a sense of being high up, among the clouds and the thermals. Such outlooks reinforce the pre-conception that art is a lonely, existential activity, where the artist confronts the universe alone.

A common motif in the later paintings of one of the more prolific artists in Cornwall, Stanhope Alexander Forbes, is that of a roadway leading into a landscape, creating an effect of distance. These roads announce the deep space that occurs in the picture, yet the entire landscape exists at the surface of the paintings. This awareness of the virtue of perspective is an illusionary device for the construction of landscape imagery which does not preclude a literal or expressive use of surface. Consequently, this meant that on the flat surface of a canvas, Forbes was able to invest his compositions with a clarity of depth and light, giving his works an emotional charge in keeping with its human subject matter. The nature of Realism, of which Forbes and the Newlyn School were quite fond, meant that many pictures wedded figurative Realism to Impressionism's highly pitched sensitivity to the behaviour of light—a theme that has always fascinated artists in Cornwall.[14] This general envelope of light is our point of departure in seeking how Cornwall most often represents itself and is represented.

According to Val Baker, a peculiar clarity of light exists in Corn-wall that throws the entire region into sharp perspective.[15] For him, this terrain exhibits a constantly shifting occurrence that reveals its large visual depth and distance. He cites many artists who claim that this peninsula's light gives everything a new meaning which redefines and enlarges the form and structure of the environment, a light that displaces the spatial relations of the canvas, whereby spaces become abstract and uniform. Consider for instance how Vyvyan grants a mystical nature to the effects that colour and light have on the quality of her environmental perception. 'It seemed as if the east wind had drained all colour from every object, large or small, from the grass at our feet to those faraway rocks; only black, brown and dull grey prevailed.'[16]

We know that light undoubtedly has a profound effect on our senses in the open countryside yet little has been written about how it affects our perception. Taking our mark from art history, we learn that the fusion of landscape elements into a total impression is achieved through the perception of light. Consequently, the rendering of light shows us that its representation in painting owes its value to it being an expression of aesthetics and love. As the light of the sun overflows the whole earth, so divinity dwells within everything and everything dwells within its mystique. This sense of the unity of creation that light provides is the basis for perception and representation. Hence, light heightens our sense of well being by enlarging the range of our physical experiences. Such an evanescent effect of light is fixed with the simplicity and certainty that gives a region an unmistakable look of cohesion to its atmosphere.[17] Perhaps nowhere else in Britain does the horizon over land and sea provide a continuous illusion of movement. Often the sky reflects an unearthly glow caused by the extraordinary disturbances that are going on in the upper air, those bubblings and convulsions of light which are entirely characteristic of Cornwall's cloudscapes. As such, this peninsula is the quintessential example of how light and shadow never stand still, where a luminous area engulfs the very centre of the landscape.

The content of the pictures sampled here reveals that this light shines mainly on an active working Cornish environment. Having stated this, we must not underestimate the importance of leisure depictions, given that almost half the sampled works combine vistas where leisure and work scenes occur together. Additionally, Jacobs reminds us that the creation of sexual analogies between the landscape and the human figure has been a typical theme in the St Ives art scene since the 1960s. This reinforces the hedonistic conception of leisure that marks the mood of the Cornish seaside .[18]

That Cornwall is accentuated as a working milieu in the landscape art of the last five generations does not necessarily translate into a heightened presence of people on the land, nor does it suggest that those present are of the working classes. Indeed, a third of the illustrations do not have any human beings in them whatsoever. An examination of the age and appearance of the figures which do occur informs us that all conceivable age groups are present with no particularly dominant age class. We can assume from their dress and appearance that people from all social classes and walks of life are present in the artworks with the exception of the physically disabled, ethnic groups (other than the Cornish) and itinerants. It is also worth mentioning that when artists have included human figures in the landscape, they have generally fore-grounded them, so that people are props in only five pictures.

Animals for their part are rare in appearance and number in the landscape art sampled. Those present are mainly domestic animals such as horses and dogs. A noteworthy absence of cattle and other farm animals occurs for reasons that are not quite clear since even though farm scenes are not customary, they are far from rare. Although a few cases depict wild animals these are equally not very diverse, consisting solely of birds and fishes. Unlike animals, buildings appear frequently. Generally, houses on their own or in conjunction with industrial constructions make up the most common forms of architecture. Surprisingly, despite the numerous references in the literature to the prominence of mines and clay-pits in representations of Cornwall, we see that industrial structures on their own do not figure prominently in these artworks.

Additionally, even though the marine environment is crucial to Cornish landscape artists, the proportion of seascapes without a hint of land is quite small. Instances that are solely inland are somewhat more common but in large part images that combine land and sea dominate. Perhaps the importance of beach scenes as a recurring theme explains this occurrence. In depicting Cornwall's human environment, the chosen artists have slightly preferred rural settings over village ones. Furthermore, they have chosen to illustrate views that are identifiable and locatable instead of generic or imagined sites. Fields and farmland are characteristic examples, representing a third of the total where land is prevalent. Sights of wilderness, on the other hand, manifest themselves infrequently and in those cases where the seascape prevails, boats prevail as the archetypal feature.

As far as the composition of these paintings is concerned, there is a balance between 'cold' and 'warm' depictions of Cornwall. This equilibrium between cold and warm representations emphasizes one of Cornwall's stereotypical paradoxes of having both a warm Mediterranean clime as well as being a wet and windy place. More generally, the paintings depict 'calm' rather than 'turbulent' interpretations of Cornish scenery. Laura Knight's style provides a good example of such sedate illustrations. On the whole her paintings are static entities that are rarely animated or in motion. Instead, they encourage the spectator to move around from different angles and experience her transparent, planar and spatially open pieces in a way that would parallel how she would move about in order to empathize with the countryside.[19]

Given that Cornwall principally takes on the form of a working environment with a moderate number of people and a considerable number of material artefacts such as boats and houses, we would presuppose that this territory generally appears as a cultural rather than a natural habitat. Indeed, the information regarding this distinction confirms such an assumption. Here it is the work of Alfred Wallis and Ben Nicholson that typify the genre of a finely controlled equilibrium between the given order of nature and the invented pattern of culture. Principally, they achieve this by creating a playful tension between the shallow, flattened space of Cubism and the evocative depth of landscape.

It might be interesting to compare these findings with Halle's study of American landscape representations in New York.[20] The pictures in the houses that he studied convey a vision where the presence of people is appropriate to the past landscapes of industrial societies or the current environs of non-industrial societies. Images of contemporary America, however, are particularly devoid of humans. Contemporary Cornwall, on the other hand, combines industrial elements with human ones. Halle's sample further divulges the exceptional preference for representations of nature that are sedate and calm. Trees are un-swept by the wind, waters are placid and the texture of snow-covered surfaces is smooth and undisturbed. In the case of his study then, landscape paintings pursue pervasive modern ideals; they are artefacts of virtual travel and vicarious experience. They stand for the imaginary achievement of free private leisure since they are unfettered by people, industrial scenes and the logistics of owning or leasing the depicted leisure space.

Despite their calm and quiet appearance, Cornish scenes differ in that they mimic a lived-in and worked-in environment. Artists in Cornwall have been fascinated by the landscape as a repository of history. Their focal aim has not been in creating pictorial illusions. Rather they have sought out a precise language of pure form where symbolic significances can articulate how the natural and the human have become metaphorical images for the material embodiment of culture onto the land. For example, Maeckelberghe sees the landscape as a metaphor for the way passion confronts reason. Like the famous Cornish painter Peter Lanyon, she searches for mythic dimensions to the countryside—not by associating landscape to the human figure as he does—but by identifying with the lost age of the pagan, barren and ancient elements of Cornwall. More recently in her career she has introduced expressionistic distortions to conventional compositions. The upshot has been to heighten the visual character of place in a body of work which represents Cornwall in a soft, milky light—where the topography turns into a dreamlike mirage in which the objects of nature no longer become clearly discernible.

The harmony in the art examined here is not a classical harmony.

Instead, it is an accord between abstract and experiential feelings for Cornwall's natural heritage. The relationship of the single to the whole, seen in overlapping as well as dispersed shapes, becomes a major theme in this landscape genre. Similarly, the viewer delights in exploring a spatial dynamic that is clearly captured in terms of a language of colour, lines and form which create the sensation of unrestricted movement and direction. Movement is, therefore, an unmistakable sub-theme throughout the sampled artworks. Cornish artists have deliberately depicted hidden links and rhythmic continuities across the countryside's topography. Indeed, they have associated a rapid calligraphy with the visual experience of an evolving scenery—the result being that the calm, tranquil environment also emerges as vibrant and unfolding.[21]

We observe from this analysis that representations of Cornwall are of a diverse nature. Granted, the view of the seascape dominates, yet this can be expected in a peninsula in which there is around 250 miles of coastal contact and where one is never more than 20 miles from shore. The diversity present comes in many forms. Landscape diversity is the first, with a variety of scenes that cover gardens, farmland, moorland, beaches, seascapes, cliffs, harbours, townscapes and industrial environments. Secondly, diversity occurs with regards to the climatic conditions so that all seasons and all types of conditions —from turbulent to tranquil—find a place. Material diversity is equally common, with artefacts that range the gamut of leisure objects and work tools. Finally, diversity exists in relation to the presence or absence of humans, the types of perspectives illustrated and the division between natural versus cultural descriptions. The one realm where diversity does not exists is in reference to ethnic diversity. Of the identifiable human figures, the large proportion seem to depict local people instead of visitors and whether insider or outsider those people portrayed are invariably Caucasian.

Although some work exists on the social forces that influence artists, we know very little of why certain pieces attain high or low levels of popularity with audiences and even less about how to construct a theory of taste for certain styles. To rectify this, Halle has argued that we need 'an understanding of art and cultural items in the audience's own terrain, namely the social life, architecture, and surroundings of the house and neighborhood'.[22] This analysis of the interplay between meaning and the material context calls for a materialist approach that goes beyond the traditional mode of the production model to encompass a focus on the mode of dwelling. Examining landscape art in the context of the house is especially relevant since historically the ties between art, abode and the area in which they coexist are extremely tight. Indeed, the very occurrence of a landscape genre in the West harks back to the country house or villa-based culture of the Renaissance. This is where the brief semiotic analysis presented here falls short. Consequently, the methodology of examining landscape art in the context of familiar settings such as homes, shops and pubs is a line of investigation that I am currently pursuing in Cornwall.

HERMENEUTICS AND CORNWALL'S LITERARY LANDSCAPE

As Raymond Williams once put it, 'we learn to see a thing by learning to describe it'.[23] He makes this point ever more lucid by adding that we do not describe things that are known since by description we discover them anew and invest them with fresh meaning. As a conceptual philosophy, hermeneutics is closely related to such a humanistic interest in subjective interpretation and description. Understanding the world of experience defines meaning as contextually located in the world, not floating around like a transcendental essence outside of experience. The hermeneutic concern with a meaningfully laden world of purposeful beings is similar to the phenomenologist's concern with the lifeworld of everyday experience. Such a mode of investigation leads to an active dialogue between different constructions of reality. Given that such discourse reveals the way in which an array of images reflect reality, it is evidence for an all-pervasive social spatiality by which places, views and scenes link to feelings, ideas and socio-political ideologies.

In this sense, we view discourse in the context of its spatial significance as opposed to the modernist's Cartesian eye which cannot penetrate the opaque and non-linear screen of rigorous subjective observation.[24] By contrast, post-modern interpretations of the world read it hermeneutically, as a divine text. They throw-up a challenge to the myopic regimes of modernity, daring the observer to read the texture of the land and the other. As such, a hermeneutic examination of Cornwall's literary landscape is not merely an interesting intellectual exercise but will actually contribute to the understanding of how Cornish images or myths form and inform environmental perceptions. In this way, such a theoretical tool is an appropriate way of rectifying the lack of attention paid to the concrete lifeworld of agrarian pastoralists and other people on the margin.

Literature can move about the environment in ways that other art forms cannot. By their very nature paintings offer static views. Literature, on the other hand, may progress through the countryside or it may hop around from one scene to another. Additionally, the literary medium can produce a feeling of vicarious insidedness with places, given that the information communicated historically contextualizes the represented locales. The novel's changing content, form, function, shape and size tell us a great deal about the society from which it originates. The evolution of the novel provides the context for examining the evolution of national environmental ideologies. In his book *Poetry, Space, Landscape* Fitter defines the literary landscape as a notion that works by metaphor to overtly ground the optical in the ideological.[25] For him, the concept of the literary landscape is intrinsically closer than art to ideation, to the world of relations, to explicit networks of thoughts.

Fitter's objective is to map certain historical varieties of environmental perception in poetry. The premise of his book is that the multiple bases of human awareness are what generate our geographical consciousness. By linking this to literary theory—where mutable interpretative communities read the countryside much as they read a text—with distinct horizons of expectation, he strengthens the connections that exist between our perceptions and the literary medium. Such links are especially prominent in Cornwall since several influential authors have graced this place with rich regional descriptions. The literature that I will examine below are prime examples of works that have animated the landscape genre in Cornwall. They are: Thomas Hardy's short poem 'Beeny Cliff'[26] and his 374-page tome *A Pair of Blue Eyes*,[27] Daphne du Maurier's autobiographical Cornish history *Vanishing Cornwall*[28] and two pieces by Virginia Woolf, her epic *To the Lighthouse*[29] as well as an extract from her early journal which describes a family holiday in Cornwall.[30]

The topographical descriptions and representations of these texts are nothing if not dynamic. Their distinctive characteristic is that they exhibit an enactment over time of the conflictual situations from which they arise. Fundamental structural oppositions such as near far, left and right, and horizontal and vertical are everywhere at work to organize and give visual coherence to the descriptive act. The process involves uncovering a system of oppositions in a set through which largely unconscious search for resolutions to conflicts occurs. Objects in nature—trees, mountains, plains, riverbanks, flowers, the sun and the moon—occupy crucial places in that oppositional system. Moreover, conflicts frequently find indirect symbolic solutions through these objects, solutions that do not appear on the more direct plane of explicit philosophical statement.[31]

By examining the landscape descriptions in the selections, we see that these three authors have favoured panoramic descriptions over detailed up-close ones. The notion of perspective is fundamental to adequate topographical readings that extend beyond traditional limits so as to provide integrated and meaningful interpretation of imagery in prose. In considering the workings of perspective, readers typically seek to discover the specific vantage point or locus from which one perceives the scene of the narrative. Extending the notion of perspective, however, and relating it to that of the 'point of view', taken in its broadest sense, provides a more complete interpretation. The broad sense refers both to the physical vision and to the mental outlook or attitudes of the protagonists who serve as the centres of interest in the fiction. These agents are in fact the focalizers of the story. As such, one can advance that it is because we consider their mental outlooks that we come across scenic descriptions in prose that are even more wide-ranging than those found in art.

A disparity with the artistic illustrations also occurs in relation to the presence of people in the literary landscape where over half the scenes (instead of one third for art) are devoid of any obvious human presence. Furthermore, even when people do manifest themselves in the citations, they are—with one exception—either as a couple in a romantic setting or on their own roaming the wilderness. This use of nature as the backdrop for romantic encounters is a common theme in pastoralist writing and it often serves as a symbolic reference to a sentimentality for the countryside and a love for the great outdoors. This use of the environment also informs us on the politics of sexuality during the epoch of writing, since the presence of couples in romantic liaisons are strictly heterosexual and thus a fairly equal sex ratio occurs in the descriptions. A difference with the art world equally takes places in relation to the fore-grounding of persons in the representations. Here the difference between whether people are marginal or central to the recollection is less pronounced.

Additionally, a significant difference exists concerning the content of the landscapes represented in art versus those in text. The latter mostly reveal leisure scenes as opposed to work environments. Moreover, the presence of wild animals is more significant in the narratives than in the artworks. The following quotation by Daphne du Maurier highlights an acute awareness of wildlife:

Birds, except for the gulls that piloted him to port, have hitherto been absent. Now they are everywhere. Oyster-catchers—seapie to the Cornish—with a quick seeping cry, swoop to the mud-banks in a flash of black and white. The smaller redshank and sanderling scurry to probe the slate. Further up-river, where a dead branch from a fallen tree, strung about with seaweed, overhangs the water, a heron stalks, prinking his way like some grave professor fearing to lose a galosh, then suddenly stands and broods, his wings humped, his head buried in his feathers. Later the tide slackens, the trees darken, the birds are hushed, and there is no sound except the wisper of water past the anchor chain until, if the yachtsman is lucky, he will hear, during the magic moments before true dusk falls, the night jar call.[32]

As far as architecture is concerned, references to the built environment occur in a little more than half the passages and the majority of these are homesteads on their own or in conjunction with industrial sites. Thomas Hardy here provides a key testimony to the portrait of a country house:

The dusk had thickened into darkness while they thus conversed, and the outline and surface of the mansion gradually disappeared. The windows, which had before been as black blots on a lighter expanse of wall, became illuminated, and were transfigured to squares of light on the general dark body of the night landscape as it absorbed the outlines of the edifice into its gloomy monochrome.[33]

As with art, narrative depictions favour the combination of landscape and seascape elements. Instances that are solely inland are somewhat less common and seascapes on their own are infrequent. For their part beaches are not uncommon, covering a third of the passages where land is prevalent. In such scenes, fields and farmland share the same amount of representations as descriptions of wilderness. In those cases where the seascape dominates, water wins over cliffs and boats as the dominant feature.

The composition and temperament of these renditions is remarkably similar to those of the artist's illustrations in which calm scenery prevails over turbulent ones. Hardy volunteers an example: 'No wind blew inside the protecting belt of evergreens, wasting its force upon the higher and stronger trees forming the outer margin of the grove.'[34] Similarly again, instances representing warm and cold climatic conditions compare to those on canvas. The use of colour in the written representations occurs in exactly half the passages. The detail and richness of this verbal coloration, however, are rather limited, with only a few hues at a time ever being mentioned. One of the most colourfully rich citations is from Virginia Woolf:

'It suddenly gets cold. The sun seems to give less heat,' she said. Looking about her, for it was bright enough, the grass still soft deep green, the house starred in its greenery with purple passion flowers, and rooks dropping cold cries from the high blue. But something moved, flashed, turned a silver wing in the air. It was September after all, the middle of September, and past six in the evening. So off they strolled down the garden in the usual direction, past the tennis lawn, past the pampas grass, to that break in the thick hedge, guarded by red hot pokers like braziers of clear burning coal, between which the blue waters of the bay looked bluer than ever.[35]

Given the high proportion of scenes that portray Cornwall as a region of leisure, we find that cultural scenes make up a relatively small number of the total. This observation emphasizes just how important the distinction between city and country is as a thematic ingredient to pastoralist writing and helps explain why, unlike the artists, the writers have dealt almost exclusively with rural as opposed to urban subject matter. Regarding the inspirations for their descriptions, authors, as opposed to artists, seem to rely more on the fabrication of generic or imaginary places than on scenes that are identifiable and locatable.

This dependence on imaginary places is definitive of the nostalgic genre.[36] Hardy went to great lengths to stress that he was writing about rural life as it was prior to industrialization. Victorian readers easily empathized with his idyllic novels and their description of a surviving pastoral culture. That he became an exemplar of the countryside ideal in his own time reflects the late Victorian unease with industrialization. Indeed, he offered an alternative, he created a detailed picture of the people and customs of simpler times. As such, he was the voice of a growing number of people whose interests were in pre-industrial folk-culture. Particularly, Hardy brought out in his writing the worldliness of a country lifestyle that was rapidly disappearing. The result is that he is now part of an enduring English tradition of country writing that has set out to chronicle—through direct experience and knowledge—the vestiges of country life. For example, Drabble notes:

Hardy observed and described the smallest details of soil, contour, crop and vegetation, and he adds to this knowledge an antiquarian interest in topography and a poet's use of language . . . he could . . . tell each tree from the distinctive rustling of leaves. His novels contain the most precise and informed descriptions of country tasks, and of man's relation to the land.[37]

The main theme that permeates Hardy's oeuvre is the ache of modernism. The polarities that give structure and coherence to his work include the shifts that occur from intuition to rationality, from land to capital, from rural to urban, and from religion to science. The driving narrative power that underlies these oppositions rests in the fluctuating individual fortunes of his protagonists who radiate a potent sense of place and who exist in the confines of rich regional descriptions. Indeed, 'Hardy's novels constitute one of the most sustained creations of place in the tradition of the English novel'.[38] In them he outlines the effects of a rural region in transition, where rich local customs confront the metropolitan homogenization of society and lifestyles.

The balancing of oppositions is a tool that Hardy frequently uses to create and maintain tension in his work. One example exists in his portrayals of the coastline. Cliffs have a dialectic symbolism, representing linkage, connectedness and relationship as well as rupture and the ultimate cut-off of death. For instance in 'Beeny Cliff' Hardy poignantly depicts these themes. Positioned on the Cornish cliffs of human tragedy, he relates how love is lost on the overhangs of the shore. His style here is to connect and contrast long-lost happiness with links between the past and the present, between man and woman, and between place and emotions. This is unquestionably a case where landscape and seascape, symbolism and function, and inner and outer all meet up on the edge of the world in order to stir up the life of the imagination.

Virginia Woolf also found herself compelled to re-enter epochs gone by. Her annual seaside visits to Cornwall had left a mark on her writing in which she was able to come to terms with that 'foreign country' of the past. Woolf's writing describes times in the past as opposed to locations in space. For example, in *To the Lighthouse* the landscapes and seascapes are overtly Cornish yet the story is said to take place on the Isle of Skye. We tolerate that the gardens full of gorse, with views of the Scilly Isles, Gurnard's Head and those white Cornish cottages built on the sea cliffs are transposed to Scotland because we understand that her main contention is that the past lives on in memory and the literary landscape just as much as it does in our actual surroundings. Such a past is not static. It mutates and shimmers as the present throws its shadow backwards. Equally—but more slowly—the environment itself changes. It is the living link between what we were and what we have become.

It is these disturbances that invade meaning as well as order. Scenic incongruities obtrude themselves upon our consciousness. Thus Woolf, by reminiscing about material culture—fishing boats, rocks, dried limpets, yellow brown seaweed and crying gulls—is able to describe the places where the dead live in her memories. In short, by the alternate medium of the materiality of the landscape, she bypasses the need for detailed regional descriptions and opts instead for a generic genre where life histories ground themselves in both tangible materials and an amorphic countryside ideology.

Godrevy Lighthouse provides a good example of Woolf's combination of material culture and nostalgia. It is enigmatic and ageless, subject neither to illness or war. After remaining in her thoughts for over a decade, this timeless monument provides the material link between the living and the dead, the present and the past. It is here that Mrs Ramsay could not help but exclaim 'Oh how beautiful!' once the blue water before her laid bare the worn Lighthouse, forbidding and shrouded in midst. And, in the same field of vision, the affiliated representation of nature, wilderness and a glorified past 'as far as the eye could see, fading and falling, in soft low pleats, the green sand dunes with wild flowing grasses on them, which always seemed to be running away into some moon country, uninhabited of men'.[39] In this instance the material form is also a shell, to be metaphorically decoded in the stripping away of sensory qualities from its symbolic core. Consequently, we can look through the Lighthouse to its interior brilliance. We can see it as an everlasting source of hope and guidance, prized for its shining role in the source of life, perhaps even as a symbol for rebirth. Paradoxically, to complement this reading we could reveal a more sinister side to the interpretation, where despair prevails given that the allusion to the matched scene seems to be evasive of, and unwelcoming to, humanity. Indeed, can this not also mean that nature can no longer support humanity, in that the Lighthouse as a reservoir of hope has failed to sow meaning into either nature, wilderness or the present?

Daphne du Maurier's bibliographical historiography again sees the Cornish landscape through the tainted spectacles of sentimentality. Her book *Vanishing Cornwall*, however, is much more self-involved and phenomenological in temperament. Hence, her book is an inward articulation of nature in sensation. It focuses on the sights and tones of common occurrence. Generally, her need to express such experiences derives from both a mistrust and desertion of the controlling faculty of human reason. Consequently, even though her direct affective engagements of sense experience are evident, we witness the descriptions of such engagements as solitary and unsubstantiated.

A concomitant contradiction arises in the association that she makes between being an inside chronicler and an outside observer. In most of her descriptions, the narrator is an anonymous persona who in some way disengages from the scene. In this sense, the descriptive voice is an avatar of that prototypical other. Indeed, authors such as Jameson argue that alienation is at the base of the landscape concept, whereby the seed of modern landscape description germinates with the rise of capitalism and the ensuing breach that occurs between land ownership and community ties. According to Jameson what occurs in the process of capitalist reification is that 'the visual features of ritual, or those practices of imagery still functional in religious ceremonies, are secularised and reorganised into ends in themselves, in easel painting and new genres like landscape'.[40] Daphne du Maurier's prose is a prime example of a middle ground between such an alienated perspective and an engaged existential narration.

CONCLUSION

According to Val Baker, Cornwall is a hearth for creativity. He postulates that this peninsula is unique in radiating a creativity that attracts a disproportionate number of craft-folk, painters, photographers, poets, sculptors and other creatively minded souls. As he claims, there seems to be a 'mysterious net in which Cornwall seems to enmesh all kinds of creative workers'.[41] While the inherent creativity of Cornwall is certainly questionable, we can accept the tenet that a large part of the Cornish countryside is revealed through its human landscape features. As such, this region is a place where it is a given to meet up with artists of all types who are themselves tightly affiliated with specific places and thus form an integral part of the environment. Basically, they act as landscape features in and of themselves; 'artmarks' as it were. It follows that creative forces can indeed exist in Cornwall, although not as an intrinsic attribute. Instead, one could advance the occurrence of a bilaterally functioning creativity whereby creative workers are part of the landscape and the landscape is a part of them. They have shared their talent with the region and in return it has provided a remarkable source of inspiration and material. Consequently, Cornish communities are immortalized vicariously by the creation of numerous works of art that encompass a sense of Cornishness.

This interweaving of creativity and environment, image and epithet is therefore one of the factors that bind the identity of this place into a true panorama of the mind. The landscape of the mind does not reveal any particular mind. Rather, it illustrates a perceived amalgam of diverse ways of looking at similar things in which we cast onto the countryside an imaginative sweep of images.[42] Seemingly then, landscapes exist in the collective mind. They act as a metaphor for the world of objects which is itself but an endless circle of mutuality reflecting metaphors. All the symbolic manipulations of body experience, starting with displacements within a mythically structured space, tend to impose the integration of the body space within cosmic space. It does so by grasping, in terms of the same concepts, the relationships between humanity and the natural world.

In Cornwall such ephemeral metaphorical relationships reveal themselves via certain icons of identity, such as art, literature, industry, Celticity and the landscape. They are points of access through which the deeper structures of the Cornish drama shine. Consequently, those images and symbols that bear identity in harmony with the past and the present tell of an inextricably interwoven existence between people, artefacts and environment. The entwining of past and present is especially visible in numerous local landmarks and named places of this peninsula. These are spatial records that partly serve to anchor myth. Hence, Gelling has argued that the vast and subtle topographical vocabularies of the Cornish population are remarkably sensitive to both diversities on the ground and to meandering socio-cultural occurrences.[43] From this we draw that landscape icons are mnemonic of social knowledge. They relate stories about the origins of how communities order their territory, demarcate unique features in the land and exoticize seemingly mundane everyday spaces. One's experiences of the environment may vary but it is just this varied overlapping and independent knowledge and experience of place and person that makes the landscape cognitively and emotionally vibrate with ongoing meaning.

NOTES AND REFERENCES

1. T. Hardy, 'In Front of the Landscape', *Satires of Circumstance*, London, 1914.
2. D. Lowenthal, 'British National Identity and the English Landscape', *Rural History* 2, 1991, pp. 205–30.
3. E. Relph, *Place and Placelessness*, London, 1976.
4. P. Howard, *Landscapes: the Artists' Vision*, London, 1991.
5. W.H. Tregellas, 'Artists Haunts I: Cornwall, the Cliffs', *Magazine of Art*, 1878, p. 8.
6. P. Davies, *St. Ives Revisited: Innovators and Followers*, Gwent, 1994.
7. L. Binyon, *Landscape in English Art and Poetry*, London, 1931.
8. M. Bunce, *The Countryside Ideal: Anglo-American Images of Landscape*, London, 1994.
9. D. Daiches and J. Flower, *Literary Landscapes of the Bristish Isles*, London, 1979.

10. M. Gottdiener, *Postmodern Semiotics: Material Culture and the Forms of Postmodern Life*, Cambridge, Mass., 1995, p. 29.
11. S. Lash and J. Urry, *Economies of Signs and Space*, London, 1994.
12. Two criteria have served to justify my choice of illustrations for this analysis: (a) the picture had to be an identifiable portrayal of a Cornish landscape, hence omitting excessively abstract works; (b) the date of the chosen item's creation had to be subsequent to 1880 (in the case of the nine artworks that are not inscribed with a date, I assume that they are post-1880 given that the artists who made them are essentially twentieth-century painters). In total, the analysis relies on forty colour plates and five black and whites. They are listed below in chronological order and were chosen from the following sources: *St. Ives Revisited: Innovators and Followers*, Davies 1994; *St Ives: 1883–1993 Portrait of an Art Colony*, Whybrow 1994; *Stanhope Forbes and the Newlyn School*, Fox 1993; *Artists from Cornwall*, Manasseh, Cross, Berlin, & Mellis 1992; and *The British Landscape 1920–1930*, Jeffrey 1984.

1. Alethea Garstin: *Penzance Harbour and St. Mary's*, n.d. Oil on panel.
2. Lawrence Isherwood: *St. Ives Harbour*, n.d. Oil on canvas.
3. Dame Laura Knight: *At the Edge of the Cliff*, n.d. Oil on canvas.
4. Charmian Leonard: *Near Zennor*, n.d. Oil on canvas.
5. Moffat Lindner: *Woman at Well*, n.d.
6. Sydney Mortimer Laurence: *Cornish Lugger*, n.d. Oil on canvas.
7. Rachel Nicholson: *Pig 'n Fish*, n.d. Oil on canvas.
8. John A. Park: *Sailing Boats St. Ives*, n.d. Oil on canvas.
9. Stanhope Alexander Forbes: *The Slip*, 1885. Oil on canvas.
10. Stanhope Alexander Forbes: *A Fish Sale on a Cornish Beach*, 1885. Oil on canvas.
11. Stanhope Alexander Forbes: *Off to the Fishing Grounds*, 1886. Oil on canvas.
12. Stanhope Alexander Forbes: *Beach Scene St. Ives*, 1886. Oil on canvas.

13. Helene Schjerfbeck: *View of St Ives*, 1887. Oil on panel.
14. Norman Garstin: *The Rain it Raineth Every Day*, 1889. Oil on canvas.
15. Walter Langley: *Disaster*, 1889. Watercolour on paper laid on stretcher.
16. W.H.Y. Titcomb: *Marguerites*, 1895.
17. Stanhope Alexander Forbes: *Across the Stream*, 1897. Oil on canvas.
18. Stanhope Alexander Forbes: *The Drinking Place*, 1900. Oil on canvas.

19. Stanhope Alexander Forbes: *Goodbye—Off to Skibereen*, 1901. Oil on canvas.
20. R. Hayley Lever: *Boats Before Smeatons Pier and Lighthouse*, 1905. Oil on canvas.
21. John A. Park: *Boats at Anchor, Late Afternoon*, 1905. Oil on canvas.
22. Stanhope Alexander Forbes: *Newlyn*, 1909. Oil on canvas.
23. Harold Harvey: *The Close of a Summer's Day*, 1909. Oil on canvas.

24. Dame Laura Knight: *The Beach*, 1909. Oil on canvas.
25. Elizabeth Forbes: *Blackberry Gatherers*, 1912. Oil on canvas.
26. Stanhope Alexander Forbes: *Going to School, Paul.* 1917. Oil on canvas.
27. Stanhope Alexander Forbes: *Market Jew, Thursday*, 1923. Oil on canvas.
28. Dame Laura Knight: *Sennen Cove, Cornwall*, 1926. Oil on canvas.
29. Alfred Wallis: *St-Ives*, 1928. Oil on panel.
30. John A. Park: *The Morning Ride (St Ives)*, 1930. Oils.
31. Ernest Procter: *Summer Holidays*, 1934. Oil on canvas.
32. Dame Laura Knight: *September Radiance*, 1937. Poster.
33. Stanhope Alexander Forbes: *Village Rendezvous*, 1938. Oil on canvas.
34. Ben Nicholson: *Mousehole*, 1947. Oil and pencil on canvas, mounted on wood.
35. Patrick Hayman: *Harbour and Fishing Boat*, 1951. Oil on canvas.
36. Joan Gillchrest: *Porthleven Setting Off*, 1975. Oil on canvas.
37. Joan Gillchrest: *Mousehole, Cornwall*, 1977. Oil on canvas.
38. Margo Maeckelberghe: *Estuary*, 1978. Oil on canvas.
39. Margo Maeckelberghe: *Scilly Blue Round*, 1987. Oil on canvas.
40. Tony Giles: *Entering Charlestown*, 1991. Oil on board.

Black and Whites
41. James Lynn Pitt: *Clodgy*, n.d.
42. John Milton: *Cornish Village*, 1945. Ink and gouache on paper.
43. Ben Nicholson: *Chytton, Cornwall*, 1949. Chalk on paper.
44. Colin Johnson: *Chalets and Sand dunes, Hayle,* 1981. Oil.
45. Gill Watkiss: *Journey Round Cape Cornwall*, 1990. Oil on canvas.

13. J.F. Weiner, *The Empty Place: Poetry, Space, and Being Among the Foi of Papua New Guinea*, Bloomington, 1991, p. 50.
14. C. Fox, *Stanhope Forbes and the Newlyn School*, Devon, 1993.
15. D. Val Baker, *The Timeless Land: the Creative Spirit in Cornwall*, Bath, 1973.
16. C.C. Vyvyan, *Letters from a Cornish Garden*, London, 1972, p. 107.
17. K. Clark, *Landscape into Art*, London, 1976.
18. M. Jacobs, *The Good and Simple Life*, Oxford, 1985.
19. M. Whybrow, *St Ives: 1883–1993 Portrait of an Art Colony*, Suffolk, 1994.
20. D. Halle, *Inside Culture: Art and Class in the American Home*, Chicago, 1993.
21. Davies, 1994.
22. Halle, 1993, p. 3.
23. R. Williams, *The Long Revolution*, London, 1961.
24. S. Lash and J. Friedman, *Modernity and Identity*, Cambridge, Mass., 1992.
25. C. Fitter, *Poetry, Space, Landscape: Toward a New Theory*, Cambridge, 1995.

26. T. Hardy, 'Beeny Cliff', 1913, in *Landscape Poets: Thomas Hardy*, (intro. by P. Porter), London, 1981.
27. T. Hardy, *A Pair of Blue Eyes*, London, 1873.
28. D. du Maurier, *Vanishing Cornwall: the Spirit and History of Cornwall*, Middlesex, 1967.
29. V. Woolf, *To the Lighthouse*, London, 1927.
30. V. Woolf, 'Diary Cornwall, 1905', in M. Leaska (ed.), *A Passionate Apprentice: the Early Journals 1897–1909 Virginia Woolf*, London, 1990.
31. Gottdiener, 1995.
32. du Maurier, 1967, p. 19.
33. Hardy, 1873, p. 40.
34. Hardy, 1873, p. 51.
35. Woolf, 1927, pp. 24–5.
36. J.R. Short, *Imagined Country: Environment, Culture and Society*, London, 1991.
37. M. Drabble, *A Writer's Britain: Landscape in Literature*, London, 1979, p. 177.
38. Drabble, 1979, p. 177.
39. Woolf, 1927, p. 17.
40. F. Jameson, *The Political Unconscious*, Ithaca, 1981, p. 63.
41. Val Baker, 1973, p. 73.
42. A. Enstice, *Thomas Hardy: Landscapes of the Mind*, London, 1979.
43. M. Gelling, *Place-names in the Landscape*, London, 1984.

CORNISH IDENTITY AND LANDSCAPE IN THE WORK OF ARTHUR CADDICK

Catherine Brace

Cornwall turns out to be many places, as perceived by different people and at different times.[1]

INTRODUCTION

This article examines the construction and representation of Cornwall in the poetry and prose of Arthur Caddick, who lived and worked in Nancledra, near St Ives, Cornwall, between 1945 and 1981. Arthur Caddick's writing made explicit the link between Cornish landscape and identity, making him a tempting subject of research for cultural geographers and those from other disciplines interested in Cornish studies. In his work Caddick argued that the unique qualities of the Cornish landscape inspired creative effort and invoked a particular sense of place. Significantly, though, he insisted that Cornishness was not a matter of birth but a state of mind realized through contact with the culture and landscape of Cornwall. As a Yorkshireman by birth, Caddick satirized those who insisted that only people born in Cornwall could feel or evoke the spirit of the place and vigorously attacked the Cornish Gorsedd's apparent claim that Cornishness was located exclusively in language and traditions. Caddick was both friend and critic of Cornish nationalism in the post-war period, occupying a complex place in recent Cornish (and Celtic) literature.

This article also contributes to the growing body of work on the cultural construction of place and brings together ideas about the relationship between landscape and identity from contemporary cultural geography and innovative new work on Cornish identity and culture from Cornish and Celtic Studies. It follows other recent work on the construction and representation of Cornish identity in 'casting place as a social and cultural process rather than an achieved state or a pre-social residue or refuge'.[2] It also seeks to challenge, as Deacon has done recently, the idea that 'outsiders were the main actors in constructing identities of the Celtic peripheries of Britain, identities which were then used by insiders as their own self-definition'.[3] Rather, this article seeks to disrupt the binary opposition of insider and outsider and show that individuals cannot be easily categorized in this way. In so doing, the chapter highlights the contested nature of identity and representation and calls attention to the specificity of place in the construction of meaning.

The article begins with a short biography of Arthur Caddick and then examines his complex response to the activities of the Gorsedd and Mebyon Kernow, and particularly the language revival. The final part of the article examines Caddick's ideas about the effect of Cornwall's landscape on creative effort.

ARTHUR CADDICK

Arthur Caddick was born in 1911 at Coatham in Yorkshire and spent a sickly childhood engrossed in books. He was educated at Sedbergh and Wadham College Oxford where he officially read Jurisprudence to please his father, but attended more English Literature lectures and secretly wished to have read English.[4] He was married to his wife Peggy in 1938 and they moved from London to Kerbournec in Brittany. When war broke out they returned to London, and by 1945 they were living in a garden flat opposite Holloway Jail. Of this time Caddick wrote: 'We were surrounded by a desolation of dirt and brick and noise and concrete and corruption. Our first three children were as much prisoners as the women locked up opposite them.'[5] In 1945 Caddick decided to move the young family to Cornwall and impulsively sold all their furniture and boarded a train to Penzance, 'the last station in England, and the genial, healthy, happy centre of the peninsula where the air is clean, the seas wash round, and the earth lies tranquil beneath the most intricate light in the kingdom'.[6] Caddick and his wife stayed in Cornwall for over thirty years until Caddick's ill health forced them to move to North Devon. Looking back at this time in 1975 whilst revising his autobiography, Caddick mused that Cornwall had given his wife and children (of whom there were five eventually) something 'weighed against which the most material lacks are pennyweights . . . cities can be jails. Their dwellers do not watch the seasons. The eight o'clock news tells them when it is spring.'[7] Caddick's own private reason for moving to Cornwall was to pursue his life-long ambition to be a writer, Caddick remarking that he 'had never wanted to do anything else, except to read' and 'imagined Cornwall as an ideal environment to write in'.[8]

It was from the family's rented cottage at Trenowin Downs, near St Ives, that Caddick had his first view of the cottage that would be their family's home for over thirty years—Windswept Cottage at Nancledra, about four miles from St Ives. The cottage came with Caddick's job of looking after an electricity sub-station in a nearby field. 'From the window of the furnished cottage', wrote Caddick:

> I first noticed, down across some rough croft, tangled with bracken and furze, and fragrant with heath and wild thyme the cottage we have made our home . . . This cottage was called Windswept, and stood by the side of the ancient bridle path from Marazion to Zennor, down which the pack mules trod with tin through ages whose history is now in-decipherable as the contours of St. Michael's Mount when the clinging wraiths of mist drift past its ancient shore.[9]

From this prose it is possible to get a hint of Caddick's ebullient character, his intense attachment to West Penwith and his particular skill in using landscape and weather to convey a sense of both place and history. Frank Ruhrmund, a fellow poet, recalled his main memory of Caddick as being an oral and visual one:

> Visually he was quite a sight! He was a good looking man— tall hawk-like man and his voice matched his appearance—I suppose that's what you remember more than anything . . . and he had . . . a marvellous booming voice . . . If you were in Penzance, in Market Jew Street—and this is no exaggeration —if Arthur was one end of the street and you were down the other, you could tell it was Arthur (laughs)—you could hear him booming away. He loved it—he loved declaiming.[10]

After settling in Cornwall, Caddick quickly published several collections of poetry including *Lyrics from Nancledra* (1950) and *Quiet Lutes and Laughter* (1955), and these were well received critically. Caddick became a well-known local figure, with a wide circle of friends and acquaintances in and around St Ives. He counted amongst his close friends Bernard Leach, Peter Lanyon and Guido Morris. He held public poetry readings on his own and with Cornishman Frank Ruhrmund and Scotsman Sydney Graham, among others. However, he never achieved commercial success with his poetry and his large family struggled to survive in their small cottage. He continued to write and publish even after he left in 1981, but was always associated with Cornwall, in particular West Penwith. Such was his renown that Derek Tangye, another well-known Cornish author, called Caddick 'the Dylan Thomas of Cornwall' in the introduction to Caddick's last collection of poetry *Call of the West*.[11]

Unfortunately, Caddick was an inveterate drinker—even publishing a pub guide to West Cornwall entitled *One Hundred Doors are Open*[12]—and what little money he earned from writing was quickly spent in his favourite pubs in St Ives or Penzance. As his wife Peggy Caddick recalled, 'I think we had a guardian angel (laughs). I really don't know looking back how we managed. We had the garden and the hens.'[13]

It soon became apparent to Caddick that he had arrived in Cornwall at a time when Cornish language, identity, culture and nationalism were being explored. The Inter-Celtic Festival was held in St Ives in 1949, and The *Cornish Review*, a magazine dedicated to the 'Cornish people and their cultural activities and Cornwall as a creative centre' was launched.[14] The fifties saw the formation of Mebyon Kernow ('Sons of Cornwall' in the Cornish language), a proto-nationalist movement later to become a political party, and the publication of new editions of Robert Morton Nance's Cornish–English, English–Cornish Dictionaries. Never shy of intellectual debate, it was on questions of Cornwall's identity that Caddick wrote some of his most incisive statements in poetry and prose.

ARTHUR CADDICK AND THE CORNISH LANGUAGE

Some of Arthur Caddick's most biting satirical verse centred on the activities of the Cornish Gorsedd (a college of Bards modelled on the Welsh Gorsedd) and Mebyon Kernow, and in particular on the attempted revival of the Cornish language by Robert Morton Nance, who also lived in the village of Nancledra. In his largely unpublished autobiography *Laughter from Land's End*,[15] Caddick argued that the activities of the Celtic Revivalists were superimposed on the Cornish background: a phrase that hinted at the atmosphere of inauthenticity that he felt pervaded Revivalism.

The 'Old Cornish Movement' had 'several layers of differing depth', he wrote. He went on:

> The most profound is Mebyon Kernow, the Cornish Underground Resistance Movement, in everything except that it publicises its rebellion. Then there is the Federation of Old Cornwall Societies which homogenises the activities, mainly historical, of parochial groupings of enthusiasts. Finally—yes,

the absolute end!—is the Gorsedd. This august and almost
metaphysical band of scholars and patriots has King Arthur as
its lodestar, but its true Patron Saint was Mordred, the late
Morton Nance, Grand Bard of Cornwall, an eagle of a man
with the flaming eyes of a fanatic.[16]

Caddick made Mebyon Kernow the subject of his opening speech
for an exhibition of the Nancledra School of Painting, arguing that
followers of Mebyon Kernow, along with the Welsh, Scots and Irish
nationalists, were determined to peel themselves away from Britain by
a process of 'Inter-Celtic striptease'.[17] 'I am one of those countless
un-Cornish who have found in Cornwall years of happiness', said
Caddick , '[and] we are bound by gratitude and affection to wish
for Cornwall not only what Cornwall wishes for itself, but more so. It is
our duty to place ourselves not solidly behind Mebyon Kernow but
foursquare in front of it.'[18] To this end he announced his humorous
vision for the future; an organisation known as Lesvebyon Kernow
or Step-Sons of Cornwall, whose manifesto 'Backward towards
Tomorrow' called for Cornwall to be given naval parity with the Isle of
Man, anti-skin-diving submarine bases at Mousehole and Mevagissey
and gazey-money for being stared at by tourists. Further, unemployment would be eradicated through three simple steps:

1. All positions held by Cornishmen shall be made
   hereditary.
2. All positions held by un-Cornishmen shall be declared
   vacant.
3. All vacant positions shall be filled with Cornishmen.[19]

In typical Caddick style he also wrote two satirical poems about
the activities of the Gorsedd, 'The Druid's Whoopee—or A Ballad of
Bards and Bonfires' and 'A Rocket for the Gorsedd'. From the former,
only two verses are reproduced here:

I sing the Bards—long may they thrive!—
Who keep the name of things alive
When all the meanings gone
Who sanctify Midsummer rites
(And what the heathen did at night)
By calling on Saint John.

They light the flames of old desire
By setting heaps of straw on fire

And baying to the stars
Strange relics of pre-Saxon runes
To ancient, atavistic tunes
In fragmentary bars.[20]

The poem continues with an account of naughty bards chasing
Aphrodite lustfully over the hills, shedding their clothes as they went
until one of their number falls down a mine shaft. In the first two
stanzas the sense of empty ceremony is compounded by the references
to a distant, half-remembered past irrelevant to contemporary Cornish
life. Similar motifs are found in the later poem 'A Rocket for the
Gorsedd', a real flight of fantasy in which Caddick imagines Cornish
Bards attempting to fly to the moon:

O Moon, what fierce magnetic lure
Is yours, that you beguile the hearts
Of men in such diversity
To probe into your death-cold parts?
Was Merlin moved by you to chase
The Bards of Cornwall into space?

For—lo!—at Lanyon Quoit upon
The Feast of Saint Penpoligoon,
At midnight's stroke, the Gorsedd met
To put Olde Cornwall on the moon,
And prove in realms outside this earth
The cosmic good of Cornish birth.[21]

'A Rocket for the Gorsedd' appeared in a book of Caddick's
humorous verse entitled *Broadsides from Bohemia*, a collection
which was received with relish by local critics. The *Cornishman* called
Caddick 'A legend in his own lifetime . . . he brings the broadside and
the barb of humour to a dull-grey society of vanity and pomposity.
He wears the jester's motley and the sage's gown.'[22] The *Sunday
Independent* noted that the 'satirical scourge of West Cornwall' had
taken 'a swing at everyone from the hippies living on the beach to
Penzance Council and the Cornish language revivalists'.[23] Finally, the
Penwith Advertiser called for 'three loud cheers for *Broadsides from
Bohemia*' and raved about Caddick's caustic comments on 'some of
the more inane happenings in our present day society which will
give people the encouragement to giggle aloud at the pompous and
pretentious elements among us'.[24]

Caddick clearly used humour in his poems to satirise the Gorsedd, but when it came to the Cornish language he mounted a systematic academic argument in prose. In *Laughter from Land's End* and an earlier four-part article in the *Cornishman*, Caddick argued mischeviously, and with examples, that Cornish was derived from Latin and could not be considered a Celtic language at all. In doing so he touched the rawest nerve of all, calling into question Cornwall's position as a Celtic nation.[25] He lampooned mercilessly the efforts of Celtic Revivalists like Robert Morton Nance, pointing out that he had 'deduced from Mordred's [Nance's] age that his formative and most impressionable years must have coincided with the Dawn of the Celtic Twilight' (Celtic Revival) and that Morton Nance's Cornish–English, English–Cornish Dictionaries represented nothing more than 'flights into the realms of poetic fantasy'.[26]

In his four-part newspaper article entitled 'The Dream of Mordred or the Cornish Tongue', Caddick argued that 'there are not six Celtic nations at all; there are 5.0001, give or take the feather-weight of one Cornish chough'.[27] His objective was not to destroy a sense of Cornish identity but to give it a foundation based on a more 'truthful' understanding of the past. 'I shall feel rewarded', he wrote,

> if I provoke many loyal Cornishmen into closing eyes blurred by sentiment and tradition, and into opening eyes clear enough to be the windows of man's unconquerable mind, so that they may probe and peer into their linguistic past as it truly was.[28]

Caddick's friend and fellow writer Denys Val Baker was less strident, calling attempts to use language to secure a degree of cultural autonomy for Cornwall equal to that of Wales and Scotland 'forlorn'. He went on to argue that:

> immense efforts are now being made to spread a knowledge of the old Cornish language. But surely this is to miss the whole point. Cornwall does not need to create differences to emphasise its apartness from the rest of England. It *is* apart, solidly and unmistakably, and in the fullest geographical sense.[29]

Current research amongst scholars interested in Cornish studies has demonstrated the importance of language to a sense of Cornish identity. Burton argues that one of the ways in which the English state attempted to achieve cultural hegemony in Cornwall was by encouraging the decline of the language, for instance by the refusal of the state to introduce a Cornish Prayer Book and Bible in the sixteenth century.[30] Cornwall's right to be considered a Celtic nation—hotly debated during the Celtic Revival in Cornwall in the late nineteenth and early twentieth centuries—depended on the condition of the Cornish language. As Amy Hale notes:

> throughout the course of the Revival, too much time and energy has been spent justifying Cornwall's 'Celticity' . . . As in most measures of 'Celticity' Cornwall has been evaluated in terms of the past—in language . . . the language issue in particular giving activists in other Celtic areas an axe to grind (if Cornwall has 'lost' its language, then is it still to be considered Celtic?).[31]

Caddick's argument about the relationship between Cornish language and identity worked on two different levels. First, he felt that in the face of disastrous economic decline in Cornwall, the last thing that ought to worry the Cornish was the revival of the language or traditions, the students of which were 'busy trying to constrict their intellectual horizons by rendering themselves incommunicado in the twentieth century'. 'This countryside', he wrote,

> punctuated by stacks of derelict mines, scarred by the gashes hacked by disused quarries, occasionally whitened by dumps of china clay at discontinued workings, farmed by marginal smallholders earning less than the labourers they used to employ, is now becoming a Geriatric Unit.[32]

These were concerns that he repeated in the poem 'Blood Transfusion' which appeared in *Broadsides from Bohemia*.

> From the close kinship of village
> And the continuing home
> And the croft and the cove
> And the firm embraces of truth,
> Gone are the young men,
> The young girls are going,
> Going is Cornwall's youth.
>
> Small holders settle for wages,
> Fisherman start frying chips,
> Old miners mend roads.
> And the family business is sold.

Out goes the true wealth, the Cornish,
In come the Pensions
Of complacent up-country old.[33]

In his poem 'Cradle-Song for Mebyon Kernow', Caddick foresaw
an even worse predicament, when Mebyon Kernow drove the 'Anglo-
Saxons' from Cornwall:

O hush thee, my handsome,
The bad days are dead!
Those gross Anglo-Saxons
Who plundered thy birthright
(Sleep safely, my baby!)
Yield back to the Cornish
The Kingdom of Cornwall—
The spoilers have fled.

Sleep deeply, my lover,
Sweet flower of the Celts,
Thou last of my litter,
My own piggy-widden,
My late twelfth-born handsome,
Thy mother, thy father,
Five sisters, six brothers,
Shall tighten their belts.

Breathe proudly, my baby,
Our clean Cornish air!
There's no bed-and-breakfast,
No trips-round-the-harbour,
No chip-shops, my lover,
To sully its essence—
O breathe it in deeply,
Its all of thy fare.[34]

The appearance of these two poems in the same collection reveal the
complexity of Caddick's attitude towards Cornwall. On the one hand,
the thought of young Cornish people being forced to leave to find work
and build lives elsewhere filled him with dismay, as did the prospect of
their replacement by 'complacent up-country old'. On the other hand,
Mebyon Kernow's brand of nationalism could not, he argued, provide
a sustainable solution to Cornwall's economic problems.[35]

The second level on which Caddick's satirical rendering of the

Gorsedd and Mebyon Kernow works is linked to the first. His treatment of Cornish Revivalism demonstrated the problem for Caddick of being what he called 'un-Cornish'—an issue of considerable significance to him. In the early fifties, Caddick's friend Guido Morris, the printer, happened to show Caddick a catalogue that he had printed for Peter Lanyon's exhibition 'Paintings from Penwith'.[36] In the preface to the catalogue two quotes had appeared. The first from Ronald Bottrall, the Director of Education for the British Council, read 'To see Cornwall as a Cornishman sees it, it is necessary not merely to have been born and brought up in the county, but to come from Cornish stock'. The second, from a Miss R. Glynn Grylls, commented that Peter Lanyon's exhibition represented:

> the work of a true Cornishman, born and bred in West Penwith, not one of the cuckoo orphans come down to claim the home where the rightful heirs belong to be . . . Peter Lanyon's work has a backbone of granite underneath its charm; when this trips up the foreigner there is a chuckle of laughter on the Downs, from knockers deep beneath the soil and ghosts, never laid, that haunt the Lanyon Quoit. You take risks here, Stranger.[37]

In response to these remarks Caddick wrote the humorous 'Cuckoo Song':

> O Auntie! Fetch the family tree!
> Have I Cornish blood in me?
> Did my forebears ever rove?
> Somewhere round by Lanyon Cove?
> Did they chase the fairies in
> The mystic darkness of the glynn?
> Did they live on Bodmin's hills
> Roasting goats for Celtic grylls?
> O Auntie! Fetch our pedigree!
> HAVE I Cornish blood in me?
> If I'm not a proper Celt.
> Do I hit below the belt
> If I say that, now and then,
> I've seen the little whimsy men,
> Leaping on the Bottrall Downs
> Laughing like demented clowns?
> The cuckoo calls! I must, I must
> Become a Cornishman or bust.

Buy up scores of family trees,
Bottrallize me, Auntie please!
And then—O then!—no cuckoo, I
Shall sing canary-like on high,
Fed on proper Celtic groundsel
From the Ancient British Council[38]

Caddick signed his poem Polarthur Trebruce Pencaddick—a clear skit on the maxim 'By Tre, Pol or Pen you shall know the Cornishmen'. In a recent interview I put it to Caddick's friend and fellow poet Frank Ruhrmund that being Cornish for Caddick was more a state of mind than a matter of birth:

> FR: That's a very good statement actually because I know a lot of artists in particular who've lived down here for thirty or forty years, they've been living and working here, and they're not Cornish artists in the sense that they were not born Cornish—I mean they've been here all this time and they've got this state of mind—they don't think of themselves as anything other. Yeah, I think that's fair. Again there are some people who have lived here all these years and they haven't got the state of mind and they never will even if they're here for a thousand years.
>
> CB: I think it was your obituary for Arthur in the *Cornishman*—when you said he was 'one of us', what did you mean?
>
> FR: I think I meant that, if you like, that although he was an Englishman he wasn't an outsider—he'd been here that long. It goes along with what we've just been saying, he had the right state of mind and I think he was—despite his satirical verse where he took the mickey out of us—you didn't have any doubt he was on our side—I always felt he was.[39]

These remarks from Frank Ruhrmund demonstrate the complexity of Caddick's position with respect to the representation of Cornwall and Cornishness. He was not easily defined as either insider or outsider and was, as Ruhrmund's comments show, accepted in West Penwith in a way that some other artists or writers were not. As I have shown, Caddick was capable of defending and attacking aspects of Cornish life and culture with equal vigour. In the next section, I turn to Caddick's representation of the Cornish landscape and show how his sense of being connected to the unique landscape of West Penwith further blurs the analytic value of insider/outsider categories or, to put it in a way that Caddick would have appreciated, Cornish or un-Cornish.

A CLEARING HOUSE FOR THE SPIRIT

Despite satirizing the Gorsedd's and Mebyon Kernow's Revivalist view of Celtic Cornwall, Arthur Caddick drew on well-understood imagery of an ancient, timeless land with deep historical roots and a distant mystical past in his lyrical poetry, and especially in his collection of poems *A Croft in Cornwall*.[40] The reviewer of this collection for the *Western Morning News* wrote that 'Mr Caddick's croft, the sights in the area of Marazion, the Cornish air and earth, provide many homing points of reference throughout the book'.[41] For Caddick, Cornishness lay not in the revival of the Gorsedd but in the landscape and its influence upon his creative effort. In this he shared the opinion of the founder and editor of the *Cornish Review*, Denys Val Baker. In the first ever edition of the *Cornish Review*, Val Baker wrote:

> What matters most is the spirit of Cornwall, of the Cornish people and their culture . . . Cornwall is the same brooding, mysterious, otherworldly place, impregnated with a sense of age and eternity. The coastline is as beautiful as ever, the sea as unpredictable . . . [and] there is the same incomparable variety of countryside.[42]

For Caddick, the creative power of Cornwall lay in the particular configuration of climate and landscape, on which he reflected in the lovely, poignant 'Lesson Learnt on Cornwall's Hills':

> Through having passed half my life among them
> I have become one with giant outcrops
> Of gaunt granite at extraordinary angles,
> Hieroglyphics which record the ravages
> Of time's unsentimental journey.
>
> One, also, with the subtle delights
> Of high places, the scent of heath, furze, bracken,
> The flowering from gale-bent blackthorn branches
> Of delicate white sprays
> Before green leaves break open
> And the omens sea-gulls cry aloud
> As they follow the plough on inland fields
> That a hurricane has crossed the horizon
> To shroud the blue bay in a pall of cloud

And scrounge the shore with whip-lashed squalls of rain
I have stood in a luminous silence
Where no one who stands alone is lonely[43]

In this poem, the configuration of soil, rock, plants, animals, sea, wind and rain make up Cornwall's particular character for Caddick. The idea of a place 'where no one who stands alone is lonely' speaks to a profound connection between people and landscape which reanimated Caddick. He was attached elementally in more ways than one, reflecting that 'A man comes here from a metropolis and finds himself face to face with the silent, unrelenting scrutiny of the eternal elements'.[44]

In 'Letter from Land's End' Caddick explained that gales and mists and the heaviness of the hills on the Land's End peninsula created 'an indolent atmosphere' that drove men in on themselves. 'And in this', he wrote:

> lies its true value to the creative worker. Writers and painters come down from great cities, or from the dominions, often from environments they have found uncongenial to the arts, and gradually this atmosphere works on them. I think it starts by calming them down and making them reflective. Then it leads to introspection.[45]

Caddick went on to describe how this process had affected different people during his years in Cornwall as it had undoubtedly affected himself:

> I knew a young painter who came down here four years ago, distracted and bewildered by life and London, where he had suddenly lost all his creative powers. He came here distraught, nervy and unsure of himself, and he took a cottage at Zennor. As the months went by, I saw the sophistication blown away from his face. He began to look younger. Gradually, after two years of adjustment, his work came alive again . . . Cornwall slowed him down and made him think, and he found out what he could do.[46]

The effect on the young painter is represented as a stripping away of a layer of artifice to achieve a more essential state. In this state, the act of creation is more purposeful and authentic because the artist has been removed from the superficiality of the modern world. For Caddick, the intangible creative force that Cornwall exercised was given material form by artists of all kinds in paint, clay, verse, prose, wood, iron and stone. The creative possibilities were endless in what Caddick called the 'clearing house' for the spirit, where life was lived closer to the elements and distant from the ceaseless buzz of metropolitan England. In 'I have booked a Cumulus' he wrote

> Yet Cornwall tempers for creative minds
> That uncouth materialism, based on greed,
> Which, by killing England's ancient tolerance
> Has changed the essence of the English breed'.[47]

To feel and understand something of Cornwall depended not on being able to trace your Cornish ancestry or speak the language but in the sense of being connected to a place unlike any other capable of inspiring creative effort. In arguing this, Caddick resisted the (to him) exclusionary practices of the Gorsedd and Mebyon Kernow which he saw as marginalizing both those 'un-Cornish' with a strong attachment to Cornwall, and ordinary Cornish people themselves.

CONCLUSION

Deacon and Payton have argued that 'Cornish culture is that meanings system adopted by the group of people who define themselves as "Cornish" . . . a dynamic process subject to constant change and re-negotiation and contested by other cultures'.[48] The work of Arthur Caddick, one of the 'un-Cornish', shows how the process of negotiation is certainly never straightforward. Caddick occupies a complex position in Cornish culture between insider and outsider and show us how it is possible to disrupt these categories.

Caddick counted amongst his close friends Bards of the Gorsedd like Peter Pool and Frank Ruhrmund, and he even welcomed Robert Morton Nance to a public reading of the 'Druid's Whoopee'. However, Caddick could not countenance the activities of the Gorsedd or Mebyon Kernow. 'I'm a sniper', he said, 'I don't belong to anything. I just don't like injustice, artifice and sham.'[49] In attempting to reveal the 'Latin roots' of the Cornish language he struck right at both the heart of the Gorsedd's claim to Cornish Celticity but also at the 'heroes of Cornish nationalism' like Morton Nance.[50] The landscape and climate of Cornwall undoubtedly inspired his creative effort, yet he was not averse to evoking Cornwall's ancient history to lend his work poetic force, as in his poem 'At Lanyon Quoit'—

> Look not aloofly
> Stranger, upon this Stone-Age scene,
> Nor let remoteness

Disguise where living men have been'.[51]

There is an apparent paradox between his own love of Cornwall (informed by a sense of Cornwall's distant past) and his view of the Gorsedd's work.

Caddick admired, loved and found a spiritual attachment to Cornwall's landscape and the observable relics of its ancient past in the landscape, such as Trencrom which was visible from Windswept. But for Caddick the Gorsedd were reviving the wrong version of Cornwall, one that made no connection to the every-day lives of contemporary Cornish people. He further contested the view that only the 'pure-bred' Cornish could have a connection to the life and landscape of Cornwall. Much attention has been paid in the contemporary literature to the construction of Cornish identity around the twin pillars of language and Celticity, both of which are contested in Caddick's work. He instead highlights the symbolic significance of landscape and climate, and his personal connection with the land and, to take the title of his second-to-last poem written at Windswept, 'Lesson Learnt on Cornwall's Hills'.[52]

ACKNOWLEDGEMENTS
My thanks are due to the following people: Mike Leyshon, Nick Ford and Alan Kent for their constructive comments on an earlier version of this paper; Dave Harvey for clarifying some of my ideas; Peggy Caddick, Ken and Di Calvert, Audrey Pool and Frank Ruhrmund for their invaluable insights into Arthur Caddick's life and work, and finally staff at the Morrab Library in Penzance. A shortened version of this paper was presented in the 'Celtic Worlds: Landscapes and Identity' session of the RGS/IBG conference in Leicester, January 1999.

NOTES AND REFERENCES
1. Ella Westland, 'Introduction', in Ella Westland (ed.), *Cornwall: The Cultural Construction of Place*, Penzance, 1997, p. 1.
2. Philip Crang, 'Regional Imaginations: An Afterword', in Westland (ed.), 1997, p. 154.
3. Bernard Deacon, 'The Hollow Jarring of the Distant Steam Engines: Images of Cornwall between West Barbary and Delectable Duchy', in Westland (ed.), 1997, p. 8.
4. 'Notes on Contributors', *Cornish Review*, First Series, 4, Spring 1950; Arthur Caddick, 'Laughter from Land's End' unpublished manuscript, University of Exeter Library, revised 1975.
5. Caddick, 1975, p. 5.
6. Caddick, 1975, p. 5.

7. Caddick, 1975, pp. 5–6.
8. Caddick, 1975, p. 6.
9. Caddick, 1975, p. 16.
10. Transcript of Interview with Frank Ruhrmund, 10 September 1998, p. 4.
11. Caddick, *Call of the West*, St Teath, 1983.
12. Caddick, *One Hundred Doors are Open*, Nancledra, 1956.
13. Transcript of Interview with Peggy Caddick, 29 August, 1998, p. 5.
14. Denys Val Baker, 'Commentary', *Cornish Review*, First Series, 1, Spring 1949, p. 4.
15. Some passages from 'Laughter from Land's End' appeared in Arthur Caddick, 'Laughter at Land's End', *Cornish Review*, Second Series, 1, 1966 and in Arthur Caddick, 'Nancledra' in Michael Williams (ed.), *My Cornwall*, St Teath, 1973.
16. Caddick, 1975, p. 115. Morton Nance's Bardic name was in fact 'Mordon'; Caddick's rendition of it as Mordred may be an ironic allusion to King Arthur's treacherous cousin, Mordred.
17. ' "Backwards Towards Tomorrow": Arthur Caddick's Manifesto for Lesvebyon Kernow', *Cornishman*. Undated article in Arthur Caddick's press cutting book.
18. 'Backwards Towards Tomorrow'.
19. 'Backwards Towards Tomorrow'.
20. Arthur Caddick, 'The Druid's Whoopee or A Ballad or Bards and Bonfires', *Quiet Lutes and Laughter*, 1955, pp. 26–7.
21. Arthur Caddick, 'A Rocket for the Gorsedd', *Broadsides from Bohemia*, St Teath, 1973, p. 32.
22. *Cornishman*, 'Broadsides from Caddick', 6 December 1973. In an ironic twist, shortly after Caddick arrived in Cornwall he won the prize for best poem in English at the Inter-Celtic Festival held at St Ives in 1949 for 'Simple Song at Morning'.
23. *Sunday Independent*, 'The Rebel Poet Hits Out Again', 16 December 1973.
24. *Penwith Advertiser*, 'Broadsides from Bohemia', December 1973.
25. For more detail on Cornwall, Cornish language and Celticity see Amy Hale, 'Genesis of the Celto-Cornish Revival? L.C. Duncombe-Jewell and the Cowethas Kelto-Kernuak', in P. Payton (ed.), *Cornish Studies: Five*, Exeter, 1997, pp. 100–11.
26. Arthur Caddick, 'The Dream of Mordred or The Cornish Tongue Part One', *Cornishman*, 2 December 1971. The timing of the article is curious. Nance and Caddick had both lived in Nancledra and had obviously attended social events such as the opening of art exhibitions at the same time, though they could not be described as friends. However, the articles in the *Cornishman* were written after Nance had died.
27. Arthur Caddick, 'The Dream of Mordred or The Cornish Tongue Part Two', *Cornishman*, 9 December 1971.
28. Arthur Caddick, 'The Dream of Mordred', *Cornishman*, 1971.
29. Denys Val Baker, *The Timeless Land*, Bath, 1973.

30. Rob Burton, 'A Passion to Exist: Cultural Hegemony and the Roots of Cornish Identity', in P. Payton (ed.), *Cornish Studies: Five*, Exeter, 1997, pp. 151–63.
31. Amy Hale, 'Rethinking Celtic Cornwall: An Ethnographic Approach', in P. Payton (ed.), *Cornish Studies: Five*, Exeter, 1997, pp. 85–99.
32. Caddick, 1975, p. 115.
33. Arthur Caddick, 'Blood Transfusion', *Broadsides from Bohemia*, St Teath, 1973, p. 18.
34. Arthur Caddick, 'Cradle-Song for Mebyon Kernow', *Broadsides from Bohemia*, St Teath, 1973, p. 30.
35. The appearance of 'Cradle-Song for Mebyon Kernow' in the *Cornishman* in 1969 solicited a response in verse from Len Truran entitled 'Song for the Cornish': Len Truran, 'A Song for the Cornish—A Reply to Polarthur Pencaddick', *Cornishman*, 8 January 1970.
36. Caddick, 1975.
37. Both quotes are reproduced in Arthur Caddick, 'Cuckoo Song', *Quiet Lutes and Laughter*, 1955, p. 22.
38. Caddick, 'Cuckoo Song', 1955, p. 22.
39. Transcript of Interview with Frank Ruhrmund, 10 September 1998, p. 8.
40. Arthur Caddick, *A Croft in Cornwall*, Marazion, 1968.
41. *Western Morning News*, 'Poems of Cornwall', 14 June 1968.
42. Denys Val Baker, 1949, pp. 3–4.
43. Arthur Caddick, 'Lesson Learnt on Cornwall's Hills', unpublished manuscript, University of Exeter Library, final draft 23 July 1983.
44. Arthur Caddick, 'Letter from Land's End', in Derek Maggs (ed.), *Zebra*, Bristol 1955, p. 13.
45. Caddick, 'Letter from Land's End', 1955, p. 13.
46. Caddick, 'Letter from Land's End', 1955, p. 14.
47. Arthur Caddick, 'I have Booked a Cumulus', unpublished manuscript, University of Exeter Library.
48. Bernard Deacon and Philip Payton, 'Re-Inventing Cornwall: Culture Change on the European Periphery', in P. Payton (ed.), *Cornish Studies: One*, Exeter, 1993, p. 63.
49. *Sunday Independent*, 1973.
50. Garry Tregidga, 'The Politics of the Celto-Cornish Revival, 1886–1939', in P. Payton (ed.), *Cornish Studies: Five*, Exeter, 1997, p. 133.
51. Arthur Caddick, 'At Lanyon Quoit', *The Call of the West*, St Teath, 1983, p. 12.
52. Arthur Caddick, 1983.

A POETRY OF DARK SOUNDS: THE MANUSCRIPTS OF CHARLES CAUSLEY

John Hurst

INTRODUCTION

There is a sense in which Charles Causley may be said to have lived, in Lord David Cecil's terminology, A Quiet Life.

The outlines of his life are well known. Born and bred at Launceston in Cornwall, where he still lives, he had never left it for any substantial period of time until pitchforked into the powerful experience of Navy life in war time, which he evokes so vividly in some of the early poems and in the volume of short stories *Hands to Dance*.[1] Despite, or because of this interruption, after the war he settled back into Launceston life, training as a school teacher, living alone with his mother until her death. He provides a touching account of her declining years, and of his devoted care of her, in the essay 'So Slowly to Harbour'.[2] Throughout this time he had been expanding his reputation as a poet, broadcaster and man of letters. Public, literary, and academic honours accrued; an Honorary Doctorate of the University of Exeter in 1977, and the CBE in 1986. There are, however, no highly publicized personal traumas such as beset his friend Ted Hughes, and no bitter political controversies such as surrounded neighbouring Devon writer Henry Williamson. Occasional poems may hint at tensions and disappointments in personal relations in the manner of Hardy; but, in the manner of Hardy, the polished craftmanship of the verse repels the impertinencies of enquiry. It is, visibly, a life dedicated firmly and steadily to his craft, rooted in his native Launceston, but with wide perspectives which his frequent trips to read, to lecture and for pleasure to many parts of the world serve to enhance.

THE ARCHIVE

This even surface may not, however, tell the whole story. There is a fuller story 'between the lines' of the poetry and the occasional writings. Much of this material is unpublished. The remarkable collection of manuscripts and documents which constitutes the Causley Archive in the University of Exeter Library provides an approach that can only be described as invaluable.

The Archive was first acquired by the University in 1970 and there have been several significant additions since. It is contained in thirty-nine numbered boxes. Material is not in chronological order nor divided by category, though there is a limited amount of grouping. Closely related material may be spread over several boxes. (For instance, working papers for the verse play *Aucassin and Nicolette*[3] are to be found in Boxes 10, 13 and 19, the annotated script for the BBC broadcast is in Box 26, and the musical setting in Box 31.) There is a valuable listing in longhand made by a member of University staff, enabling the contents of each box to be readily seen, but no index to the Archive. Users need, therefore, to make a personal index of material most directly relevant to their interests. The collection contains work from very early in his career through to 1984. The earliest work is the play *Benedict* published by Muller in 1938, but here present as a broadcast script dated 27 April 1939, the only pre-World War II item. His writing resumed immediately on his return from the Royal Navy, the first poems to find their way into print written while a student at Peterborough Training College and included in the College Magazine, *St Peter's Chapbook*, for 1946. There appears to be an almost complete run of working papers from this date, with the exception of those for *Hands to Dance*, to some of the poems included in *A Field of Vision*[4] and the volume of children's verse *Jack the Treacle Eater*[5] and the occasional broadcast script from the early 1980s. The genesis and development of most of the poems written between 1946 and the late 1970s can, therefore, be traced, as can that of the verse plays. There is an important dossier of scripts, often with detailed working notes, of BBC Radio broadcasts, and later, of a little work for television. (See Appendix I.) Much of this remains unpublished, though some broadcasts were printed in the *Listener*. There are also numerous work-sheets for critical articles, reviews and for editorial material for the various anthologies. There is much evidence about the criteria and processes of selection of items for inclusion in the anthologies. There is much correspondence about the details of the art-work. (This is mainly correspondence to Dr Causley, there are comparatively few letters from him.) The Archive also bears eloquent testimony to the breadth and range of his contacts in the literary world, particularly to his close and supportive friendships with Jack Clemo and Frances Bellerby. It is here, perhaps, that one senses most closely what he has referred to as the 'hidden agenda' below the surface of the poetry.

THE DARK SOUNDS OF LORCA

Early in his career, while stationed in Gibraltar in the course of his Naval service, he became aware of 'the day to day sounds and cadences of Spanish language',[6] and particularly of the work of the poet Lorca. Lorca was to become an important figure in his perception of how poetry worked. One of his earliest poems 'Serenade' was dedicated to him, and at the opposite end of his career he has translated Lorca's 'Casida del Herido por el agua' as 'Song of One Wounded by Water'. There are recurrent references to him in the prose and broadcasts, particularly to Lorca's memorable phrase 'sonidos negros'—a phrase to which Causley would often refer in his public readings. The phrase is used as an important element of definition in the broadcast 'The Making of a Poem', and in the introduction to the anthology *Dawn and Dusk*. Lorca's own characterization of these 'dark sounds' is significant. They are 'the mystery, the roots thrusting into the fertile loam known to all of us, ignored by all of us, but from which we get what is real in art'.[7]

This might be seen as a definition of Causley's own poetic practice—a poetry apparently simple, into which 'the roots thrust from the dark below'. 'It is important that all works of art keep some of their secrets in order that they may go on giving out what the Spanish poet Lorca has called sonidos negros, black sounds.'[8]

WORKING METHODS

Often the pages of the Archive will point us towards aspects of Causley's practice as a poet. Two small but significant jottings among sketches for poems in Box 25 are striking. The first is a quotation from Valéry—'a poem is never finished, only abandoned'. The second is attributed to Eliot; rhymes are 'accidental stars with a talent for squad drill'. Taken together these phrases—apparently casual jottings in a notebook—lead us close to the heart of Causley's poetic practice.

The notebooks and work-sheets reveal time after time the painstaking and prolonged craftmanship that goes to the making of even a poem as apparently simple as, for instance, 'I saw a Jolly Hunter'. He speaks of himself as always writing 'slowly and arduously'[9] throughout his career. The Archive reveals, at almost every turn, moreover, the detailed and scrupulous research, the concern for accuracy and context, which underlines the making of poetry and prose. Behind, for instance, the creation of the narrative poem 'St Martha and the Dragon'[10] lies not only detailed scholarly reading but also a significant body of correspondence with scholarly authorities, notably Professor E.O. James and Peter Levi. (See Box 2). The poems written out of his experience of travel reveal a different form of care. The notes for the poem 'Bugis Street' are a series of impressions of the street scene, such as could be used for a high-class travel article.

These are processed in the crucible of the poet's imagination. Some are retained, some rejected, as the focus of the poem, its final disturbing vision emerges from his awareness of the 'terrible innocence' of this apparently corrupt setting.

> A peddler blocks our path;
> Reads every word I do not say,
> Pushes an orchid dunked in gold
> Across the dirty tablecloth
> And my hand shakes, but not with cold.[11]

The 'black sounds' have pushed through the plethora of surface detail. The assiduous note-taking behind what might be termed the 'Poems of Travel' is consistently clear—even to the disturbance of the normally immaculate handwriting by the shaking of the vehicle in which he is travelling. And always there is the careful balancing of phrase against phrase, of rhyme against rhyme, so that even when a poem may appear to have reached a stage at which it is ready for publication its future in precisely that form may not be fixed. It is not uncommon, and again careful use of the Archive reveals this, for there to be alteration between typescript and first printing (normally in an appropriate literary journal) and between that format and *Collected Poems*. Even having reached an advanced stage the future of a poem may not be assured. Occasionally, though rarely, the manuscripts show a poem not having been taken to the point where it can be submitted for publication. Occasionally, though this is more often true of the earlier poems, a poem having reached publication may not be taken forward to hardback or collected form. A notable instance is the poem 'A Visit to Van Gogh', printed in the volume *Johnny Alleluia*,[12] after earlier periodical publication, which was not included in *Collected Poems*. It is a poem which the Archive reveals as the product of careful research and extensive reworking, and several changes of title, but which, nevertheless, the author does not wish to see established in the format of the *Collected Poems*.

LITERARY FRIENDSHIPS

The poet's care does not, however, stop with the nurturing of his own work. The Archive provides us with detailed and moving evidence of his partnership with and support for his fellow writers Jack Clemo and Frances Bellerby: support which was expressed in the most concrete of ways. Jack Clemo was becoming established on the Cornish and UK literary scene very much at the same time as Causley was beginning to be widely published and known. Clemo's first published novel *Wilding Graft*,[13] appeared in 1948, and the early collection of poems *The Clay Verge*[14] in 1951. Wide recognition was afforded by his inclusion in *Penguin Modern Poets 6* in 1964, following on the collection *The Map of Clay* in 1961.[15] Causley's career had developed in close parallel with the publication of *Hands to Dance* in 1951, of *Survivor's Leave*[16] in 1953 and inclusion in *Penguin Modern Poets 3* in 1962. Causley had expressed his admiration for Clemo's powerful if unfashionable work in the poem 'Homage to Jack Clemo' included in *Survivor's Leave*. An article in the *London Magazine*, 'The World of Jack Clemo',[17] and the introduction to *The Map of Clay* under the same title reinforced a bond which had been building through the 1950s. Clemo gives an appreciative and affectionate account of the part which Causley played in a TV programme featuring Clemo himself and his mother during the late 1950s in *The Marriage of a Rebel*.[18] Clemo speaks warmly of Causley's exuberance and spontaneity, of his intellectual independence and integrity, his refusal to belong to a 'School', Cornish or otherwise. There was a clear friendship which could reconcile difference of approach with respect and affection. The bond was made even firmer by Causley's introduction to a BBC broadcast in April 1962. (BBC script in Archive Box 23.)

The friendship with Frances Bellerby was equally remarkable and the documentation in the Archive is even more extensive. A poet, short-story writer and, to a lesser degree, a novelist, she came to live in Cornwall—known well for many holidays—in 1940, settling at Plash Mill near Upton Cross. She was writing steadily throughout her stay at Plash Mill. Causley became aware of her work which he regarded with great admiration, and they became friends. (Her work, too, is conspicuously marked by its 'dark sounds'.) Never robust, after a spinal injury in her early thirties, life-threatening illness struck in 1950. On recovery she found her beloved Plash Mill both too isolated and too impregnated with memories of her illness, and she left to live in Devon, first, unhappily at Clearbrook near Yelverton, subsequently settling at Goveton near Kingsbridge where she lived until her death in 1975. Although this was a period of great physical and spiritual suffering, it is clear that throughout she was sustained by a small number of close friendships, not least of these being that of Charles Causley. On her death she appointed him her literary executor. The Exeter Archive of her work is divided into two collections—both under the trusteeship of Charles Causley. There is a substantial body of material included in the Causley Archive itself, particularly Boxes 2 and 35. In addition there is a separate Archive consisting for the most part of extensive correspondence with friends other than Causley. Taken together they constitute a remarkable record of a writer of great intensity and perceptiveness, continuing to create despite immense personal difficulties. The papers in the Causley Archive itself detail a literary association that was mutually productive and a friendship that was deeply enriching.

Causley had been reading her poems in broadcasts and including them in anthologies (e.g. *Dawn and Dusk*[19] in 1962 and *The Puffin Book of Magic Verse*[20] in 1974). Both had been contributing regularly to the *Westcountry Magazine*. As Causley and others, particularly Alan Clodd of the Enitharmon Press, became more and more convinced of the stature of her work, a proposal for an anthology developed and Causley agreed to edit such a collection with a brief introduction. The Archive contains extensive correspondence both about the poems to be included and the material to be included in the Introduction. For this Frances Bellerby supplied a statement of her beliefs—a term she did not find entirely satisfactory. This statement in her own hand, and significantly amended at points—is to be found in Box 2. It is, in some ways, a singular document. In some ways profoundly revealing of her inner convictions, it is in other ways deeply impersonal. It contains, for instance, nothing about her uneasy relations with her clergyman father or her despair at her mother's suicide. Nothing about her grief for her only brother killed in France a few months after enlisting in 1915. Her marriage and its breakdown are not mentioned, nor her continuing and recurrent illnesses. Causley respects this impersonality in his introduction, giving only the barest details of her life, but focuses most sensitively on the character of her poetry and her vision. The book was published under the title *Frances Bellerby; Selected Poems* by Enitharmon Press[21] in a limited Edition of 300 copies.

The calculated impersonality of the statement provided for this purpose is not, however, characteristic of this part of the Archive. There is, for instance, a sketch towards a biography (Box 2) which despite certain reticencies, is open, frank and detailed. It provides the basis for much subsequent writing about her, such as Robert Gittings' introduction to her *Selected Poems*.[22] Of particular interest also are the working papers for many of her poems, and her correspondence with Charles Causley about the wording of many of his poems. They would exchange manuscripts for comment and it is clear that serious consideration was given by each to the perceptions of the other. Particularly interesting is the correspondence about the poems to be included in the collection *Underneath the Water*.[23] Frances Bellerby argues a very strong case for the inclusion without hesitation of 'Death of a Poet' and 'By St Thomas Water'.

The Archive contains many indications of friendships with writers. There are fascinating glimpses of correspondence with, for instance, Seamus Heaney (Box 29) and Vernon Watkins (Box 14)—the latter making supportive criticism of particular poems. Inevitably, there is much correspondence with editors, including valuable material about the details of dust-jackets of illustrations, in which he is seen as taking an active and informed interest. (Ron Tamplin in his introduction to *Charles Causley—A Tribute from the Artists*[24] draws attention to Causley's active interest in and awareness of the visual arts). A picture emerges of a writer deeply, though unsentimentally, aware of the vocation of the artist and of the particular ways in which 'life's cold truth' affects them.

THE MAKING OF A POEM

It is in this context that one of the most significant groupings of material in the Archive can be seen to be relevant—the body of documentation relating to the poem 'A Short Life of Nevil Northey Burnard', the associated broadcast and periodical material, and the remarkable range of correspondence that goes with it. These are to be found in Boxes 27 and 29.

Causley's interest in Burnard focuses a wide range of his concerns, and the extensive work-sheets for the poem, often dated so that its evolution can be closely followed, give perhaps the clearest insight into his working methods that the Archive affords.

It is difficult to date the origin of Causley's awareness of Burnard. All the evidence leads one to think that Burnard's story was, in fact, well known in East Cornwall. A poor boy from Altarnun, a handful of miles to the west of Launceston, he showed a remarkable talent as a sculptor from an early age. The memorial stone for his grandparents in Altarnun churchyard carved by him at the age of 14 is a work of obvious distinction in an area notable for the quality of its slate carving. He rapidly found recognition within his native Cornwall, and thence, with the assistance of such well-placed Cornishmen as Sir Charles Lemon, to a career in London, working in the atelier of Sir Francis Chantrey, before establishing himself independently and successfully. The facts of what happened subsequently are clear enough; the underlying causes are less so. At the height of his success (attracting even a Royal Commission), apparently after increasing drinking, less and less care for his work, and the death of his daughter Lottie, he closed his studio, left his wife and walked back to Cornwall. Three years spent wandering, staying from time to time with friends, led to his death in Redruth Workhouse and burial in a pauper's grave in Camborne churchyard. The broad outline of the story seems to have been well known in Cornwall. Descendants of Burnard and friends of descendants still lived in the area, and there were many anecdotes. There was a readily accessible and well-documented account of his life written by Hamilton Davey,[25] and subsequently an article by Lawrence Maker in *Doidge's Annual* for 1940. Maker also gave an address at the Burnard Memorial Day ceremonies in Camborne in 1954. (It is not clear from the Archive whether Causley attended this or not, but there is a copy of the proceedings in the Archive.) Causley's interest then appeared to take an increasingly active form. There are copies of the Camborne Church Guide (1959) and the Altarnun Church Guide (1961) in the Archive, both containing material relating to Burnard. He worked intensively on the poem during June 1962 and it was published in the *New Statesman* in the edition dated 2 November 1962. This was rapidly followed by an article on Burnard in the local East Cornwall weekly paper, the *Cornish and Devon Post* dated 10 November. This induced several local people to contact Causley with memories and memorabilia of Burnard. Interest was maintained by his broadcast talk 'The Stone Man', which went out over the air a year later on 5 December 1963, the text being published in the *Listener* of 2 January 1964, both broadcast and article again provoking further correspondence and leading to more information. The poem reached a wider audience by its inclusion in the hardback volume *Underneath the Water* in 1968, the year of the Burnard Sesquicentenary. Causley was much involved in the celebrations and a further broadcast, 'The Man from Altarnun', was timed for that date. The poem obtained even wider circulation by its inclusion both in *Collected Poems 1951–1975* and its updated form *Collected Poems 1951–1997*. It is also included in his taped selection from the *Collected Poems* 'Causley reads Causley'[26] and was widely used by him in public readings. His continuing commitment to the poem is indicated by the presence of an unusually high number of differences between the first periodical publication and the appearance in the first hardback printing in *Underneath the Water*. At that point the poem appears to have reached a form in which the poet was satisfied by it as there is only one minor rewording in its appearance in *Collected Poems*.

A Short Life of
Nevil Northey Burnard

Cornish sculptor, 1818–1878

HERE lived Burnard who with his finger's bone
Broke syllables of light from the moorstone,
Spat on the genesis of dust and clay,
Rubbed with sure hands the blinded eyes of day,
And through the seasons of the talking sun
Walked, calm as God, the fields of Altarnun.

Here, where St Nonna with a holy reed
Hit the bare granite, made the waters bleed,
Madmen swam to their wits in her clear well,
Young Burnard fasted, watched, learned how to tell
Stone beads under the stream, and at its knock
Quietly lifted out his prize of rock.

As Michelangelo by stone possessed
Sucked the green marble from his mother's breast
So Burnard, at his shoulder the earth's weight,
Received on his child's tongue wafers of slate
And when he heard his granite hour strike
Murdered Christ's hangman with a mason's spike.

The village sprawled white as a marriage bed,
Gulls from the north coast stumbled overhead
As Burnard, standing in the churchyard hay,
Leaned on the stiff light, hacked childhood away,
On the tomb slabs watched bugler, saint, dove,
Under his beating fists grow big with love.

The boy with the Laocoön's snake crown
Caught with a six-inch nail the stinking town.
He turned, as Midas, men to stone, then gold.
Forgot, he said, what it was to be cold.
Birds rang like coins. He spread his fingers wide.
Wider the gulfs of love as his child died.

Packing only his heart, a half-hewn stone,
He left house, clothes, goods, blundered off alone:
London to Cornwall and the spinning moor,
Slept in stacks, hedges, barns, retraced the spoor

Of innocence; through the lost shallows walked,
Of his dead child, they say, for ever talked.

At last, the dragged November sun on high,
Burnard lay in a mumpers' inn to die.
At Redruth Workhouse, with the stripped, insane,
Banged on death's door and did not bang in vain;
Rocked in a gig to sleep in paupers' clay
Where three more warmed his side till judgement day.

No mourner stood to tuck him in God's bed,
Only the coffin-pusher. Overhead,
The fishing rooks unravelling the house,
Two men, a boy, restored Camborne Church tower.
'This box,' the clerk said, 'holds your man in place.'
'We come,' they said, 'to smooth dirt from his face.'

No cross marks the spot where he first saw day.
Time with a knife wears the dull flesh away,
Peels the soft skin of blocks cut on the green
Signed by a boy, *Burnard. Sculptor. Thirteen.*
Slowly the land shakes as the ocean's gun
Sounds over Cornwall. He stares from the sun.

The torn tramp, rough with talents, walks the park.
Children have swift stones ready. Men, dogs, bark.
The light falls on the bay, the cold sea leaks,
The slate face flushes, opens its lips, speaks.
In from the moor the pointing shadows flock,
Finger, beneath the river, the pure rock.

Causley's presentation of Burnard's story in no way departs from the basic outline presented by Hamilton Davey and Lawrence Maker and clearly well known in East Cornwall. The focus of his interest is, however, very much his own, and taken together, the work-sheets for the poem and its modifications between periodical and hardback publication and the two broadcast talks, 'The Stone Man', and 'The Man from Altarnun' make clear his developing definition of that focus.

The first sketches for the poem show that, while the general direction is already established, there are significant differences in the 'mounting' of the poem and even its verse form.

In its earliest form the poem is called 'The Visit', or, alternatively, 'My Friend Burnard'. The poet speaks in the first person, as if recounting a visit to Burnard's Altarnun home after his death. The verse form is significantly different—a pattern of alternating three or four stress lines and two stress lines. In this form the poem moves more quickly, but the adoption quite early in the poem's evolution of a regular five stress lines gives greater gravitas. Equally significant are the alterations of detail. At a very early stage the directly personal voice—'my friend Burnard'—disappears ensuring that the poem's focus is directly on Burnard. As the poem evolves, the nature of that focus also shifts and sharpens so that it is Burnard the artist, and the nature and costs of his artistic vocation, that is seen as the subject of the poem. All details, however potentially attractive or significant that do not serve to underline that theme are eliminated. So the details of his family background are removed;

> Father stonemason
> Mother kept the school
>   Made the straw bonnets
> Knew the golden rule
>   Gazed uncomprehending
> At her fighting son . . .

Other appealing details drawn from Hamilton Davey and Lawrence Maker are rejected, for instance Caroline Fox's much quoted reference to his rustic simplicity: 'Mouth wide/All sort of rustic simplicities flowing from inside'. All reference to his marriage and London life other than the ironic reference to his temporary success are removed, 'Turned, as Midas, men to stone, then gold', retaining only the salient fact of his daughter's death. The developing theme of the hazards of the artist's vocation becomes clear, but it is presented with objectivity. Details which might imply a moral verdict are carefully excised: 'I rush across, seize your hand, speak of society's crimes/ Speak of your art, but like Peter you deny it thrice'. (The marginal note 'cock' indicates the poet's ongoing interest.) The poet's attempt at exculpation, still at this stage presented in the first person, is removed as is Burnard's guilty denial. Our compassionate verdict as readers on Burnard is to arise from the complex of fact and imagery with which we are presented, not from explicit authorial judgment. Causley's attitude to Burnard is spelt out more explicitly in the article (originally a broadcast talk) 'The Stone Man' and later in the text of the broadcast 'The Man from Altarnun'. Taken together they provide an important definition. Underneath the assumptions of Hamilton Davey's key article there can be seen, as might be expected, an element of moral judgment. Statements made by Lawrence Maker about

Burnard's relationship with his wife also provoked surviving relatives of the Burnard family to write to Causley setting out a more measured and compassionate picture. So, in the later of the broadcasts Causley concludes:

> The temptation must be resisted . . . to view Burnard's career in terms of the Victorian moral fable to see it as a stern cautionary tale. Burnard was an artist; a man of complex and complicated personality, who even in his last and perhaps most difficult days seems to have shown remarkable resilience and independence of spirit.[27]

In 'The Stone Man' the point is underlined:

> No writer or painter, composer, or poet—particularly if he lives, as I do, in Cornwall—can remain unhaunted by Burnard's story; its triumphs and disasters, its demonstration of the loneliness that is the essential condition of all artistic creation . . . I have tried to lay Burnard's fierce shade by writing a poem about his life.[28]

All the revisions and changes of emphasis, through version after version of the poem, go in precisely that direction, the evocation of the 'loneliness of the artist.' It is a theme of which Causley is hauntingly aware from his earliest writing, from his fascination with Lorca, haunted by 'dark sounds' through the powerful poem, particularly admired as the manuscripts show by Frances Bellerby, 'Death of a Poet'[29] and on to the late, haunting poem 'Red'.[30]

There is, however, a further nearness of Burnard's story to Causley himself. 'No poet, particularly if he lives, as I do, in Cornwall, can remain unhaunted by Burnard's story.' Burnard's story is for him almost an exemplary one, for to a great degree Burnard's background was his too. Stone cutting and the life of the quarryman was in his blood. The poem 'Richard Bartlett'[31] tells of the death of his grandfather in a quarry accident. As he was trying to insert a wedge, a sliver of flying stone pierced his skull. He never spoke again. Causley's poem tries to 'find a place to insert the wedge'. His vocation is rooted in and springs from the land of stone that shaped Burnard too. Theirs is a common vocation. In retelling Burnard's story he is telling how 'the loneliness of the poet' can lead as Wordsworth tells us in a famous phrase:

We poets in our youth begin in gladness
But thereof comes in the end despondency and madness.[32]

'The Short Life' is, of course, in no way unique in Causley's work for
the detailed and extensive care which went to its making—the process
so well described by Jack Clemo:

The thrust through wordy torrents until
The apt phrase was shaped and shining.[33]

It does, however, exemplify particularly clearly not only his rootedness
in the environment of East Cornwall, but also the deep link between
that rootedness and his work.

BROADCASTING, JOURNALISM, MUSIC

There is, however, a further important feature. The 'spin-off', to use a
current phrase, into broadcast and periodical publication is an aspect of
his work which, while never to be seen as other than secondary to the
poetry, is nevertheless an aspect of his work of considerable interest,
and one of which the Archive provides evidence not otherwise readily
available. A selective list of the broadcast talks of which the scripts are
to be found in the Archive is attached as an Appendix. The range of
topics is worth noting. The material on Jack Clemo and Burnard has
already been noted, but there is a wide range of considerable interest.
For the most part the broadcasts went out from the Plymouth studio of
BBC Home Service for the South and West. They are often carefully
timed to take place in school vacations—a small indication of the
disciplined balancing between work and his vocation. Some work is for
the Schools Service. For the most part subjects are related to the South
West, but there is a good deal of work on poetry and poets (e.g. Louis
McNeice, Roy Campbell) and many contributions to verse programmes
such as 'Poetry Please' and 'Time for Verse'. Particularly important is
the memorial programme on the life and work of Frances Bellerby
'The Desperate Day', (a phrase from her poem 'Deep Snow'). Of
particular South Western interest are talks and features on R.S.
Hawker and Sandys Wason, those two outstanding eccentrics among
Cornish parsons, on Sir Cloudesley Shovell, and a variety of topics
about the life and topography of Devon and Cornwall. There are
discussions with other writers, such as A.L. Rowse. Though for the
most part scripts can be found anywhere within the Archive they are
helpfully concentrated in Boxes 21 and 23. In turn they relate closely to
much printed work in periodical or anthology form. They provide
important additional evidence as to Causley's interests as well as

casting a light into the life of regional radio at a time of marked intellectual and cultural vigour, particularly in the late fifties and early sixties.

The Archive points us also to other significant areas of interest. There is much evidence, for instance, in the assemblage of material from specialized educational periodicals of Causley's ongoing though refreshingly non-doctrinaire interest in the education of children, and the place of poetry in that development. There is his careful concern over the artwork for the books, very fully documented, and a particularly fine collection of the attractive, but elusive, Poetry Cards, Posters and Pamphlets. Perhaps more surprisingly there are a significant number of manuscripts of musical settings of his work. Particularly noteworthy is the score for the verse play *Aucassin and Nicolette* by Stephen McNeff which is included in short score form in the printed version. There are other elaborate scores of some length, particularly noteworthy being those for the narrative poem 'St Martha and the Dragon' by Phyllis Tate and for his adaptation of Dylan Thomas's *The Doctor and the Devils*. A variety of shorter poems have also attracted musical settings, for instance 'Timothy Winters', 'The Seasons in North Cornwall' and 'Nursery Rhyme of Innocence and Experience'. It is here that the user would particularly welcome an extension to the Archive in the form of recordings, in whatever form possible, whether tape or, in the case of the plays CD-ROM. That the process of setting is continuing is both unsurprising and welcome. A recent news item indicates a setting of the poem 'Riverside' by Launceston-based musician Elizabeth Ashford.[34] A poet whose verse is both so intrinsically musical and so dramatic will inevitably attract musical setting. A list of music in the Archive is to be found in Appendix II.

CONCLUSION

It is commonplace in writing about Charles Causley to say that the apparent simplicity of his words and verse forms conceals depths, evokes 'dark sounds' that can be profoundly disturbing: the superficial simplicity of 'What has happened to Lulu?' or the wry compassion of 'Ten Types of Hospital Visitor'. It is an art that never hectors, never seeks to convert, never burdens the reader with the poet's own pressing personal concerns. It is a poetry that keeps its profound truths, like Mary's baby 'safe inside'.[35] In his poem 'Letter to W S Graham' he comments:

> . . . Like
> All poets, you were

In disguise; a
Good one, too.[36]

To be able to approach this work through the richness of the manuscripts is to be able, to some small extent, to understand that good
disguise.

APPENDIX I. BROADCAST TALKS, PLAYS ETC; ALL BBC SOUTH AND WEST UNLESS INDICATED

Box 15
John Clare; undated

Box 20
Secret Destinations—introduction with readings to new volume of
    verse 16.5.84

Box 21
On Being a Cornish Bard 18.2.55
The Stroud Guitar (re Laurie Lee) 14.12.55
(with readings by Laurie Lee and Desmond McCarthy)
Dear to the Heart (re Launceston) 21.12.56
Sandys Wason 15.3.57
Primitive Physic—John Wesley's Book of Old Fashioned Cures 3.11.58
Return to Moscow 1.1.59
Pictures from Italy 10.10.59
Interview with A.L. Rowse September 61

Narrative Verse:
The Dragon of Dunborough 30.12.55

Undated:
Portrait of Ivan Kenny—Plymouth Painter
Dearest Robert—Portrait of R.S. Hawker
A Devon Village—Poetry Anthology
Daphne Du Maurier's Infernal World of Branwell Brontë—review
Crowndale Farm (re Tavistock area)
Magic on the Moor

Box 23
Song of Samuel Sweet—a dramatic Ballad 18.10.52
Sassoon's Progress February 55 (National Network)
A.L. Rowse—a Discussion 26.2.59

The Making of a Poem 26.6.61
Jack Clemo 26.4.62

Undated:
Admiral Sir Cloudesley Shovell
Mayflower Sails again (Film commentary)

Box 26
The Ballad of Aucassin and Nicolette—Monday Play 12.5.80
(National Network)
Scripts of 'Poetry Please' nos. 36 and 50–55 1980/81
The Desperate Day—poems by Frances Bellerby chosen and intro-
    duced by Charles Causley 16.3.79

Box 27
Benedict—a Play 27.4.39
Frontier Y—a Play 4.10.50
Who Lived Here? (re Norman Castle) BBC Schools Service 14.6.54
Apollo in the West 8.12.54
Return to the Rock 3.1.56
Review of Halliday's History of Cornwall June 59
The Stone Man 5.12.63
The Man from Altarnun 11.10.68

Undated:
Talk on Plymouth caricaturist Percy Dollery

APPENDIX II. MUSICAL SETTINGS

Box 23
Mervyn Horder   I Saw a Jolly Hunter

Box 31
Stephen Dodgson   Innocent's Song
T.W. Southern   Timothy Winters
                       Nursery Rhyme of Innocence and
                           Experience
                       Sheep on the Blackening Fields
                       (another copy in Box 34)
                       The Seasons in North Cornwall

Box 31

Unsigned Manuscript	Three Masts
Stephen McNeff	Palmer's Songs—songs from *Aucassin and Nicolette*

Box 34

Anthony Castro	Early in the Morning (Song Cycle)
Adrian Vernon Fish	Christ at the Cheesewring
Norman Fulton	A Norman Diary (Song Cycle)
Stephen McNeff	The Doctor and the Devils—score

Box 39

Phyllis Tate; St Martha and the Dragon—printed score

There is correspondence in Box 19 with Anthony Castro concerning his settings for *Early in the Morning*.

ACKNOWLEDGEMENTS

I would like to express my thanks to the Trustees of the Caroline Kemp Fund for a grant towards the preparation of this article; to Mrs J. Pyne and her colleague Miss Teresa Robinson of the Staff of the University of Exeter Library for their unfailing and cheerful help, to my colleague Mrs H. Blake for much patient and detailed assistance, and to my colleague Mrs J. Comben for word-processing of the manuscript. And particularly, I should like to thank Dr Causley himself for his help, encouragement and permission to use his material.

NOTES AND REFERENCES

1. Charles Causley, *Hands to Dance and Skylark*, London, 1951. The reprint in The Cornish Library (London, 1979) contains a valuable Introduction and concluding autobiographical essay.
2. Originally a broadcast talk (*Listener*, 17 March 1997, pp. 337–8), a slightly shortened version is to be found in *Causley at 70*, Calstock, 1987, pp. 106–11.
3. Charles Causley, *Aucassin and Nicolette*, London, 1981.
4. Charles Causley, *A Field of Vision*, London, 1988.
5. Charles Causley, *Jack the Treacle Eater*, London, 1987.
6. Unpublished broadcast talk 'Time for Verse' 16.3.79, Archive Box 12.
7. The original of Lorca's phrase is to found in his essay, 'The Theory and Function of the Duende' to be found in *The Penguin Poets* edition of Lorca; London, 1960, pp. 127–39.
8. Charles Causley, *Dusk and Dawn*, Leicester, 1962, p. 11.
9. *Causley at 70*, p. 106

10. *Collected Poems, 1951–1997*, London,1997, pp. 197–210; Subsequently referred to here as C.P.
11. C.P. p. 335.
12. Charles Causley, *Johnny Alleluia*, London, 1961.
13. Jack Clemo, *Wilding Graft*, London, 1948.
14. Jack Clemo, *The Clay Verge*, London, 1951.
15. Jack Clemo, *The Map of Clay*, London, 1961.
16. Charles Causley, *Survivor's Leave*, Adlington (Kent), 1963.
17. 'The World of Jack Clemo', *London Magazine*, October 1960, pp. 41–4.
18. Jack Clemo, *The Marriage of a Rebel*, London, 1980, pp. 99–100.
19. Charles Causley, *Dawn and Dusk*, London, 1962.
20. *The Puffin Book of Magic Verse*, London, 1974.
21. *Frances Bellerby: Selected Poems*, London, 1970.
22. Anne Stevenson (ed.), *Selected Poems*, London, 1986.
23. *Underneath the Water*, London, 1968.
24. Ron Tamplin, *Charles Causley—A Tribute to the Artists*, University of Exeter Press, 1987.
25. *Royal Cornwall Polytechnic Society Annual Report*, Vol. 1, Part 2, 1910.
26. *Sentinel Records*, Newlyn, Penzance, 1975.
27. Archive Box 27.
28. *Listener* 2 January 1964, pp. 15–16. Broadcast script in Archive Box 27.
29. C.P. p. 144.
30. C.P. p. 383.
31. C.P. p. 277.
32. Wordsworth, 'Resolution and Independence', lines 49–50.
33. 'Meeting-Points (for Charles Causley)' in Jack Clemo, *Approach to Murano*, Newcastle-upon-Tyne, 1993.
34. *Western Morning News*, 1 May 1999.
35. 'Ballard of the Bread Man', C.P. pp. 154–6.
36. C.P. pp. 371–4.

MAXIMILLA, THE CORNISH MONTANIST: THE FINAL SCENES OF *ORIGO MUNDI*

Jim Hall

INTRODUCTION

This study takes a 'cultural studies' approach to excerpts from the *Ordinalia*, the fourteenth-century Cornish mystery cycle. It derives from a seminar with literature and cultural studies undergraduates which set out with a resolutely literary and historical approach that was rapidly overturned by the students themselves. The local references and some of the radically 'strange' values and attitudes that underlie the text combined to produce contradictions that excited a range of problematic interventions.

An initial discussion around the problems of historicism was not enough to dissuade students from attempting to apply very modern paradigms such as humanism and feminism to the representations of the medieval that comprise the cycle. Many of their criticisms were quite clearly inappropriate to a medieval context. Our notions of class, for instance, are so determined by Marxist ideas around industrialized systems of production that they are of little help in considering relations between the bishop and his servants in the play, or, for that matter, between God and humanity. Equally, modern ideas of gender are heavily predicated on a 'separate spheres' model of development which is quite anachronic here. The students did go on to make other provocative and productive evaluations of the text, several of which this study attempts to extend.

Commencing with an overview of the text (in translation, from the original Cornish to English), the study goes on to review critical work that has been done on the *Ordinalia*, as well as some contextualizing material. As might be anticipated, those works are largely literary and historical. The second part of the study takes the final scene of the first play, *Origo Mundi*, and applies a reading that is rather more 'against the grain' and which attempts to locate the text within a more firmly historicized cultural arena than previous more literary readings have done. Textual analysis suggests that a likely period for the plays might begin with an economy still shattered by the Black Death and closes with the Church forced onto the defensive against the Lollard controversy.

The study returns the plays to the seminar with a much wider agenda. Unquestionably, the material has much to disclose to Cornish or regional studies on cultural syncretism. It can also illuminate ideas around gendered positions before the advent of the 'subjectivity' which is the defining product of post-medieval systems of production and consumption in the West. The relationship of religion and culture in medieval Cornwall, in addition, informs us about a time before ideology and might also be instructive in an era that is considered by some to be post-ideological.

DOCTRINE AND SYNCRETISM

The *Ordinalia* comprises three scripts composed in strophic or lyric verse, probably intended for performance on consecutive days: *Origo Mundi* (The Beginning of the World), *Passio Domini Nostri* (The Passion of Our Lord) and *Resurrexio Domini Nostri* (The Resurrection of Our Lord). While this study is concerned specifically with the penultimate passage in *Origo Mundi* it is useful to locate it briefly within the first play. The *Passio* and the *Resurrexio* are largely omitted from this account.

The play opens with God the Father[1] and the Genesis story. Importantly for the Maximilla sequence, and as an addition to the biblical account and perhaps anachronistically, as he works on Adam's form God pronounces the Trinitarian formula:

Del ony onen ha try
tas ha map yn trynyte, . . .
(As we are one and three,
Father and Son in Trinity, . . .)[2]

The plays' repeated declarations of doctrine[3] seem to substantiate Gloria Betcher's[4] assessment in dating them at the end of the fourteenth century. They refer to a time when the Church's teachings were clearly under attack, perhaps especially in the 'wilds' of Cornwall, although Exeter, the episcopal centre, had yet to identify the rising tide of dissent, as the first murmurings of Protestantism and unrest could only be understood through obsolete paradigms of heresy and superstitious reversion. Textual analysis of the *Ordinalia* points back to a popular pagan afterglow, perhaps amounting on occasions to formal apostasy, as well as forward to the rise of Lollardy, Wycliffe and the seeds of Reformation. I am not, of course, suggesting even the most tentative evidence for a pagan underground or non-Christian religious movement in the plays.

Eve, immediately upon her appearance, is tempted by the Serpent to eat of the fruit of the tree of knowledge, so that, in Edwards' translation, she might 'rise up to heaven just like a goddess'.[5] While the play dates from nearly a millennium after the introduction of Christianity to Cornwall, it seems to contain many echoes and insinuations which are neither biblical nor apocryphal but which admonish against pagan reversion, or, read not too violently against the grain, seem to accommodate it with, to a modern sensibility, an unnerving complacency. Both this direct equation of the 'getting of knowledge' with the godhead and the suggestion of witchery in the 'rising to heaven like a goddess' suggest a popular currency in the fourteenth century for the myths and understandings of Christianity's antecedents in Cornwall. The introduction of material from *The Legend of the Holy Rood*, with its veneration of the tree that was to bear the body of Christ and which prefigures him in medieval Christian iconography, is of course a major instance of this and that text may even propose, if not a victory, at least a stand-off for pre-Christian survivals against the Church during the late medieval period, at least in the land to the west of the Tamar.[6] *The Legend* is employed as the primary structural support or spine of the three plays in that it is used as a linking narrative, one which would have been well known to its audiences, for an assortment of biblical and apocryphal episodes. In the *Origo Mundi* these are mostly from the Old Testament (the Vulgate) and they will culminate in the crucifixion and resurrection in the following plays.

Adam's negotiations with God over how he is to fare outside the Garden of Eden are conducted in a burlesque which is succeeded by the story of Cain and Abel. The play continues with the legend of the Holy Rood (beginning with Seth's return to the Garden seeking the Oil of Mercy which will redeem Adam and Eve). The surviving English *Rood* narratives regularly include Maximilla's own story,[7] and, perhaps appropriately for Cornwall, Noah's ark. The narrative of the Holy Rood sees Seth take three pips from the fruit that Adam ate and place them between his dead father's tongue and teeth. Three saplings grow from the seeds which are later cut by Moses as the Staves of Grace. He plants them in the ground on Mount Tabor where they take root. Later, King David will cut them again and, upon the order of God, take them to Jerusalem where they once more take root. David binds the staves together with a 'garland of silver' (*vos garlont gureys a arhans*).[8] His adultery with Bathsheba demands a penance in the form of a 'shining temple' but also prevents him from completing it.

SOLOMON'S TEMPLE

It is left to Solomon to raise the temple in a further burlesque passage featuring groups of rustic masons and carpenters, both, on the face of it, capable enough. It seems clear, especially through Jane Bakere's[9] mapping of the local references and David's exhortation to his messenger to 'make a noble wall of stones and of lime in the middle of the town . . . create a temple',[10] that medieval audiences would have made an immediate connection between this account of the building of Solomon's Temple and Bishop Branscombe's foundation of the Collegiate Church of St Thomas of Canterbury at Glasney (Glasney College). The image of the 'noble wall' was recalled in Glasney's last days by Leland in his *Itinerary*. He described the college as 'wel walled and dyked defensabley', and again as 'strongly wallid and incastellid, having 3 strong towers and gunnes at the but of the creke'.[11] Clearly, the college was one of the most significant medieval buildings in Cornwall. The establishment of Glasney in 1265 inevitably had a major impact upon both the life and the economy of the town and while the play probably appeared a century or two[12] later the foundation must still have been recalled as decisive in Penryn's fortunes.

Solomon rewards the masons and carpenters who have worked on the temple with benefices which heavily deplete the Bishop of Exeter's lands in the locality. Bakere observes that the rewards, appropriately, are localities of significant medieval quarries, and, of course, the Seal Rock itself, as well as wooded demesnes such as 'the whole wood of Penryn'. The carpenters do noticeably better from Solomon's generosity than the masons, who, 'because your work is so good (*wheyl tek*)', receive merely the 'parish of Budock and the Seal Rock with its land'.[13] Now known as Black Rock, it lies midway across the entrance to the Fal and is mostly only revealed at low tide. Many commentators remark on the irony underlying the paucity of the gift. Perhaps that, and the qualification *wheyl tek*, reflect the, by the time of our manuscript, notoriously shoddy workmanship of the masons.

> The fabric of Glasney seems to have been a constant source of trouble. As we have already seen, no less than £13 6s. 8d. (about £260 in our money [in 1903]) a year was in 1316 assigned to its expense. In about a hundred years from its foundation the church was in course of reconstruction; in 1379

Wm. Carslake, one of the canons, bequeathed twenty pounds to the new work on the church (*nove fabrice ecclesie*), and a gift similarly expressed occurs in Bishop Grandisson's will . . . in 1404 the choir was newly vaulted and other repairs executed, in accordance with the bishop's order after his visitation of 1400.[14]

While there were many additions during the 300 years of its existence, the main buildings of Glasney were completed in only two years,[15] with a precipitousness which, by medieval standards, must have verged on the reckless. The further possibility that the gift of Seal Rock represented a subtle attack on an emergent Freemasonry cannot be entirely dismissed. There is some medieval evidence for Masonic guilds, including more than a hundred versions of English *Old Charges* from as early as 1390, outlining the duties of masons to God, their masters, the craft and brother masons.[16] The search for the temple roof's master joist takes the carpenters to the Holy Rood, the 'one tree with garlands of silver around it . . . straight as a spear-shaft'[17] which, imbued with some eldritch power, when cut keeps changing its shape to prevent (or protect) itself from being used as intended. Instead, as a holy object, it is 'taken with great honour to lie in the temple'. A replacement joist is found, miraculously ready-cut to shape and size.

On the consecration of Solomon's Temple, his chief counsellor is anointed bishop, in a parallel of which Phyllis Harris finds several historical antecedents at Glasney, with 'keepers of the Privy Seal', all of whom, as Gloria Betcher points out, would have been clerics in the fourteenth century, finding advancement to bishop. Her suggestion that the reference is to Edmund Stafford, who was keeper of the Privy Seal for Richard II (1389–96) before becoming Bishop of Exeter (1395–1419) as well as Chancellor of the realm (1396–99 and 1401–3)[18] places the plays (or the surviving draft of them) neatly at the end of the fourteenth century. The writers of the *Ordinalia* would have had many reasons to celebrate his advancement, not least in order to align Exeter and Penryn with the metropolitan Church. The reference also strengthens the notion that contemporary audiences would have unequivocally understood Solomon's Temple as representing Glasney. There is a contradiction here, compounded of resistance to a colonizing (English) language and culture and a complicity with one of the chief agents of that culture which may well have contributed to the college's complete destruction at the time of the dissolution. Both Peter[19] and Whetter[20] suggest, largely on the evidence of the *Ordinalia*, that the Collegiate Church at Glasney was a bastion of the Cornish language and culture, and that may well have been the case as local solutions were sought within the church to meet the rising tide of incipient Protestantism and antipathy to the Church, the former meeting popular resistance in Cornwall but, paradoxically, the latter felt just as strongly in Cornwall as elsewhere. On the evidence of the plays alone we should treat the idea of Glasney as a redoubt of Cornish identity with some care. Their macaronic language, in which Middle Cornish is only one of several elements, speaks more of Cornwall's frontier status, and even Jane Bakere's claim that God at least always speaks pure Cornish does not entirely hold up to examination. However, the Bishops of Exeter and many of the canons and prebendaries of the college were undoubtedly metropolitan in outlook, and looked to Oxford and to Catholic Europe in their thinking. On both counts they would have fared badly at the hands of Henry's commissioners. The collegiate church survived until the time of Edward VI when it was seized and, against the advice of the commissioners—'This ys a mete place to establyshe a learned man to teache scollers and to be a precher'[21]—and the desires of the borough, which supported the foundation of a grammar school, the very stones were sold off.

MAXIMILLA AND THE ROOD

With a perfunctory service of consecration the new bishop, an apparently not unworldly appointment, intends that 'each one of us all around [should] drink a draught of wine to comfort his heart'.[22] Maximilla enters the temple and seats herself on the Rood. Her clothes catch fire and she cries out, in an anachronistic plea to Jesus, that the flames should be quelled. The bishop, scenting heresy, enquires where she has heard God called Christ. Maximilla compounds her heresy by suggesting that the nature of Christ is anticipated in the three staves bound into one by David 'as a symbol of the three persons in the Trinity'.[23] The bishop then calls for the wretched Maximilla to be taken from the temple and stoned till she is dead. Her death is represented in explicit and apparently gratuitous action and her executioners are rewarded with Bohelland,[24] Bosaneth and the town (Penryn itself) together with the Canonry and the Close; that is, in contrast to the temple carpenters who were given lands further away from the college,[25] the immediate environs of the college itself and the area where many of the contemporary clerics would have lived. For the audience, these benefices cement the association between the executioners or inquisition and the churchmen of Glasney.

The Rood is removed from the temple and sunk in the pool of Bethsaida by two of the bishop's servants, Amalek and Gebal. The naming of these two, in a passage where masons, carpenters and executioners remain anonymous, and in the context of desecrating that most numinous of objects, was significant for medieval audiences. Amalek and Gebal led the confederacy of nations mobilized against Israel in the Song of Asaph (Psalm 83).[26] The Psalms comprehend the war as a confrontation of cosmic proportions between good and evil, 'between those who fear God and those who fear only men',[27] one in which 'The Lord will be at war with Amalek throughout the ages'.[28] The writer of the Psalm prays that a fate oddly reminiscent of Maximilla's own experience descend upon his enemies.

> O My God, make them like a wheel; as stubble in the wind
> As the fire burneth the wood, and as the flame setteth the
> mountain on fire
> So persecute them with thy tempest. (Psalm 83. 13–15)

That Amalek and Gebal are here the servants of the bishop might suggest that the sympathies of the audience are expected to lie with Maximilla and the Rood itself. However, Sally Joyce Cross proposes that they are better understood in terms of the carnivalesque,[29] as an outburst of repressed impulses in popular culture. While they find it heavy, Amalek and Gebal meet none of the difficulties with the rood that so perplexed Solomon's carpenters or the deflagration that startled Maximilla. As representative of what Bakhtin describes as 'material bodily principle' and pure physicality it is as though they are immune to those properties of the Rood which are related to the spirit and the intellect but are weighed down by the sheer physical mass which apparently went unnoticed by the carpenters. Gretchen A. Shapiro suggests readings from the Torah in which Amalek stands not only as the evil human 'other' in the Old Testament battle between good and evil but also, on the evidence of the worship of the golden calf by the multitude of the Israelites, as the evil seed which lies in wait within all humanity. This fatal ambivalence which makes humanity its own worst enemy was a powerful ingredient in the medieval conception of the self and an important constituent of Bakhtin's notion of the 'grotesque.'

The pool rapidly gains a reputation for curing the sick,[30] which would not have surprised contemporary audiences since it is recorded in the New Testament as the site of many of Jesus' miracles. Nonetheless, in the ecclesiastical economy of the medieval period, the pool's power, with its pagan associations, had to be either arrogated or suppressed, and the bishop finally resorts to using the Rood as the main member of the bridge over the Cedron, where 'it will be trodden under foot and its virtue unfailingly reduced by the dirt'.[31] I will return to the problem of Glasney's construction of a bridge over the River Antron at Penryn and its reception by the various local communities.

In the *Passio* the 'accursed timber' will finally be cut in two by Jesus' torturers to make the upright and transom of the cross. The *Origo Mundi* closes with Solomon inviting the audience to return the next day to see the Passion of Jesus.

THE *ORDINALIA* AND PERFORMANCE

That the *Ordinalia* is available in print at all is due to the survival of a single manuscript, now held in the Bodleian Library (Bodl. MS. 791), of which there are several copies. It comprises eighty-three folios of parchment and appears to be the work of two scribes working, in David C. Fowler's opinion, in the third quarter of the fourteenth century, and at least a further two later hands making corrections to the mostly Middle Cornish text[32] and adding stage directions in Latin. The title *Ordinalia* comes from the rubrics at the head of the *Origo Mundi* and the *Resurrexio* (*hic incipit ordinale de origine mundi* and *hic incipit ordinale de resurrexione Domini Nostri Jhesu Christi*).[33] *Ordinale* is glossed as 'a book that prescribes the manner of saying and celebrating the divine office',[34] and Longsworth, correctly I feel, comprehends the manuscript as 'a kind of stage manager's guide to the rites and ceremonies of the church'.[35] That seems to be corroborated by the later additions of Latin, and thus clerical, stage directions to Bodl. MS. 791. This notion of the Bodleian manuscript as the stage manager's personal, marked-up script forces the existence of an earlier master-copy. This more valuable manuscript was evidently lost to Glasney and to posterity by the time of the final inventory at the suppression of the college. Markham Harris points to further evidence for the earlier manuscript in the stage direction after line 48 (OM), 'Here God comes down from the upper stage and God says:- [Here Lucifer from heaven appears on the stage.]' (*Hic descendit Deus de pulpito et dicit Deus [hic ludit Lucifer de celo]*).[36] There is no obvious reason for Lucifer to appear at this point in the script, although Harris takes the direction to indicate a passage including the angel which existed in some earlier draft of the *Origo Mundi*, but which is omitted here.[37]

The prompt copy brings the historical document to colourful, even frantic life. The college man who used this manuscript organized the fifty-six characters of the *dramatis personae* of the *Origo Mundi* upon an arena the size of a football pitch[38] as the culmination of one of the major ecclesiastical feasts of the year. The *Passio Domini* manuscript includes a stage plan which indicates the *domii* or stations (of the cross) which will locate the scenes of the play around the perimeter of the *plen-an-gwarry* or playing place. Over the three days of the spectacle the cycle features 125 characters in all,[39] as well as many 'special effects' and pieces of elaborate theatrical business. Much more depended on his success than the edification and entertainment of the community and its participation in the festival. More than a dramatization of doctrine, the play made a determining political and economic statement for the area while it held the faithful to their creed, and reminded the burghers of Penryn and Helston of what Exeter had enabled and continued to promise for them, and the country-folk of the indisputable fact that there was only one Church, and that it was, increasingly, a metropolitan Church.

While it is not my purpose to criticize Gloria Betcher's reassessment of the provenance of the *Ordinalia* in this study, this might be an appropriate juncture to suggest that, while I am sure that her dating is sound, I see no reason to move the authorship to Bodmin, at least not on her demographic evidence.[40] She suggests, on a reading of John Maclean's 'Poll Tax Account for the County of Cornwall', that the (tax-paying) population of the Kerrier hundred in 1381 was 3,274. The performances at Penryn would have also drawn parishioners from Penwith (1381 population 4,459) parishes attached to the College. Even if we are to account for those who would have evaded the Poll Tax registers, she is correct in that these numbers do not amount to a very promising constituency for a modern theatrical audience, especially when we have subtracted the 10 per cent or so of the local population required for the production. But Betcher fails to consider that the *Ordinalia* operated in a very different economy to that supporting modern theatrical productions. While the plays take dramatic form they were consummately liturgical events and an integral element of the community's devotional life rather than spectacles of public worship. As such, they were performed to the greater glory of God and their lay audiences must be construed in an altogether different light. As has already been suggested here, in terms of their impact upon the local community they might be compared more appropriately to the modern carnivals of Notting Hill or Rio de Janeiro, which, rather than theatre, are their formal descendants. Dunn furthers the comparison by setting the preparation in the community:

> Although the plays . . . did not consume more than two or three days, the enterprise involved months of preparation and rehearsal, the whole season of Lent often serving as the interval of long-range training for the great event. Such an immersion in the Biblical narrative and assumption of the roles by actors meant an exposure to the story of creative and redeeming love that must have operated as a theocentric force in the lives of the participants.[41]

Bakhtin construes such a period as having been experienced with violent intensity erupting through and producing forms of its own in flamboyant excess of the 'official' narratives which bound both participants and audience to the routine of the community: sowing, harvest, trade and the long reach of the See of Exeter. It was a 'second life of the people, who for a time entered the utopian realm of community, freedom, equality and abundance'.[42] I will return to the implications of Bakhtin's understanding of the carnivalesque. For the present, the consequential intensity of even a secular theatrical entertainment might be gauged from a local legend cited by James Whetter which describes an attack upon Penryn by a band of Spanish sailors in 1567.

> A company of actors was playing late at night in the town when . . . certaine Spaniards were landed the same night . . . with intent to take the towne, spoyle and burn it; when suddenly even upon their entrance, the players (ignorant as the towne's men of any such attempt) presenting a battle on the stage, with their drums and trumpets strooke up a lowde alarme: which the enemy hearing, and fearing they were discovered, amazedly retired, made some few idle shots in a bravado, and so in a hurly-burly fled disorderly to their boats. At the report of this tumult, the towne's men were immediately armed, and pursued them to the sea.[43]

How much more absorbing must have been the effects of a playing of the *Ordinalia* for the inhabitants of pre-Reformation Cornwall. Bakhtin makes it clear that while the plays were being performed they would have completely displaced everyday life; for the people of Penryn and its environs they were a kind of lived hyper-reality. 'Carnival is not a spectacle seen by the people: they live in it and everyone participates because its very idea embraces all the people. While carnival lasts there is no life outside it.'[44]

Commentators on the plays since before Norris have described the *plen-an-gwarry* or 'playing places': circular arenas surrounded by tiers of turfed seating capable of accommodating more than 3,000 spectators. They were capable of seating the entire population of the area because it was expected that everyone would attend. While many commentators on the cycle point to *plen-an-gwarry* some distance from Penryn, a more immediate possibility for the town's own 'playing place' lies in the area called 'Playing Place' about five miles from Penryn on the road to Truro. A situation half-way between the two local centres of population would seem to be a very suitable location for such a site.

A more intriguing possibility lies in the place called Round Ring in 'the fields of Behethlen (Bohelland Fields)',[45] the location that is the first of the rewards to have been bestowed by Solomon upon the carpenters. Both Roddis and Wingfield consider the Round Ring to have been 'a pre-Christian place of worship on the site now occupied by St Gluvias church'. Lord Burghley's map of 1580 (British Museum MS. Royal 18 D.111, f.15) clearly indicates the concentric outer circles of the ring immediately adjacent to the church between it and the river. If Denny's supposition is correct, and the *domii* or pavilions of the *plen-an-gwarry* representing heaven and the other stations of the cross were more or less permanent structures,[46] they would most certainly have been the contribution and responsibility of Penryn's woodworkers' guild. As the builders and renovators of the playing place's 'scenery', the carpenters would have been fitting beneficiaries for the gift of the site.

While Denny suggests that these medieval amphitheatres were 'improvised from prehistoric fortifications or early cattle enclosures',[47] it should be recalled here that the mystery sites of the pre-Christian faiths in Britain were also circular enclosures. Given the provisional nature of early medieval Cornish Christianity it seems quite likely that the original function of the *plen-an-gwarry* was not secular. John D. Niles alludes to St Gregory's 'policy of gently weaning the pagan English from their repugnant practices',[48] by encouraging pagan mystery sites, including pools, trees and groves, to be incorporated into Christian faith and practices. The present study suggests that, in Cornwall, that syncretism was both persistent and pervasive, permeating much more than the disposal of a few local spiritual centres.

THE SMITH'S WIFE

We can recognize four social groups in late fourteenth-century Penryn which might have been exercised around performances of the *Ordinalia*: clerics (a fairly large category when all those in the service of the Collegiate Church or the See of Exeter are included), the burghers of Penryn (many of 'foreign', specifically Breton, extraction), the indigenous, mostly rural, population and women. To offer women as a separate category here might seem perverse to modern thinking; however, by the late medieval period their position in most Western European societies was becoming increasingly constrained by ecclesiastical and civil practice. In *Mont Saint Michel and Chartres* Henry Adams describes the roles that women such as Eleanor of Guienne and her daughters were able to play during the High Medieval period, the age of Eleanor's Court of Love, but 200 years later the independence and authority of women across the whole social continuum had been radically curtailed. The trend continued, certainly into the following century, and Karen Winstead[49] points out that fifteenth-century female exempla are represented to be generally modest, even repressed, and certainly less outrageously self-confident than women such as St Margaret of Antioch or St Catherine of Alexandria. The women of the *Ordinalia*, including Eve, the smith's wife and Maximilla herself are far from diffident.

Women were increasingly understood to be not only frivolous but the social and cultural repositories of all that was bodily, material and carnal. Intellectual and spiritual principles were the exclusive domain of men. Married women were, by definition, submissive and subordinate, and beatings, abuse and death secured their status. The *Ordinalia*'s audiences would have been unsurprised by Maximilla's brutal treatment. Women continued to engage in commercial affairs, as is clearly the case for the smith's wife in the *Passio*, and were indeed active in trade and religious guilds. However, men made the determining decisions and, wherever possible, including in the administration of convents, formal authority had been wrested from women as being inconsistent with a femininity that was at best unstable and more likely depraved. The heavily sexual innuendo in the *Passio* through which the smith, his wife and the torturer negotiate the manufacture of the nails for Christ's crucifixion goes to some lengths to propose that women engaged in trade or commerce, that is to say male roles, are specifically prone to depravity.[50] The smith's wife's readiness to take up his hammer speaks against any idea of fixed 'separate spheres' which was to become the key metaphor for understanding gender difference in later centuries. A female proclivity for sensual gratification is made explicit in Eve's insistence that the Serpent should tell her the 'one thing that would delight [me]', when she adds, 'You can tell me because I am a woman'.[51] Both positions indicate a construction of gender roles and difference as a moral process rather than one that is understood though sexuality and the body. By striking the smith's hands with leprosy, God has prevented him from implicating himself in Christ's death.

Since the medieval construction of gender was in many respects more fluid than our own, female depravity was not entirely unrecuperable. Vern L. Bullough suggests that it was constructed along a continuum centred upon an Adamic hermaphroditism. A general acceptance of Galen and Aristotle comprehended that male genitalia, displayed externally, were mirrored by those of the female which were enclosed within the body. While the male body, after Adam and Christ, remained, as Caroline Walker Bynum has it, 'paradigmatic', 'a permeability or interchangeability of the sexes' was considered as being within the bounds of the model, and in the case of the woman

who lived a chaste and devout life, quite possible.[52] Veronica in the
Resurrexio, manifests this continuity in a robust spirituality which
masculinizes her whole persona. Her 'good and perfect counsel'[53]
arranges the disposal of Pilate's body for the Emperor in a hard-
headed and businesslike manner. In the late fourteenth century, by way
of contrast, Julian of Norwich, writing at the bounds of orthodoxy,
represented Jesus as mother.[54] Bynum points out that Julian regularly
feminized humanity itself as woman, thus accentuating the distinction
with 'the father', the receptacle of reason, spirit and the soul. And, of
course, the church itself was more generally comprehended as 'the
Bride of Christ'.

DISSENT AND HERESY

By the end of the fourteenth century the European Church was beginning to sense the seeds of a variety of species of dissent. Prior to the
Counter-Reformation it attempted to comprehend and deal with them
as heresy and, at first, its wildly anachronistic models for heresy were
taken directly from the patristic writings including the records of the
First Council of Constantinople (the Second Ecumenical Council),
Hippolytus' *Refutatio* and the texts of the Ante-Nicene Fathers, all
from a millennium before. The Church understood both the word of
God and the heresies which strove to corrupt it to be immutable
polarities, eternal and unchanging. While the cults and beliefs pro-
scribed in AD 381 (the Second Ecumenical Council) had died out long
before the fourteenth century, many were revived in the medieval
Church's demonology, along with their histories and prophets, to
prosecute those who had become unsure about the Catholic faith.
Maximilla returns in just such a vehicle.

As Phyllis Harris indicates, Maximilla (re)appears, abruptly
and seemingly without provenance, in the eleventh-century *Legend*.[55]
Harris remarks on Villemarque's assertion in *Le Grand Mystere* that
the figure is *une masque transparent* for Jeanne La Pucelle (the Virgin)
or Joan of Arc. While I will consider the symbolic parallels their
relative chronologies seem to refute the derivation. La Pucelle was
burnt in 1431. Esther Quinn's suggestion that the Montanist prophetess
martyred around AD 179 is a more likely source for the *Ordinalia*'s
Maximilla is much more productive. I suggest that the prophetess,
repeatedly placed under anathema by the early Church Fathers, was
reinvented by the medieval Church in Cornwall as a precise instrument of dialectic. Montanus insisted upon a higher standard for the
Patristic Church, greater discipline and a sharper separation between
the secular and ecclesiastical domains. Similar demands were being
echoed by Wycliffe in fourteenth-century England. Montanus and his

prophetess believed that their testament, witnessed in a state of ecstasy brought on through dancing and speaking in tongues, superseded the word of the Bible and the Church. The notion that the Holy Spirit, through them, could supplement the revelation of Christ and displace a decayed and corrupt clergy (and even the Pope) was one that, to the medieval Church, must have seemingly revived in the doctrine of John Wycliffe and Lollardy. Wycliffe's influence, which was to prepare the ground for the English Reformation,[56] was mainly centred around Oxford at this time and it must be recalled that one of the colleges where it was prevalent was Exeter College, the *alma mater* of many of the masters of Glasney.[57]

Chapter XII of Volume V of the Ante-Nicene Fathers,[58] concerning 'The Montanists; Priscilla and Maximilla Their Prophetesses . . .' is the source of the *Origo Mundi*'s martyr. Maximilla provides a highly productive model for a Church which is being harried by Rome and Canterbury to vigorously hunt out heresy. Walter Wakefield quotes Robert Grosseteste, the Bishop of Lincoln and one of the most eminent European churchmen of the age, as asserting that 'prelates who failed to protect their flocks from "wolves" were themselves guilty of heresy'.[59] It was important that Exeter should be seen to be addressing the problem of heresy since the crisis that it betokened was more than spiritual. The coherence of feudal society depended on the oath of fealty to one's lords, spiritual and temporal. David Christie Murray suggests that second century 'Montanism . . . was a revolt against the increasing organisation of the church'[60] and its concerns with the secular. Its imaginary revival, especially when it implicates Lollardy, has the same preoccupations. As the Church became the underlying organizing principle in society, which it was in fourteenth-century Cornwall, that revolt is simultaneously turned against both the Church and the state. Any denial of the oath to the God of the Catholic Church threatened to undermine the whole basis of secular society. Phyllis Harrris's translation makes clear how, through his dramatic investment in her recantation, the bishop comprehends just what is at stake in Maximilla's heresy. It is Grosseteste's decree which stands him in personal danger of being 'hanged by the thews' without Maximilla's expiation.

> Nor do we say there to be any other God
> Save the Father in heaven above;
> And thou, jade girl, another
> Will make God for thyself.
> May I be hanged by the thews
> If ever thou goest hence

Until thou expiate it abjectly
And clean forswear all thy talk.[61]

While there is little evidence to substantiate this, it would have been naturally assumed that the most susceptible conduits for heresy into a community would be its weakest members: women.[62] As the more apocalyptic and extreme religious movements of the thirteenth century appeared—the Beguines, the Brethren of the Free Spirit, the Albigensians and flagellants of various schools—the Church redoubled its repression, even resorting to crusade. Adventist heresies, anticipating the imminent return of the Saviour, were particularly dangerous to the Church since they

> sapped missionary enterprise and far-sighted planning for the extension of Christ's kingdom . . . made the faithful neurotically excited and discontented with the quiet virtues of everyday Christian living [and produced] a lust for martyrdom which, carried to its logical conclusion, would have destroyed the Church.[63]

The Fourth Lateran Council in 1215 decreed that 'Catholics who have girded themselves with the cross for the extermination of heretics shall enjoy the indulgences and privileges granted to those who go in defence of the Holy Land'.[64] While none of these movements appeared in England, much less Cornwall, it must be recalled that the Church was international and its ministers travelled freely in Western Europe and received their guidance as well as their authority from Rome. When Wycliffe's teachings appeared in Cornwall during the decade or so preceding Bodl. MS. 791 they would have been read in a context that was already well and truly panicked.

THE SUDDEN FLAME
Maximilla appears in the *Origo Mundi* at line 2628 with the stage direction '. . . *et veniet maximilla in templo et sedent super stuppam et vestes ejus concremantur a stuppa et ipsa clamat dicens* . . . (. . . and Maximilla shall come into the temple, and she sits upon the timber and her clothes are set on fire by the timber and she cries out, saying . . .).

> O Father God, through your mercy, send me a cure for my disease with which I am afflicted. Oh! Oh! Oh! alas! woe is me! My clothes are blazing from the wood of Christ, I believe.[65]

Her dramatic manifestation at this moment, in a piece of business which is pure pantomime, radically upsets the anagnorisis which had appeared to be about to culminate in the consecration of Solomon's Temple and the anointing of the bishop. The flames themselves propose a range of interpretations, not least, if we accept Betcher's dating of the manuscript, through the fact that in 1401 the English statute *de heretico comburendo*, enabling the burning of heretics, was enacted.[66] Before Wycliffe the English Church usually considered that confession and reconversion of the heretic to the true faith was the most effective way of dealing with heresy.[67]

The following from Robert Hunt's nineteenth-century anthology of Cornish lore suggests a very different interpretation for the flames that scorch at Maximilla.

> At the close of the fireworks in Penzance, a great number of persons of both sexes, chiefly from the neighbourhood of the quay, used always, until within the last few years, to join hand in hand, forming a long string, and run through the streets, playing 'thread the needle,' heedless of the fireworks showered upon them, and oftentimes leaping over the yet glowing embers. I have on these occasions seen boys following one another, jumping through flames higher than themselves. But whilst this is now done innocently in every sense of the word, we all know that the act of passing children through fire was a very common act of idolatry; and the heathen believed that all persons, and all living things, submitted to this ordeal, would be preserved from evil throughout the ensuing year. A similar blessing was supposed to be imparted to their fields by running around them with flaming torches.[68]

Hunt offers other examples from a Cornish folk-lore which clearly associated flames with cleansing, innocence and purity, and it is in that light that the audience of the *Ordinalia* would have perceived Maximilla. She has 'passed through the fire' and appears at first to have emerged unscathed. Equally evidently, she is not to be preserved from evil which is perhaps intended as the final proof positive of the collapse and failure of the old religion. The detail of the text would have further led the audience to associate Maximilla with Brigid the Irish triple goddess and saint (Breaca, Crowan and Germoe in her Cornish manifestation) who was said to have landed at Hayle around AD 500 as one of the 800 Irish saints who were supposed to have 're-christianised' Cornwall. The oblique reference to Brigid (Breaca) must be read in the context of the medieval Church's strategy through which, by 'transmitting older myths as anecdotes or isolated legends within the context of a Christian system of faith, they contributed to the breaking up of an integrated system of pagan beliefs'.[69] The scope of this long game of atomization was finally realized in the Vatican II modernization of the 1960s when, declaring that there was insufficient proof of both Brigid's sanctity and her historical existence, one and half millennia after she had been adopted and christianized by the church and in the face of lay opposition from the faithful of two continents, Brigid was decanonized. In *Origo Mundi* the British fire-goddess, saint of metalwork, healing and poetry, clearly recognizable through the trope of the 'sudden flame' and the nature of her triple death is deliberately conflated with a much more obscure figure and geared towards the new religious economy.

The notion of the Trinity itself may have arisen from the pre-Christian 'Three Blessed Ladies of Britain', the goddess who had three identities, and, indeed, the *Ordinalia*'s preoccupation with Trinitarian dogma can be seen as being advanced by the introduction of the figure. Paradoxically it was the third-century Montanist, Tertullian, who first articulated the doctrine, finally being sedimented into medieval popular theology through the trope of the Throne of Grace,[70] of the Holy Ghost in the Trinity. Brigid is associated with fire, hence metalwork, the hearth and healing, and illumination and poetry.[71] As the patron of smithing she forged the iron cooking pots which fed and nurtured the community. She guaranteed both heat and light through which her people would prosper, and rituals devoted to her kept the hearth fire alight. Her fire cult was accommodated by Christianity and kept alive in Kildare (meaning Church of the Oak) where Brigid's fire burned until at least AD 1220 when the cult was described by the Welsh cleric Giraldus Cambrensis. She was characterized by the nuns who kept her shrine as 'sudden flame'.

It is clear that the flame of the Rood does not harm Maximilla except in so far as it forces attention to her heresy. Accordingly, the flame would have been understood as the fire of the Holy Spirit. The details of her death are also significant in that she suffered wounds by mallet, bludgeon and stoning (delivered by four, not three, torturers). She is killed by blows to the forehead and jaw (her intellect and speech), to her skin and bones (body) and her breast and heart-blood (spirit) which runs out onto the earth. Joan Radnor argues that the 'threefold death . . . is in Celtic tradition an explicitly Christian narrative device'.[72] In another of the paradoxes of which the authors of the *Ordinalia* are so fond, while such a death would have been very specifically understood by the medieval audience as one in which God is punishing a particular evil, in this context it also serves, along with the Rood narrative itself, to preface the death of Christ in the *Passio*. The scene closes with Maximilla's 'heart-blood' 'running out' as she is stoned with pieces of granite. Another pagan fragment, this image dramatizes the belief that the blood of a divine or royal sacrifice must fall upon the ground to nourish it. The stoning confirms that sense as the heretic's body is buried or re-incorporated with the earth in the stoning. While the passage refuses any fixed meaning the audience would nevertheless have read much of social significance into such a spectacular punishment. The Church is defining a set of boundaries for (still provisional) believers in which Maximilla's body becomes the site of cultural confrontation around faith, superstition and heresy.

At the same time, and paradoxically, a sacred moral order that lies beyond Catholicism, one which stands at the heart of an earlier popular identity and solidarity, is reaffirmed and restored. Medieval myth constantly returns to the pre-Christian dogma of the Dying God, one who guarantees continual life and fertility for the world, in figures such as Jeanne La Pucelle, William Rufus, who was said to have dripped blood all the way from the New Forest to his burial place at Winchester, and Thomas à Becket (Glasney's patron) who was hacked to death and who bled upon the ground even though his body was alleged to bear no wounds. The idea is implicit in grotesque realism where death is always ambivalent. 'It is pregnant death, a death that gives birth.'[73] This reading compromises *de heretico comburendo* itself with the taint of vestigial paganism. In 1428 Wycliffe's remains were exhumed and burnt in accordance with the Statute. Significantly, they were then dispersed upon the ground. What Joan of Arc, William Rufus and Becket also have in common with Maximilla is that they were all said to have fore-knowledge of their deaths which they refused to act upon. While Maximilla's Montanism forbade her the option of flight in the face of persecution her refusal to accept the bishop's offer of expiation, in what could well be a reference to Becket and his association with Glasney, is similarly tantamount to suicide. For Catholicism nature was the creation of God, designed to speak his Glory, but for the mass of the laity it was still understood through the grotesque body, as a macrocosm of body and the self. There were no fixed boundaries between the body and nature and it was constantly at risk of decay or collapse back into its primordial form. That collapse, through the Dying God in her/his protean manifestations, is what guaranteed its renewal.

ST THOMAS BRIDGE

After the Maximilla episode the Rood is taken from the temple to be sunk temporarily in the pool of Bethsaida. Given miraculous powers by the Rood the pool becomes a votive site whereupon the tree is recovered to end the play as a bridge over the Cedron. The Cedron[74] carries a wealth of meaning for the medieval Church. Firstly it is the stream over which Jesus will pass on his way to Gethsemane. In the *Passio*, once he has crossed over the Cedron, he is made to carry the Rood when his torturers have taken it up and placed it on his back. In the Old Testament the Cedron is repeatedly mentioned as a depository of idols and pagan relics.[75] The Rood, here quite literally the bridge which allows the Church to transcend or pass over idolatry and the pagan, is itself here placed under anathema in the same way. In some versions of the legend the Queen of Sheba refuses to pass across the bridge, saying that to do so would prove the ruin of Israel.

Deborah Wingfield suggests that, roughly contemporary to the foundation of the Collegiate Church, 'St Thomas Bridge, over the River Antron, Antre or Anter, existed by 1275 and possibly as early as 1260 . . . It must have been a hump-backed bridge and, if compared with the one still existing at Gweek, of considerable length'. The bridge, 10 or 20 metres distant from the main gate of Glasney in St Thomas Street, must have been fairly substantial as it had its own adjoining chantry, the *Cantaria de Ponte*.[76] The construction of roads and especially of bridges was accounted as the work of God during the whole medieval period and indulgences were regularly granted to those who built them. The bishop of the *Origo Mundi* would have been doubly blessed for taking a sacred pagan object and turning it to God's work. The allusion to the Cedron may well imply that the River Antron was considered to be a site of some significance for pre-Christian Penryn (Polsethow).

In the fourteenth century the journey to London took at least a fortnight and most of the roads in Cornwall ran north–south from coast to coast, rather than towards England. They were used both to transport goods to hundreds of tiny harbours (as well as to more important ports such as Penryn) and by travellers who did not wish to make the dangerous voyage round Cape Cornwall. Most of the Cornish, including the Breton merchants who had settled in Cornwall, would have travelled by water for preference. River and coastal traffic was both safer and faster than road and by far the best way to transport Cornwall's chief exports, stone, tin and fish. Accordingly, the Cornish were prejudiced against the building of bridges since they not only obstructed the free passage of river and creek traffic except at lowest water but also cost those who used them a toll (pontage). The bridge in St Thomas Street would have been one of many sources of funds for the Collegiate Church and seen as another reason for resenting a rapacious church. Towards the end of its existence the canons of Glasney are also said to have built a drawbridge on the site of the twentieth-century bridge.[77] Presumably they would have charged both those who crossed it and seafarers who wished to have it raised so that they could enter the harbour.

CONCLUSION

Considerations of the *Ordinalia* in context demand a wholesale rejection of modern thinking, including that upon authorship and text. The plays would have been understood by their audiences as a 'tradition' and been revised from production to production, perhaps like modern pantomimes, to meet the exigencies of the moment. The clerics who undertook such reworking dealt with a range of social, religious and economic issues through a prescribed array of plots which could be reorganized, omitted (as in the case of the fall of the angels), or re-incorporated and returned to popular culture in what C.S. Lewis described as a 'living continuity'.[78] The cycle is clearly not so much a dramatization of scripture as a cultural enterprise geared specifically to contemporaneous concerns. Major issues such as the redemption of humanity were argued alongside vitriol upon the builders for the disintegration of the fabric of the collegiate church, particulars of dogma and celebration of the advancement of eminent collegiate brethren. Fudge notes that the final scenes of the *Origo Mundi* entirely replace biblical with apocryphal material, and I suggest that the author is here using the play as a vehicle to comment upon (or to fulminate against) contemporary religious and social trends.

We have to base our reading of the cycle in an economy that, for many, has yet to adopt money as its primary means of exchange. An economy of 'natural husbandry' would still have met the needs of the rural population in mid and west Cornwall during the late fourteenth century. At the same time the foundations of a new social structure and regional economy were being laid by the burghers, the town dwellers of Penryn, Truro and Helston. Elliott-Binns suggests that the populations of these towns would each have been around 300 in 1377 and that, throughout the period, a high proportion of town dwellers comprised Breton merchants and traders.[79] As they were important patrons of the cycle we must expect to find evidence of these alien settlers in the texts, and of course, the ideas and values that they would have brought with them. Outside of the towns the feudal economy still held sway, with the bulk of the land either in the hands of the Church or other local magnates. Court records indicate that land rights were jealously guarded by both parties, with free people, who perhaps out of the range of living memory but well within folk memory had held much of that land, deriving their subsistence from a new ruling class and the Church.

An essential significance of the *Ordinalia* for contemporary audiences is the demarcation of the landscape of Cornwall, much of which, three or four generations previously, had been either held in common or as family lands, as parish and ecclesiastic demesnes. Kim McCone makes it clear that before the Anglo-Saxon and Norman regimes land was inviolable. Even in war it was 'hedged around with taboos . . . one did not annex the enemy's territory or confiscate their lands'.[80] For audiences whose identities were still tightly bound to specific plots of ancestral holding, the plays emphasize above all else the fact that the land of Cornwall has been irrecoverably transformed into a kind of capital or instrument of exchange; one that largely accrues to, and is at the disposal of, the Church. The townlands and parishes which are so freely bestowed in the plays would have carried the livelihoods and the histories of many of the audience with them. In Penryn itself the charter conferring the town on its burghers seems to be signified by a change in the town's name. The plays clearly identify those who are to be the winning factions in the new political economy of Cornwall.

The plays, then, must be read in the context of a struggle for political power. They seem to propose a Church that was far from monolithic, tensioned between the conflicting demands of Exeter, Canterbury, Rome and the court. It was attempting to increase both its institutional effectiveness and to underpin a pattern of centralized and increasingly invasive techniques of control over a population which was by no means subdued while at the same time mobilizing against the contrivances of a state already seeking ways of disinvesting it. A fourth front had already opened with the appearance of clerical dissent, rapidly spreading to the laity, in the form of John Wycliffe's teachings and Lollardy.

The *Ordinalia* stand as a complex and multi-layered text for a culture which was being drawn inexorably into metropolitan England through a range of influences: its bishop (based across the Tamar in Exeter), its trading contacts and exports, and its gentry. Clearly the Church, a continental Church, had its own view on that process. The cycle's careful ambiguities speak of an unstable and fractious audience whose faith, while it had not succumbed to the apostasy of contemporary Brittany, was often heavily compromised with persistent superstition and pagan vestiges. The intensity of popular Cornish Catholicism, which was to meet its greatest test in the Prayer Book Rebellion of 1549, was adamantine, but the plays suggest that there was often considerable distance between that grass-roots religion and the doctrine that was promulgated from the cathedral at Exeter.

NOTES AND REFERENCES

1. As in other medieval liturgical texts God the Father (Deus Pater) is here conflated with the 'Creator God,' the Demiurge of the Gnostic cults and some heretical Christianities, also with the 'jealous god' of the Old Testament.
2. Edwin Norris (editor and translator), *The Ancient Cornish Drama* (2 vols), New York and London, 1968, pp. 6–7.
3. C. Fudge, 'Aspects of form in the Cornish *Ordinalia*, with special reference to *Origo Mundi*,' *Old Cornwall*, Vol. 8, 1979, pp. 457–98. Fudge points out that in the *Origo Mundi* 'the Trinitarian formula is repeated by Adam, Moses, David and Maximilla; the playwright is concerned to express by this anachronistic phrase God's eternal Trinity'. p. 460.
4. Gloria J. Betcher, 'A Reassessment of the Date and Provenance of the Cornish *Ordinalia*', *Comparative Drama*, Vol. 29, 1996, pp. 436–53. Betcher's reassessment of the historical evidence to suggest a date towards the end of the century seems very plausible, especially in the light of rising resistance to the Church at that time. As I will suggest, her reallocation of the provenance of the plays, moving them from Penryn to Bodmin largely on demographic evidence and a reassessment of place-names within the text seems much weaker.
5. '*Kepar yn beys ha dves the 'n nef grusses yskynne*', Ray Edwards (ed.), *Origo Mundi*, Sutton Coldfield, 1998, p. 6, line 155.
6. Lower Brittany (most of the country west of Morlaix including the area known as Cornouaille) was not fully Christianized until a determined mission by the Jesuits in the seventeenth century reconverted the indiugenous population (E. Werner, *Pauperes Christi*, p. 180). A stronger central policy forced Cornwall to bow to its metropolitan economy rather earlier in Britain but in the late medieval period its people were deeply superstitious and a constant worry to the Bishop of Exeter, their spiritual shepherd.
7. Sometimes as Sibyl, Sibilla or the Queen of Sheba, as well as a range of other variants. The woman is often a harlot and Phyllis Pier Harris refers (after Ester Quinn) to a 'whole complex of legends which developed about the sibyl . . . there is, moreover, a well established tradition that the Queen of Sheba and one of the Sibyls were merged.' Phyllis Pier Harris, (ed. and trans.) '*Origo Mundi*', *First Play of the Cornish Mystery Cycle, the 'Ordinalia': A New Edition*, University of Washington, 1964 (Ph.D. thesis on loan to the Courtney Library, Royal Institution of Cornwall, Truro) p. 394.
8. In some versions of the Rood legend David binds the staves with a premonitory thirty rings of silver.
9. Jane A. Bakere, *The Cornish Ordinalia: A Critical Study*, Cardiff, 1980, is heavily dependent for her mapping of the place-names on E. Hoblyn

Pedler's 'Notes on the names of places etc. mentioned in the preceding dramas', an appendix of Norris.

10. I am using Ray Edwards' 1998 translation of the *Origo Mundi*, based on Norris' 1859 edition. Ray Edwards (ed. and trans.), *Origo Mundi*, Sutton Coldfield, 1998, p. 86.

11. Cited in C.R. Sewell, 'The Collegiate Church of St Thomas of Glasney', in the *Journal of the Royal Institution of Cornwall*. No. 3, 1865, p. 27.

12. Bakere's assessment (p. 1). Betcher is more precise and the present essay seems to find good textual and historical evidence to support her dating.

13. Edwards, p. 93.

14. Thurstan C. Peter, *The History of Glasney Collegiate Church, Cornwall*, Camborne, 1903, p. 40.

15. Deborah E. Wingfield, *Special Report No. 5: Penryn: Archaeology and Development—A Survey*, Truro and Redruth, 1979, p. 4 (from Glasney Cartulary).

16. From http://internet.lodge.org.uk/masonic.UGLE/history/early.html (1/7/98). Modern Freemasons are 'non-operative'. Their medieval forbears were patently operative. The surviving *Old Charges* comprise: 'parchment rolls up to nine feet in length or paper sheets formed into notebooks containing a legendary history of the mason trade and *Charges* reciting the duties of a mason.'

17. Edwards, p. 94.

18. Betcher, pp. 441–2.

19. Thurstan C. Peter.

20. James Whetter, *The History of Glasney College*, Padstow, 1988.

21. Chantry Certificate 9 cited in Roland J. Roddis, *Penryn: The History of an Ancient Cornish Borough*, Penryn, 1964, p. 128.

22. Edwards, p. 100.

23. Edwards, p. 101. Norris indicates that the following stanza was added to the manuscript by a later hand . . .

onan yw an tas a neff	(One is the Father of heaven,
arall crist y vn vaaw eff	Another, Christ his one Son,
a vyth a wyrghas genys	Who shall be born of a virgin,
ha'n sperys sans yw tressa	And the Holy Ghost is the third;
try hag onan ow trega	Three and one, dwelling
yn vn dewsys me a grys.	In one Godhead, I believe.)

The second writer has rendered Maximilla's initial rather obscure reference to the Trinity in explicit and didactic terms.

24. Before the establishment of Penryn by Bishop Simon of Exeter in 1216 the parish was called Behethlan (dwelling by the monastery?) or Bohelland. Fowler suggests (p. 100) that the name Penryn was not commonly used until after 1388 (after Pedlar). This is not to place Bodl. MS. 791 before 1388 since such an antique usage employed by a cleric would have carried its own connotation for the audience.

25. 'The field of Bohelland [note that the executioners are given Bohelland

itself] and the whole wood of Penryn [Pedlar suggests that this is probably the Bishop's Wood which reinforces the suggestion of a conflation of bishop and builders], I give them now to you; and all the water courses. The island (*enys*) and Arwinnack, Tregenver and Kegillik, Make of them a charter to you.' Norris p. 197.

26. Robert Longsworth, *The Cornish Ordinalia: Religion and Dramaturgy*, Cambridge, Mass., 1967, p. 63. Malcolm Godden (1991) points out the importance of the psalms to the medieval liturgy.

27. Gretchen A. Shapiro, '*Then came Amalek*: An Analysis of Amalek in the Torah in light of the Commentaries and the Zohar', http://users.qual.net/ ~alyza/Jewish/amalek.htm, 1997, p. 1.

28. Exodus 17: 16 cited in Shapiro.

29. Sally Joyce Cross, 'Torturers as Tricksters in the Cornish *Ordinalia*,' *Neuphilologische Mitteilungen*, Vol. 84, 1983, pp. 448–55.

30. Bethsaida in the Vulgate and Bethesda in the King James version; the site would have been recognized by medieval audiences as the site of the feeding of the multitudes, the healing of the blind man and where Jesus was reported to have walked upon the water. Perhaps the very fact that the location was lost to contemporaneous scholarship, which through the discoveries of crusaders and pilgrims had recovered much of biblical Palestine, made it so very evocative in the context of the Temple in Penryn. The Bronze Age city was rediscovered in 1985 by a Benedictine monk, Father Bargil Pixner, at el-Tell, near the Sea of Galilee.

31. Edwards, 1998, p. 107.

32. All three *Ordinalia* comprise heteroglossia of passages and interventions in Middle Cornish, English, French and Latin.

33. The *Passio* merely begins *hic incipit passio Domini Nostri Jhesu Christi*. While it is interesting that the *Origo Mundi* and the *Resurrexio* are offered as *ordinalia* or scripts and the *Passio* is not, it seems unlikely that we can read more into the fact than evidence of a scribe's carelessness.

34. Quoted in Longsworth, p. 105, '*liber in quo ordinatur modus dicendi et solemnizandi divinum officium*,' from Linwodus, *Glossarium mediae et infimae latinitatis*, 10 vols, Paris, 1937–8.

35. Longsworth, p. 105.

36. Norris, p. 5.

37. Markham Harris, *The Cornish Ordinalia: A Medieval Dramatic Trilogy*, Washington D.C., 1969, p. 250, n. 'I have omitted from this stage direction a final clause, written in a later hand [as they all were in Bodl. MS. 791] which reads *hic ludit Lucifer de celo* 'here Lucifer plays his part from heaven'. Although wholly inoperative as it stands, it should not be passed over in silence because it implies the onetime presence in O.M. of an episode or episodes still to be found in the English cycles and in the Cornish *Gwreans an Bys*. These episodes deal with the creation of angels and the fall of Lucifer.'

38. Neville Denny, 'Arena Staging and Dramatic Quality in the Cornish Passion Play', *Stratford Upon Avon Studies*, Vol. 16. pp. 125–54: '. . . an eathern amphitheatre some 100 feet in diameter comprising a circular flat

glass *plateau* or 'place' surrounded by an embankment ten to twelve feet high, terraced into seven or eight rows of seating. Set upon this embankment in the eastern quadrant would be Heaven, a grand and commanding presence, as splendid and radiant as the dawn, the dominating visual in the entire theatrical environment. Opposed to this as a visual and thematic (even psychological) element would be *Infernum*—at ground level almost certainly—an enormous monster's head, 'hell-mouth', the Leviathan of *Isiah 27 . . .*' p. '133. Joseph Campbell suggests that this round platform also figures in the Grail romance and in the story of the Fisher King. His six realms of the 'round of being' comprise 'the gods, titans, ghosts, hell, animals and men' which seem to closely parallel the *domii* or stations of the *plan-an-gwarry*. *The Masks of God: Creative Mythology*, New York and London, 1976, p. 416.

39. After Neville Denny, 'The Staging of Medieval Drama', in *The Proceedings of the Colloquium Held at the University of Leeds 10–13 September 1974: The Drama of Medieval Europe*, Leeds Medieval Studies Ser. 1, 1975. Betcher suggests that, even allowing for actors doubling up where possible, a staging of the *Ordinalia* would require at least 100 performers and crew, a demanding logistic problem by any standards. The problem is compounded when we consider that while those of his actors who were clerics or members of religious guilds were mostly literate this was a culture still firmly anchored in an oral tradition and others would have been unable to read.

40. The appearance of Joseph of Arimathea in the *Passio* and the *Resurrexio* might also tie the cycle to Penryn. The legend claims that Joseph was a tin merchant who brought the young Jesus to the Fal, specifically St Just. The parish, including the new church consecrated by Bishop Bronescombe in 1261, was given to Glasney on its foundation.

41. E. Catherine Dunn, 'Popular Devotion in the Vernacular Drama of Medieval England', *Medievalia et Humanistica*, No. 4, 1973, p. 58.

42. Mikhail Bakhtin, *Rabelais and his World*, translated by Helene Iswolsky, Cambridge, Mass., 1968, p. 9.

43. Whetter, pp. 103–4. Sandys (1865) gives a longer account of this (from Leland I think) in which he says that the play was *Sampson* and that it was set in 'a barn in Penryn'. Deborah Wingfield (1979) suggests (after Peter) that there was a sixteenth-century theatre at No. 44 Bohill, which seems to make some sense as the Spaniards would have easily heard any uproar in the auditorium from the wharf, less than 100 metres distant. Courtney traces the anecdote to a piece entitled 'Strange Occurance at Penryn' in *Gosson's School of Abuse* (1579).

44. Bakhtin, p. 7.

45. Roddis, p. 61. Deborah Wingfield suggests that the site is either late Iron Age or Romano-British.

46. Denny, pp. 130–1.

47. Denny, p. 130.

48. John D. Niles, 'Pagan Survivals and Popular Belief', in Malcolm Godden and Michael Lapidge (eds), *The Cambridge Companion to Old English*

Literature, Cambridge, 1991, p. 129. Of course this was 800 years before Bodl. MS. 791 was written.

49. Karen A. Winstead, *Virgin Martyrs: Legends of Sainthood in Late Medieval England*, Ithaca and London, 1998.

50. Graham Sandercock (ed.), *The Cornish Ordinalia, Second Play: Christ's Passion*, Sutton Coldfield, 1982, pp. 179–81 (the smith's sudden attack of leprosy preventing him from using his tools, his wife has taken up his hammer and anvil and instructed the torturer to work the bellows):

> FIRST TORTURER
> I will blow like a good fellow:
> there is no-one better in this country
> who will blow better:
> I don't know a smith in all Cornwall
> who blows with bellows,
> indeed, any better.
>
> WIFE
> You blow like a careless fellow!
> Blow easy, vengeance on thy maw,
> not a spark will stay in the forge!
> Stop now, good-for-nothing,
> and beat the iron stroke for stroke:
> if thou does not, thou shalt be hanged!
>
> FIRST TORTURER
> I will strike, so God me catch,
> and that with great care,
> so that it shall stretch out like wax!
> There is not a smith's boy in this land
> who will strike certainly as well,
> and that everyone knows.
>
> WIFE
> Strike on the point, may thou get ill
> punishment thou very rogue!
> Strike in the right place: if it is cold
> it will not come right.
> But though they should be hammer dinted,
> the worse they will be for the toad,
> and rough in His hands.
> See how he strikes this way and that!
> Thou vile lubber, strike steadily
> and evenly, ill may thou thrive!

51. Edwards, p. 6.

52. Caroline Walker Bynum, *Fragmentation and Redemption: Essays on*

Gender and the Human Body in Medieval Religion, New York, 1992, p. 220.

53. Graham Sandercock (ed.), *The Cornish Ordinalia, Third Play: Resurrection*, Sutton Coldfield, 1984, p. 131.

54. One of the Montanist heresies found most objectionable by the Byzantine religious authorities that suppressed the sect was Priscilla's prophesy that Christ would return as a woman.

55. Phyllis Pier Harris, p. 395.

56. Wycliffe was described in the sixteenth century as 'The Morning Star of the Reformation'.

57. Peter.

58. Ante-Nicene Fathers, Volume V. http://ccel.wheaton.edu/fathers2/ ANF-05-12.htm (25/6/98), Chapter XII. 'These [heretics] have been rendered victims of error from being previously captivated by wretched women, called a certain Priscilla and Maximilla, whom they supposed prophetesses. And they assert that into these the Paraclete Spirit had departed; and antecedently to them, they in like manner consider Montanus as a prophet . . . and [the Phrygian heretics] allege that they have learned something more through these, than from law, the prophets and the Gospels. But they magnify these wretched women above the Apostles and every gift of Grace, so that some of them presume to assert that there is in them a something superior to Christ. These acknowledge God to be the Father of the universe, and Creator of all things, similarly with the Church, and as many things as the Gospel testifies concerning Christ. They introduce, however, the novelties of fasts, and feasts, and meals of parched food, and repasts of radishes, alleging that they have been instructed by [the] women.' In many ways this gloss of Montanism, with its emphasis on personal revelation, also works as an excellent prototype for Lollardy. With reference to both the Maximilla of *Origo Mundi* and the Lollard martyrs it is noteworthy that in the suppression of the second century CE all Montanists in the Empire were gathered and burned alive in their temples. In the fourth century Justinian continued to take robust measures against the movement. Four hundred years later the bones of Montanus, Priscilla and Maximilla were exhumed and burned by John of Ephesus 'lest their spirits walk the earth seeking vengeance'. C.S. Clifton, *Encyclopedia of Heresies and Heretics*, Santa Barbara, 1992, p. 99.

59. Walter L. Wakefield and Austin P. Evans (translators and annotators), *Heresies of the High Middle Ages: Selected Sources*, New York, 1991, p. 640. (from Matthew Paris, *Chronica majora*).

60. David Christie-Murray, *A History of Heresy*, London, 1976, p. 10.

61. Phyllis Pier Harris, p. 299.

62.. 'It was often remarked by medieval observers that women were particularly susceptible to heretical teaching.' Walter L. Wakefield, *Heresy, Crusade and Inquisition in Southern France, 1100–1250*, Berkeley, 1974, p. 74. Richard Abels and Ellen Harrison, 'The Participation of Women in Languedocian Catharism', *Medieval Studies*, No. 41, 1979, pp. 215–51, note that Wakefield himself sees no need to document the statement.

63. Christie-Murray, p. 36.
64. H.J. Schroeder (trans. and ed.), *The Disciplinary Decrees of the Ecumenical Councils*, St. Louis, 1937, pp. 242–3.
65. Edwards, p. 100.
66. Christie-Murray, p. 110, points out that this was some 130 years after the statute became law in France.
67. M.D. Lambert, *Medieval Heresy: Popular Movements from Bogomil to Hus*, London, 1977, p. 248.
68. Robert Hunt, *Popular Romances of the West of England or the Drolls, Traditions and Superstitions of Old Cornwall*, London, 1916, p. 207.
69. J.M. Picard, 'The Strange Death of Guaire mac Aedain', from D. Howlett (ed.) *Sages, Saints and Storytellers: Celtic Studies in Honour of Professor James Carney*, quoted in Kim McCone, *Pagan Past and Christian Present in Early Irish Literature*, Maynooth, 1990, p. 180.
70. The Throne of Grace is the seat of God's judgement. Medieval theology proposed that Christ's sacrifice offered redemption for humanity and any refusal of that redemption incurred God's curse. The overriding theme of the *Ordinalia* is redemption through Christ's crucifixion.
71. Gilbert H. Doble, *The Saints of Cornwall: Part III. Saints of the Fal and its neighbourhood*, Oxford, 1964.
72. Joan N. Radnor, 'The significance of the threefold death in Celtic tradition', in O. Hehir (ed.), *Celtic Folklore and Christianity*, quoted in McCone, p. 147.
73. Bakhtin, p. 25.
74. The name derives from the Hebrew for 'dark' or 'turgid'. It was a seasonal stream that had its source near Jerusalem and flowed past the Mount of Olives, through the Valley of Cedron into the Dead Sea.
75. Kings 15:13, Kings 23:4, 6 and 12 (from Phyllis Harris).
76. Wingfield, p. 5. She includes Baptista Boazio's *Map of Parte of Cornwall* of 1597 which clearly indicates the bridge still remaining.
77. The drawbridge is shown on *Lord Burghley's Map* (1580) British Museum MS. Royal 18.D.111,f.15 reproduced in both Peter and Wingfield.
78. C.S. Lewis, *The Allegory of Love*, Oxford, 1936 (cited in Fudge).
79. L.E. Elliott-Binns, *Medieval Cornwall*, London, 1955, p. 59.
80. McCone, p. 8.

RECONSTRUCTIVE PHONOLOGY AND CONTRASTIVE LEXICOLOGY: PROBLEMS WITH THE *GERLYVER KERNEWEK KEMMYN*

Jon Mills

INTRODUCTION

In July 1988 the Cornish Language Board adopted the orthography known as Kernewek Kemmyn. This shift in orthography brought about a need for new pedagogical materials including a new dictionary. In 1993 the Cornish Language Board published the *Gerlyver Kernewek Kemmyn*.[1] Does this dictionary really provide a suitable pedagogical basis for the revival of Cornish today? Since its publication, there has been a great deal of controversy concerning the new orthography.[2] Some people might argue that, on the one hand, Kernewek Kemmyn is to be preferred since its phonemic nature makes it pedagogically advantageous; and that, on the other hand, the reconstructed phonology on which Kernewek Kemmyn is based has a sound scholarly foundation grounded in the study of the traditional historic corpus of Cornish literature. However, it is clear that neither of these claims stands up to scrutiny. Not only is George's reconstructed phonology academically unsound but the phonemic nature of Kernewek Kemmyn, together with the respelling of place names according to their putative etymologies, actually entails certain disadvantages. Furthermore, the English translation equivalents and neologisms given in the *Gerlyver Kernewek Kemmyn* entail a contrastive lexicology that is at odds with traditional practice as attested in the historical corpus of Cornish. It is clear that the prescribed canon encoded in the *Gerlyver*

Kernewek Kemmyn is linguistically naïve and is, therefore, not a suitable pedagogical basis for Revived Cornish.

STANDARDIZATION

The orthography of traditional Cornish
The inconsistent orthography that is prevalent in the corpus of traditional Cornish is a common problem for the Cornish linguist; a multiplicity of spelling variants causes problems for the study of syntax or lexis. In their original form, the Cornish texts reflect the variety of orthographic styles that prevailed during the various chronological episodes of the period they represent. The original spelling of the texts is not consistent, even normally within a single text. For example, we find the following orthographic variants of the Cornish word for 'flesh': *chîc, cîg, cyc, gîc, gyc, gyke, kig, kìg, kîg, kyc, kych, kyek, kyg, kyk, kyke.* For the purposes of pedagogy a standardized orthography is clearly beneficial.

George, however, goes further than rejecting the traditional orthography on grounds of inconsistent spelling. George[3] offers no evidence for his assertion that Cornish scribes 'learned to write and read in English, and wrote Cornish "on the side" '. Yet George[4] maintains that, 'Cornish has little or no historical spelling tradition of its own; since the fourteenth century, it has almost always been written using contemporary English orthography'. This is not entirely true; like English, Cornish has enriched its vocabulary by borrowing from Latin and Norman French and where this is the case, orthographic practice has a lot in common with Romance languages in general. Where Cornish has borrowed from English, Cornish spelling frequently resembles that found in the works of Chaucer. But there are differences between English and Cornish spelling tradition. With the exception of the *Ordinalia* (*c.* 1500) which uses, <th>, Cornish (up to and including *Gwreans an Bys* dated 1607) uses a character resembling a long-tailed-<z>. This character has a similar form to the Old English character yogh. However it is clearly not the same character since yogh corresponds to modern-day English <g> or <y> whereas Cornish long-tailed-<z> is used to represent dental fricatives. George[5] observes that 'As in MidE, <c> tended to be used before <a,o,u; l,r> and <k> otherwise'. This should not be taken as evidence, however, of Cornish borrowing orthographic practice from English since this alternation of <c> and <k> is not peculiar only to English and Cornish. One finds in French, for example, *képi, kyste, caste, clos, cristal, costume, cuisse*; and in Spanish: *keniano, kilate, cabal, clamor, crÿpula, cosa, cuba.* Similarly,

George[6] is of the opinion that '<qu> and <wh> are English gra-phemes.' Again, however, <qu> and <wh> are not exclusive to English. One finds in French, for example, *quand, que, quitter* and *quolibet*; in Spanish: *quebrada* and *quico*; and in Latin: *quadra, quercus, quies, quo* and *quum*. One finds in Welsh, for example, *whado* and *whimbil* and in Middle Welsh, *lawhethyr* ('fetter'). One is not justified in concluding, as George does, that Cornish has borrowed its orthography from English and has no historical spelling tradition of its own.

George is not unique in naïvely assuming that Late Cornish is corrupted by English.[7] However Late Cornish orthography continued to evolve independently of English. A good example of this is that, in the Late Cornish period, several writers adopted diacritics so that circumflex, acute and grave accents are found over vowels. Further-more, if one compares Lhuyd's[8] phonetic transcription of lexical items with their spellings by Late Cornish writers the link between Late Cornish spelling and contemporary English orthographic practice seems to be not so strong. For example, in Late Cornish we frequently find <ea> representing /e/ or /e:/.[9] English visitors to Cornwall often erroneously pronounce the place-name St Teath as if it rhymes with 'teeth'. Similarly, English visitors are usually totally at a loss as to how the place-names Meneage and Breage should be pronounced.

Need to standardize spelling

The necessity for a standardized spelling system for Cornish has been recognized since the nineteenth century. Williams[10] made a start on tackling the problem of variable orthography by amalgamation. Williams' reforms, which include diacritics, the adoption Lhuyd's <dh> for voiced <th>, and the substitution of <c> for the letter <k> in all cases, met with a mixed response. Stokes[11] criticizes Williams' dictionary, saying that 'Mr. Williams has throughout his *Lexicon* been misled by Welsh analogy'. In particular, Stokes[12] is critical of Williams' orthography, maintaining that analogy with Welsh misled Williams into distinguishing between <dh> and <th>. As Stokes points out, this separation is not borne out by the Middle Cornish texts. Williams' dictionary was similarly criticized by Bonaparte[13] and Loth[14] and more recently Gendall.[15] Jenner based his Revived Cornish on Late Cornish. In other words, he chose to take up the language where it had left off. In his *A Handbook of the Cornish Language*,[16] Jenner employs a regular and fairly closely phonemic orthography. Jenner's phonology is largely derived from Edward Lhuyd.[17] The shift to Middle Cornish as basis for the revival was instigated by Robert Morton Nance and A.S.D. Smith. Their sources were mainly Robert Williams' *Lexicon Cornu-Britannicum*[18] and Henry Lewis' *Llawlyfr Cernyweg Canol*.[19]

Smith in fact initially learnt his Cornish from Lewis' *Llawlyfr*. This would explain why Smith favoured Middle Cornish. Smith did not understand that Late Cornish has its own grammar and orthography and saw any deviation from Middle Cornish as evidence of corruption and decay. Morton Nance[20] explains that he standardized the spelling to make it more consistent, 'with occasionally a re-spelling to show the derivation of the word, and a desirable distinction between the sounds of *dh* and *th*, *g* and *j*, which it did not make'. George's dictionary perpetuates and adds to the errors of Williams, Lewis, Smith and Nance.

Late Cornish vs. Middle Cornish
There has been some contention over whether Middle or Late Cornish provides the better basis for Revived Cornish. George[21] cites examples of Late Cornish syntax as evidence of the influence of English. However, it is virtually impossible to ascertain what is normal, unmarked syntax in Middle Cornish because the corpus of Middle Cornish is virtually entirely in verse. Consider this line from the English poem, 'The Charge of the Light Brigade':[22]

(a) All in the valley of Death
     Rode the six hundred.

In normal unmarked English we would say,

(b) The six hundred rode all in the valley of death.

In verse, sentence constituents are moved around in order to make the verse scan and rhyme. Now sentence (a) is not ungrammatical in English; however, it is stylistically marked. Contrary to George's[23] assertion, one cannot ascertain the most normal structures by looking at their frequency of occurrence in a corpus of verse. The structures which most frequently occur in verse are not the same as those which most frequently occur in prose or in conversation. The inadequacies of the Middle Cornish texts as a basis for Revived Cornish are evident. The Middle Cornish texts are full of Latin, French and English loanwords. They are not grammatically accurate: Smith,[24] for example, notes that one mutation is missed every nine or ten lines in *Beunans Meriasek*. The Middle Cornish texts are of a highly marked stylistic nature. Since they are entirely in verse it is not possible to determine from them which syntactic structures are the normal unmarked structures. We do not know who the writers of the Middle Cornish texts were and, consequently, cannot even be sure that they were mother-tongue speakers of Cornish. Late Cornish, on the other hand, provides us with the only detailed description of Cornish pronunciation,[25] a description of Cornish grammar,[26] and a wide variety of genres. We know something about the writers of Late Cornish and we are, therefore, better able to distinguish between those who were mother-tongue speakers of Cornish and those who learned Cornish as a second language.

THE PHONOLOGICAL BASIS OF KERNEWEK KEMMYN

George[27] writes, 'a proper examination of Cornish phonology was required, indeed overdue. After an appropriate period of background study in linguistics, I executed this task.' When considering George's reconstruction of Cornish phonology, it is vital to understand the distinction between phonetics and phonology and between the notions of phone and phoneme. A 'phone' is the smallest unit in phonetics and refers to the smallest perceptible discrete segment of sound in a stream of speech. This contrasts with the term 'phoneme' which refers to the minimal unit in phonology, the sound system of a language. Phones are the physical realizations of phonemes. A phoneme may have several phonic variants; these are known as allophones.

In order to determine the phonological basis for Cornish the phonemes have to be distinguished. The following short extract[28] explains how this is normally accomplished.

In order to ascertain whether sounds belong to the same phoneme, three criteria may be employed; complementary distribution, free variation and phonetic similarity.

Complementary distribution involves the mutual exclusiveness of a pair of sounds in a given phonetic environment. For example the differing articulations of the phoneme /k/ in the English words 'kit' and 'cat' results from the tongue anticipating the posture required for the following vowel (Abercrombie 1967: 87). Where we find one type of /k/ in English, we do not find the other. Since they never occur in the same phonetic environment, they are mutually exclusive.

Free variation involves substitutability of one sound for another in a given phonetic environment. If there is no change of meaning then the sounds belong to the same phoneme. For example whether the final plosive /t/, in the English word 'hat', is released or unreleased, there is no change of meaning.

Phonetic similarity involves adequate physical semblance between sounds if they are to realise the same phoneme. For example the two allophones of /t/ described above are both voiceless alveolar plosives.

Sounds are only given the same phonemic status if there is no change of meaning when they are substituted. A **minimal contrast** set is a group of words in any given language, distinguished by each having only one sound different from the others (Rockey 1973; Hyman 1975: Ch. 3; Bolinger and Sears 1981: Ch. 2; Ladefoged 1982: 24). The exploration of minimal sets provide a discovery procedure to determine the phonemes of a language.

If one wanted, for example, to determine the vowel phonemes of English, a minimal contrast set would have to be constructed. The following set of words contrast by having only one sound different.

beat	b i ː t
bit	b ɪ t
bait	b e ɪ t
bet	b ɛ t
bat	b æ t
bought	b ɔ ː t
boat	b o ʊ t
boot	b u ː t
butt	b ʌ t
bite	b a ɪ t
bout	b a ʊ t

This gives us most but not all of the vowel phonemes of English. Another minimal contrast set will complete the set of English vowel phonemes.

part	p ɑ ː t
pot	p ɒ t
put	p ʊ t
pert	p ɜ ː t

In order to perform this task you have to know how the words are pronounced. It is not enough to know only how they are written. Thus one can perform this task for English vowel phonemes with one's own language intuition if one is a first language speaker of English. For a

language of which one is not a first language speaker it is necessary to
have an informant who is a first language speaker of that language.

George's methodology
George[29] defines a phonemic orthography as 'one in which each
phoneme . . . is represented by a separate grapheme . . . ; and each
grapheme represents a separate phoneme'. George[30] maintains that,
'The orthography of Kernewek Kemmyn is an improvement on that of
Nance, so as to fit the phonological base, at the same epoch'. Kernewek
Kemmyn is an attempt to create a phonemic orthography based on
George's reconstruction of Cornish phonology. A thorough analysis of
Cornish phonology was thus considered by George to be a prerequisite
for the development of Kernewek Kemmyn.

The underlying problem with George's[31] reconstructed Cornish
phonology is his methodology. George began with Jackson's[32] hypothetical reconstruction of Early Breton and Jackson's[33] equally
hypothetical reconstruction of Early British. George then adopts these
as a foundation on which to build a hypothetical reconstruction of
Middle Cornish phonology—hypothetical because his analysis of
the texts was based on Jackson's hypotheses. A further fundamental
difficulty with George's phonology of Cornish is that no demonstrable
connections exist between the phonology in Breton and hypothetical
Early Breton, and between hypothetical Early Breton phonology and
Middle Cornish, and hypothetical Early British and Middle Cornish.
Since no sources exist in the long periods between these hypothetical
postulations, no logical connections can be demonstrated between
them.

George[34] makes much of a supposed 'Great Prosodic Shift' and
cites several instances of change in spelling to support this notion.
However, it does not follow logically that because the orthography
changed, this was necessarily accompanied by a simultaneous change in
pronunciation. The evidence only shows a change in orthographic
practice and there is no associated evidence regarding pronunciation of
Cornish.

George[35] cites one of his sources as Lhuyd but is rather dismissive
of Lhuyd's work, describing it as 'contradictory' and opining that
'There is insufficient evidence to be sure about many of the phonemes'.
It is a shame that George is so dismissive of Lhuyd's work because it is
the only detailed account we have of the pronunciation of Cornish. As
Gendall[36] notes, 'the only indications that we have for the pronunciation of our living language refer to its latest, most modern stage, and
any other system proposed from an earlier period must necessarily be
theoretical and open to doubt'.

Lhuyd was Welsh but spent some months in Cornwall in 1700 collecting Cornish. He devised his own phonetic system of transcription. His *Archaeologia Britannica* is, therefore, of great interest to anyone who is interested in how Cornish was pronounced. It is true that by today's standards his phonetic transcription is rather crude, but in its time it was revolutionary. It is important to distinguish between Lhuyd's system, which is essentially phonetic, and Kernewek Kemmyn, which is phonemic. Lhuyd recorded the sounds he heard in his visit to Cornwall; in other words, Lhuyd's symbols represent phones and should not be confused with the graphemes of other writers. Lhuyd[37] explains the phonetic basis of his system in his *Archaeologia Britannica*. Thus Lhuyd's [y] represents the sound of English <i> 'in the word Hil, &c' (i.e. the English word 'hill'). There remain some problems, however, in the interpretation of Lhuyd. For example, although Lhuyd writes that his symbol 'y' represents the sound of the vowel in English 'Hil', we do not know to which variety of English he is referring. Furthermore, we need to know how that variety of English was pronounced in Lhuyd's time. So we can only speculate on the phonetic values of the phones listed in Lhuyd's phonetic inventory of Cornish. Charles Thomas, former Director of the Institute of Cornish Studies, suggests Cornish dialect as a possible source, 'the true phonetic range is still just recoverable from an area west of an isogloss that cuts off the Land's End and part of the south side of the Lizard'.[38] It might make a very interesting study to see what minimal contrast sets can be obtained from *Archaeologia Britannica*. However, Lhuyd collected his data from several sources and complementary distribution refers to distribution within a single idiolect spoken by a single individual.[39] It is, therefore, impossible to determine whether variation recorded by Lhuyd is the result of free variation, allophonic variation or idiolectal difference between Lhuyd's informants.

As we have seen, the phonology of a language can be investigated by the employment of minimal contrast sets. George does not employ this method; he has not constructed minimal contrast sets from the corpus of traditional Cornish. Indeed, it is not possible to produce any real minimal contrast sets from Middle Cornish texts because one has only the written form of the language. George's study is, therefore, based on conjecture and so, despite his claims, he has not reconstructed the phonology of Cornish. It must be concluded that George's phonology of Cornish is largely invention.

Some people might argue that it is not necessary to adhere to traditional written forms simply because they are traditional and that invention is a valid procedure by which to investigate the phonology of Cornish. They might argue that one has to invent a phonology and then test this invention against the available data. If it does not fit very well, then one modifies the invented phonology or proposes a better one. Although it may be possible to get such a phonology to fit the facts arbitrarily well by making it sufficiently complex, one can never prove such a phonology. This sort of approach will almost certainly permit the generation of several equally plausible phonologies. A disadvantage with a phonemic spelling system is that it has to be changed every time a new phonological theory comes along. Take, for example, the phonemes /s/ and /z/; these were not distinguished in Kernewek Kemmyn. George[40] now recognizes this distinction. If one wanted to introduce this distinction into Kernewek Kemmyn now, it would entail the extremely costly and time-consuming replacement of all dictionaries, grammars and pedagogical materials. Consensus for an orthography for Revived Cornish will only be reached if that orthography can be demonstrated to be academically sound. It is not for an individual to propose an orthography based on his putative reconstruction of Cornish phonology and then shift the burden of proof by requiring that others demonstrate its shortcomings.

Some problems with George's analyses
We have seen how George's methodology does not determine the phonemic inventory of Cornish. However, it might be argued that it is not helpful to reject George's reconstructed Cornish phonology without indicating where George's analyses are wrong. To demonstrate individually that each of George's analyses is wrong would take a very long time, simply because there are a lot of analyses and there is very little that could be said to be right about any of them. So a few examples only will have to serve.

In his discussion of pre-occlusion, George[41] maintains that the items *kana* (to sing) and *kanna* (to bleach) form a minimal pair. However *kanna* is not attested in the corpus of traditional Cornish. *kanna* is first found in Morton Nance and Smith's[42] *An English – Cornish Dictionary* as *canna*, where it is marked with an asterisk to indicate that it is a borrowing from Welsh and Breton. Any phonological distinction between *kana* and *kanna* is, therefore, an invention.

George frequently omits attestations from his analyses. For example, in his[43] orthographic profile of the diphthong /ɛɪ/, he acknowledges no attestations of *keyn* (back) in Jordan's *Gwreans an Bys*. Examination of *Gwreans an Bys*, however, reveals,

*Me a thog ran war ow **hyen***   'I will carry some on my back'
(Jordan 1385).

Similarly George[44] does not acknowledge the <ey> in *seyth* attested in
Gwreans an Bys:

*Eve an gevyth **seyth** kemmys*	'he shall have sevenfold' (Jordan 1178)
*Ef astevyth **seyth** plague moy*	'he shall sevenfold more' (Jordan 1376)
***Seyth** gwythe y wra acquyttya*	'he will requite seven times' (Jordan 1535)
*Ha **seyth** plag te hath flehys a vyth plagys*	'and sevenfold you and your children shall be afflicted' (Jordan 1613)

The grapheme <y> that George[45] ascribes to the attestations of *treys*
(feet) in *Gwreans an Bys* is not attested; instead we find <ye>:

*Pyw a thysqwethas thyso tha vos noth **tryes** corf ha bregh*	'Who has shown you that you were naked, feet, body and arm?' (Jordan 872)
*Ty a weall allow ow **thryes***	'You will see the tracks of my feet' (Jordan 1746)
*Me a weall ooll **tryes** ow thas*	'I see the track of my father's feet' (Jordan 1762)

Such omissions and inaccuracies are typical and not the exception
in George's analyses. Consequently, one can have little confidence in
George's conclusions.

Some people might argue that although it is not possible to ascertain the precise manner in which Cornish was pronounced at any given
point in history, George's work at least gives the broad principles of
Cornish phonology. However, George's proposed phonology does not
restrict itself to broad principles; George claims to perceive some very
fine phonological distinctions such as those between /iw/, /ɛw/, /ɪw/ and
/y/, which are represented in Kernewek Kemmyn as <iw>, <ew>, <yw>
and <u> respectively.

Let us consider the first of these proposed diphthongs. George[46]
maintains that the Kernewek Kemmyn grapheme <iw> represents a
distinct phoneme in Cornish and that this is somehow supported by
evidence from the medieval texts. He shows us an orthographic profile
of his proposed phoneme /iw/ as attested by the lexical items *diw* 'two'
(f); *gwiw* 'fit'; *liw* 'colour'; and *piw* 'who'. This profile, George maintains, shows how the vowel sound in these items is variously attested in
the classical texts as <u,v>, <yv>, <yw> and <ew>.

Let us deal with the first of these lexical items. According to Kernewek Kemmyn, *diw* is the feminine form of *dew*. However, this masculine/feminine distinction is not born out by attestation. In *Pascon agan Arluth* only one form, *dew*, is attested for number 2. In the *Ordinalia* two forms are attested, *dew* and *dyw*. However they are not distinguished by gender. Thus we find the feminine noun *luef*, 'a hand' collocating with both forms, *dyw-luef* (*Origo Mundi* 1346) and *dew luef* (*Origo Mundi* 1534); we find the masculine noun *dorn*, 'a fist', collocating with *dyw* (*Resurrexio Domini* 2178) and the masculine noun *adla*, 'a rogue', collocating with *dew* (*Resurrexio Domini* 1479). In *Gwreans an Bys*, Jordan uses three forms *deaw*, *dew* and *thyw*. All three are used for both masculine and feminine. Thus we find both the feminine noun *gweth* (Jordan 966), 'a garment', and the masculine noun *vabe* (Jordan 1054, 1232), 'a son' collocating with *deaw*; we find both the feminine noun *wreag* (Jordan 1452), 'a wife', and the masculine noun *ran* (Jordan 1707), 'a part', collocating with *dew*; we find the masculine noun *fridg* or *freyge*, 'nostril', collocating both with *thyw* (Jordan 1854) and with *thew* (Jordan 1933).

Let us move on to the second lexeme in George's orthographic profile. *gwiw* has the following attestations:

gyw	(*Pascon agan Arluth* 68, 129, 226)
gwyw	(*Origo Mundi* 2242, 2601; *Passio Domini* 284, 2358)
gweff	(*Pascon agan Arluth* 95)
gwef	(Jordan 1833)
gweve	(Jordan 2138)
gweffe	(Jordan 588)

Now in the medieval texts <u> and <v> are written the same way and are thus indistinguishable. <w> is frequently found to alternate with <f> in the texts. Considering the presence of the <f> (not noted by George) it is remarkable, to say the least, that George considers this item to exemplify his proposed phoneme /iw/.

liw is the third item in George's orthographic profile. *liw* has the following attestations:

lyw	(*Pascon agan Arluth* 68,226; *Passio Domini* 3083, 3123; *Resurrexio Domini* 2101)
lew	(Jordan 1049).

The final item in George's orthographic profile is *piw*. *piw* has the following attestations:

pu	(*Pascon agan Arluth* 69, 81, 160, 253)
pyu	(*Pascon agan Arluth* 190)
pew	(Jordan 549, 1460, 1591, 2347)
pewa	(Jordan 435, 1599)
pyw	(*Origo Mundi* 261,1368, 1874; *Passio Domini* 771, 798, 2853; *Resurrexio Domini* 106, 196, 1640, 2486; Jordan 163, 871).

It can seen that there are more spellings for the vowel in these four lexical items than the four vowel graphemes given by George. His data simply does not fit the facts. There are not four graphemes only that are attested but nine: <u,v>, <yv>, <yw>, <ew>. <eaw>. <ef>, <eff>, <eve>, <effe>. Not all four lexical items can be found with all nine of these graphemes. Nor is it true that these four lexical items share the same vowel graphemes within a single text. In *Pascon agan Arluth*, for example, we find *dew*; *gyw, gweff*; *lyw*; *pv, pyv*. It must be concluded, therefore, that there is no evidence to suppose that *diw, gwiw, liw* and *piw* share the same vowel phoneme.

George[47] writes that 'One of the useful features of Lhuyd's orthography was the consistent distinction between /δ/ [sic, presumably George means /ð/] and /θ/ whereas the Newlyn School tended to use the English grapheme <th> for both phonemes'. However there are several examples where Lhuyd's <dh> and <th> are in variation:

Kernewek Kemmyn	Lhuyd (1707)	
dydh	*deyth, dedh*	(Lhuyd 1707: 227b)
	Dêdh	(Lhuyd 1707: 229b, 230c)
	Deth	(Lhuyd 1707: 229b)
fordh	*Fordh*	(Lhuyd 1707: 230c, 241c)
	Forth, Fordh	(Lhuyd 1707: 229b)
	Fordh	(Lhuyd 1707: 173b)
fydh	*Fyth, Fydh*	(Lhuyd 1707: 229b)
kynyav	*Kidniadh*	(Lhuyd 1707: 44b)
	Kidniath	(Lhuyd 1707: 90a)

On the basis of Lhuyd's (1707) evidence, it would appear that the phones [ð] and [θ] are in free variation in Cornish and, therefore, share a single phoneme. This might explain why, in the Middle Cornish texts, the graphemes, long-tailed-<z>, <dh> and <th> are found in free variation. A good example of this are the attestations of *dhodho* and *dhedha* to be found in *Pascon agan Arluth*: 'dhodho', 'doʒo', 'thoʒo', 'ʒoʒo', 'thethe', 'theʒe', 'ʒethe', 'ʒeʒa', 'ʒeʒe'. The assumption made by George that [ð] and [θ] are discrete phonemes in Cornish cannot, therefore, be confirmed by the evidence.

In Kernewek Kemmyn <i> and <y> represent separate phonemes, so that *gwynn* (meaning white) rhymes with standard English 'bin' and *gwin* (meaning wine) rhymes with standard English 'been'. KK<i> thus has the value [i:] and KK<y> has the value [ɪ].[48] Speakers of Kernewek Kemmyn often distinguish between these phonemes when pronouncing words like *gwynn* and *gwin*. However, the distinction between the vowel sound in *ty* and *hwi* is not so marked in the pronunciation of today's Kernewek Kemmyn speakers. It is not clear whether the vowels in *ty* and *hwi* ought really to be considered different phonemes on the basis of the historical corpus of Cornish since they are not distinguished in any minimal sets. Furthermore *ty*, if pronounced with short [ɪ], as in English 'bin', feels somewhat unnatural especially if followed by a vowel, as in the following phrase:

Ty a lever gwir.

In the traditional texts we find *ty* spelled,

ty	(*Charter Endorsement*)
te, se, ty	(*Pascon agan Arluth*)
ty, sy	(*Ordinalia*)
che	(James Jenkins)
te, tee, ty	(William Jordan)
che, chee, chy	(Wella Kerew)
ti	(Nicholas Boson)
ti, tî	(Lhuyd 1707)
chee	(Borlase 1769)

The vowel in Lhuyd's phonetic transcriptions of *ty* is noted variously as Lh[i] and [î]. Lhuyd[49] describes the phonetic value of Lh[i] as '*Ee*', and writes[50] that the circumflex, <^>, indicates a long vowel. This together with the <ee> found in Jordan, Kerew and Borlase[51] suggests that the phonetic value of the vowel in *ty* might be [i:] rather than [ɪ].

In the traditional texts we find *hwi* spelled

why, wy	(*Pascon agan Arluth*)
why	(*Ordinalia*)
why	(Andrew Boorde)
why	(William Jordan)

why	(Wella Kerew)
why, whi, whey	(Nicholas Boson)
wei, whei	(John Boson)
huei	(Lhuyd 1707)
whye, why	(James Jenkins)
why	(Borlase 1769)

The [ei] in Lhuyd's transcription of *hwi* suggests that the phonetic value of the vowel in *hwi* might be a diphthong.

The *Gerlyver Kernewek Kemmyn* gives three homonyms:

bys MN: *finger, digit*;
bys PP: *until*;
bys MN: *world*.

They are homonyms because they are at the same time homographs (i.e. they share the same spelling) and homophones (i.e. they share the same pronunciation). Lhuyd[52] gives

bêz, bez, beaz: *finger*
byz: *until*
bêz, vez: *world*

From this it would seem reasonable to conclude that Lhuyd's *bêz* is a homophone that shares the English equivalents 'finger' and 'world'. Lhuyd's *byz*, however, does not share the same vowel phone. Thus *bêz* and *byz* form a minimal set as recorded by Lhuyd. From this it can be seen that the phonology represented by Kernewek Kemmyn does not concur with the sounds of Cornish as recorded by Lhuyd.

How is Kernewek Kemmyn actually pronounced by its users?
Some people might argue that it is not necessary that the pedagogical basis on which Cornish is revived be true to traditional forms found in the historical corpus. They might argue that when a relatively stable pool of native speakers with a relatively stable spoken norm is established, with a literature of its own, then 'Cornish' will mean the sort of Cornish spoken and written by these speakers. If the protoform of Revived Cornish as spoken by them was based upon an imperfect reconstruction, it will be of little importance, provided that their Cornish is similar enough to classical Cornish to enable them to read classical texts and sense a linguistic continuity there. If, however, it is true that it is of little importance that the protoform for Revived Cornish may be based upon an imperfect reconstruction, then it

logically follows that the switch from Unified Cornish to Kernewek Kemmyn was a complete waste of time and energy. If at some point in the future there does exist such a relatively stable pool of native speakers with a relatively stable spoken norm, then it would be possible to study and record the phonology of the variety of Cornish spoken by this pool of native speakers. And from that phonological study it would be possible to construct a phonemic orthography.

In the meantime, however, one thing that I notice when I listen to people who have adopted Kernewek Kemmyn is just how far their pronunciation is from George's recommended pronunciation. There are tendencies amongst users of Kernewek Kemmyn

- to pronounce <u> as /u/,
- to pronounce <r> as rhotic rather than trilled,
- to omit post vocalic <r>,
- not to distinguish between <iw>, <u>, <ew>, <iw>, <yw> and <yu>.
- to pronounce all unstressed vowels as schwa,
- to pronounce <ll> as <l> (i.e. as a short consonant rather than a geminate).

In fact Kernewek Kemmyn speakers tend not to pronounce any double consonant graphemes as geminates. If they make a distinction at all between the single and double consonants, it is usually marked by the realization of <mm> and <nn> as pre-occlusions. Gemination is the term usually used for syllable timed languages in which a geminate consonant is normally accompanied by an adjacent short vowel and a short con- sonant by an adjacent long vowel. Gemination of Kernewek Kemmyn <mm> is realized as [mm]. A geminate consonant is not quite the same as a long consonant which phoneticians usually write as [m:]. Pre-occlusion is slightly different from gemination. In pre-occlusion of nasal consonants, the stop is formed before the velum is lowered to allow egression through the nasal passage. Thus pre-occlusion of Kernewek Kemmyn <mm> is realized as [bm] and pre-occlusion of <nn> is realized as [dn]. George usually uses the term pre-occlusion where Nicholas Williams uses the term gemination, though it should be noted that use of the term pre-occlusion is usually restricted to nasal consonants. So one cannot have pre-occlusion of, for example, <tt> or <pp>.

CONTRASTIVE LEXICOLOGY

The provision of English translation equivalents in *Gerlyver Kernewek Kemmyn* falls within the domain of contrastive lexicology, which is concerned with similarities and divergences between the lexical systems of Cornish and English. Languages structure their vocabulary differently. An individual language, such as Cornish, thus embodies a pattern of thought, an entire world-view, which is at times very different from that which English carries. This is sometimes referred to as 'linguistic determinism' or the 'Sapir-Whorf hypothesis'.[53] Cornish and English provide many examples of the way that languages structure their respective vocabularies differently. A comparison of colour terms in Cornish and English serves as a good example. Cornish has one lexeme, *glas* where English has three, *blue, green* and *grey*. Another example are the words *dorn* and *leuv*: Cornish has two words where English has only one word *hand*. *dorn* does not have an English equivalent that expresses all that is entailed by *dorn*, though the English *fist* might serve in some (but not all) contexts.[54] Those who maintain that Late Cornish is an Anglicized form of Cornish or that it is some way more Anglicized than Middle Cornish should take note that Late Cornish clearly distinguishes between *dorn* and *leuv*.

George[55] writes, 'Nance tended to give a large number of meanings, even to words which appear only once in the texts. In *Gerlyver Kernewek Kemmyn*, the number of meanings has in general been limited to three or less.' Now a 'meaning' is not the same thing as a 'translation equivalent', a vital distinction that George clearly does not understand. Furthermore, there is no good reason why the number of English equivalents should be limited to three. The *Collins Spanish Dictionary*,[56] for example, includes the following Spanish translation equivalents of the English word *run* as a noun:

> *acarraladura, asedio, carrera, carrerilla, corral, corrida, corriendo, excursión, fermata, gallinero, migración, paseo, pista, recorrido, serie, singladura, tendencia, terreno, tirada, trayecto,*

and as a verb:

> *administrar, andar, apresurarse, cazar, circular, competir, controlar, correr, correrse, dar caza, darse prisa, derretirse, desteñirse, dirigir, ejecutar, estar en marcha, fluir, gobernar, gotear, hacer, hacer funcionar, huir, introducir, ir, llevar, manejar, marchar, ofrecer, organizar, pasar, poseer, regir, seguir, supurar, tener, tomar parte, transportar, traspasar.*

As can be seen, a lexeme can have many more translation equivalents than three. Morton Nance[57] gives the following equivalents for *denythy*: *to give birth to*, *beget*, *bring forth*, and *generate*. George[58] gives only *give birth*. George has decided to drop *beget*, *bring forth* and *generate*. Now, if we examine the medieval texts we find,

hag ef a wra **dynythy** vn   'and he shall *beget* a goodly son
map de hep falladow   undoubtedly' (*Origo Mundi* 638),

and,

ny a **thynyth** vn flogh da   'we will **beget** a goodly child'
                                      (*Origo Mundi* 664).

The one equivalent given by George is clearly not satisfactory for these examples. What George appears to have done is take the translation equivalents given by Nance and reduce the number without any recourse to historical usage.

Cornish has one word, *nija*, where English has two words, *swim* and *fly*. This might appear rather poetic, viewing 'swimming' as 'flying in the water' or seeing 'flying' as 'swimming in air'. However I suspect this appears poetic only if you speak a first language that structures its vocabulary in the way that English does. To a first-language speaker of Cornish in the middle ages, *nija* possibly meant something like 'move the body through a medium or substance such as air or water'. Morton Nance[59] gives, **swim** v. *nyja y'n dowr*. The earlier 1934[60] dictionary brackets 'y'n dowr' thus: **swim** v. *nyja (yn dour)*. However, the 1934 dictionary also recommends *nüfya* which it marks with an asterisk to show that it is a neologism borrowed from English, Welsh or Breton (*nüfya* is adapted from Breton *neuñviñ and* Welsh *nofio*). In fact it is in this 1934 dictionary that *nüfya* seems to be first attested in Cornish. Nance and Smith appear to be influenced by the lexical structure of English, Welsh and Breton. In other words, they felt uncomfortable that *nija* could translate both *fly* and *swim*. Hence their perceived need to append *yn dour* to *nija* or use the neologism *nüfya*. Earlier lexicographic tradition gives *nija* without *yn dour*:

Lhuyd gives[61] *nyidzha* for *to swim*.
Borlase[62] gives 'Niedga (ga pron. as, ja) *to fly*; *swim*.'
Pryce[63] gives '*NYIDZHA*, dho nyidzha, *to swim*; also, *to fly*.'
    (Note that Pryce gives *swim* before *fly*.)
Jago[64] gives 'SWIM, *v*. Nyge/, nija, W.; nijay, nizhea, P.;
    niedza, B.; nyidzha, nyse/, W.; nys, renygia, P'swim, v nyja'
    (Allin-Collins 1927:62)
Lhuyd[65] and Pryce[66] also give *tarneidzha* for *swim over*.

Another example of an unnecessary neologism has to do with language attitude. Revivalists have adopted the neologism *pennskol* as equivalent for the English *university*. Cornish already has the word *universite* which is attested in *Beunans Meriasek* (line 78).

MAGISTER	'*MASTER*
My yu mayster a gramer	*I am a grammar-master*
gurys yn bonilapper	*made at Bonilapper,*
universite vyen	*a small university.*

The problem for the revivalists is that *universite* looks too much like its English equivalent. As George writes in his *Gerlyver Kernewek Kemmyn* '**pennskol** is more Celtic'. The term used for *university* in Breton is *skol-veur*[67] and in Welsh is *pryfysgol*.[68] George[69] maintains that the etymology of Cornish *universite* is from Middle English which in turn comes from Old French. In fact Cornish, French and English all share the Latin etymon *universitas* and, though cognate with English *university*, the Cornish *universite* need not, therefore, have been necessarily borrowed from English at all. The adoption by George of a neologism in favour of an attested lexeme, is another example of Revived Cornish being influenced by English; the rule being, if a word closely resembles its English equivalent, replace it with neologism that appears more Celtic. The creation of unnecessary neologisms such as *neuvya* and *pennskol* supports the arguments of those who view Revived Cornish as being a semi-artificial language.

It might be argued that the Cornish language should retain the original Cornish elements that make it Celtic and/or unique since, if revivalists do not 'reincarnate' the Celtic 'soul' of Cornish, the language will lose its 'raison d'être'. Only the Cornish language, the Celtic language of Cornwall, embodies the fullness of the Cornish world-view, and one would hope, capture the essence which was lost when the language disappeared from general use as an everyday language. This, of course, is one important reason for Cornish people to learn Cornish. This is certainly a reason for studying the medieval Cornish texts. However, the case for Kernewek Kemmyn is less certain, since, sadly, the way that Kernewek Kemmyn structures its vocabulary is largely influenced by English. In order for the 'Celtic Cornish world-view' to be carried over into the speaker of Revived Cornish, pedagogic materials need to be more closely based on the historical texts than they appear to be at present.

RESPELLING OF PLACE-NAMES

It is common practice amongst writers of the various forms of Revived Cornish to respell Cornish place-names. Thus in *Gerlyver Kernewek Kemmyn*[70] we find

Bosveneghi {1:P:0} *NP* Bodmin
[C: BOS<abode>2MENEGHI]

For me, there are a number of problems with this convention. First of all, it assumes that the etymology given *must* be correct. However, as with most attempts at place-name etymology, there exists a large measure of conjecture. Attested etyma for *Bodmin include,*

Bodmine *c.*975, 1086[71]
Botmenei *c.*1200[72]
Bodmen 1253
Bodminie 1260
Bodman 1337
Bodmyn 1522

I know of no etyma of *Bodmin* that begin 'Bos'. The respelling of 'Bod-' as 'Bos-' takes for granted that it does indeed derive from the Cornish word for 'abode'. That the second element '-min' derives from *meneghi*, the Cornish word for 'monks', is even more conjectural. It is not that I wish to contest this putative though widely accepted etymology of *Bodmin*. I do, however, wish to emphasize that place-name etymology is not an exact science.

A second worry that I have with this practice concerns the semantics involved. The expression *Bodmin* does not mean 'monk's abode'. That might possibly be its etymology, but it is not its meaning. Consider these two sentences:

This morning I went to Bodmin.
This morning I went to a monk's abode.

They clearly have quite different meanings. *Bodmin* is a referring expression. It refers to a particular locality, a particular town. Similarly,

I went to Camborne yesterday

does not mean the same as

I went to a crooked hill yesterday.

Camborne has deixis to a particular town, a particular geographical location. 'A crooked hill' means something quite different.

The Kernewek Kemmyn respelling 'Kammbronn' is based on the assumption that *Camborne* somehow derives from *kamm + bronn*. Whilst this is one plausible etymology of *Camborne*, it is not the only one. The earliest known form, *Camberon* (1182), suggests Late Cornish *cambern* 'a dog-leg'. This could refer to the course of a road or stream. In 1700, a stone called 'The Camburn' stood in the churchtown. So *kamm + bronn* is not an undisputed etymology for this place name. Camborne people still make reference to the town sign, and it is one of the things that they mention if you talk to people about the language. They remember two things, the controversy that raged about erection of the sign, and the fact that it looks nothing like 'Camborne'.

Etymology is not an exact science and for many, if not most, Cornish place-names, conflicting etymologies exist. This, of course, leads to considerable problems if one wishes to respell place-names to conform with Kernewek Kemmyn. It is quite unnecessary to respell a place-name in order that some putative etymology is transparent. It is unreasonable for one group of Cornish speakers to insist that Cornish place-names are respelled according to their spelling system and their putative etymologies, and that these respellings must be accepted by the rest of the Cornish-speaking community. Respelling is not even necessary: English speakers do not feel that it is necessary to respell English place-names. My own view then is that it neither necessary nor wise to go about respelling place-names in Revived Cornish.

IS A PHONEMIC ORTHOGRAPHY REALLY NECESSARY?

Whilst it is recognized that a need exists to standardize the spellings of Cornish words, a phonological approach is not necessarily the best way to go about this. Some languages, such as Irish, Welsh, Breton and Dutch, have undergone spelling reform. However, the change has not always been to make them more phonemic. Hebrew is an example of a language which has been successfully revived in this century. However, Hebrew was not revived by first constructing a conjectural phonology and then deciding how that phonology should be represented orthographically. Consider the case of the English language. Spelling reform for English has been frequently recommended. But it is not only cost that obstructs English spelling reform. Not everybody pronounces English in the same way. A decision would have to be made concerning which of many varieties of spoken English would be chosen as a basis for a phonemic English orthography. If a single state, such as the United Kingdom, were to respell English, this could have disastrous consequences. Written British English might then be no longer mutually intelligible with other world varieties of English. English orthography is only very loosely phonemic. However, English is the most widely spoken language in the world. Furthermore, most of the English speakers in the world have learned English as a second language. There are in fact more people learning English in China than there are native speakers of English in the USA! So a closely phonemic orthography is not a prerequisite for language learning. If it were, German and Spanish would be more widely spoken than English as a second language. People will learn Cornish because they want to and not because a phonemic orthography exists for it.

Central Ladin is a minority Romance language spoken in the Dolomites. There has recently been an attempt to create a standardized Central Ladin to serve as a basis for the creation of linguistic resources for local communities and institutions. This attempt adopts the strategy of building a new communicative code from the various existing local varieties. Four criteria are used to select forms for use in the standardized variety:[73]

(a) *frequency* preference is to be given to the most frequent
    forms among the varieties;
(b) *systematicity* forms are given preference which enhance
    the regularity and coherence of the whole system;
(c) *transparency*: preference is given to 'full' forms, more
    readily comprehensible than shortened ones;
(d) *typicality*: forms are chosen which distinguish Ladin from
    competing languages.

Some people might argue that, since the spelling of Kernewek Kemmyn denotes the pronunciation of Cornish, it is easier to learn. A fairly closely phonemic spelling system might help the learner who knows both the meaning of a word and how it is spelt but has not heard it pronounced. However, this is not a very usual path of lexical acquisition. If a learner encounters a new word in a written text, they will need to look it up in the dictionary anyway and, therefore, have access to the pronunciation. Language-teaching methodology and materials possibly have a far greater impact on second language acquisition than does a phonemic orthography.

One of the problems that is associated with Kernewek Kemmyn is that it is phonemic only for those who pronounce Cornish as prescribed by George's putative phonology. There are many speakers of Cornish who prefer some other theory of Cornish phonology. Even those who have learned Kernewek Kemmyn do not usually pronounce Cornish as prescribed in George's phonology.

With regard to making reading easier, it is possible that phonemic spelling has no appreciable effect. If a learner is proficient enough to read the Middle Cornish texts in a standardized spelling system such as Unified or Kemmyn, they are unlikely to have very much difficulty in reading them in their original spelling. By way of illustration, here are the opening lines of *Origo Mundi* in their original spelling in Unified[74] and in Kernewek Kemmyn.[75]

Original	Unified	Kernewek Kemmyn
DEUS PATER	DEUS PATER	DEUS PATER
En tas a nef y'm gylwyr	An Tas a Nef y'm gylwyr,	An Tas a nev y'm gelwir,
formyer pup tra a vyt gurys	Formyer pup tra a vyth gwrys.	formyer puptra a vydh gwrys.
Onan ha try on yn guyr	Onen ha Try on yn gwyr—	Onan ha tri on yn hwir,
en tas ha'n map ha'n spyrys	an Tas ha'n Map ha'n Spyrys;	an Tas ha'n Mab ha'n Spyrys;
ha hethyu me a thesyr	ha hedhyu my a dhesyr	ha hedhyw my a dhesir
dre ou grath dalleth an beys	dre ow gras dalleth an bys.	dre ow gras dalleth an bys.
y lavaraf nef ha tyr	Y lavaraf—nef ha tyr	Y lavarav, nev ha tir
bethens formyys orth ou brys	bedhens formyes orth ow brys.	Bedhens formyes orth ow brys.
lemmen pan yu nef thyn gwrys	Lemmyn yu nef dhym gwrys	Lemmyn pan yw nev dhyn gwrys
ha lenwys a eleth splan	ha lenwys a eleth splan,	ha lenwys a eledh splann,
ny a vyn formye an bys	ny a vyn formya an bys.	ny a vynn formya an bys.
par del on try hag onan	Par del on Try hag Onen—	Par dell on Tri hag Onan,

It can be seen that if a student of Cornish can read either the Unified or the Kernewek Kemmyn transcriptions, they should be able to read the original orthography without too much difficulty. It can also be seen that the Unified transcription is a little closer to the original than the Kernewek Kemmyn transcription.

CONCLUSION

Whilst a standardized spelling system may be beneficial for the pedagogical basis of Revived Cornish, it is vital that this is based on the scholarly study of the historic Cornish texts. George's methods cannot determine the phonology of historical Cornish; they only provide a basis for speculation. Furthermore, when one compares the data reported by George with the primary sources, they do not match. His results and conclusions are, therefore, spurious. George's work thus makes claims about Cornish phonology which are not really justified. Since George's investigation of Cornish phonology is badly flawed, the switch to Kernewek Kemmyn seems to have been an expensive waste of time and energy. If one is content with an orthography which is based on a broad approximation of Cornish phonology, then Unified Cornish provides this; and if one goes along with that viewpoint, then there was never any need to replace Unified with Kemmyn. People who start to learn Cornish need the assurance that the form that they are being taught is indeed Cornish and not the product of some individual's fertile imagination. Systems which respell Cornish words, such as Kernewek Kemmyn and Unified Cornish, are liable to be criticized by some people as being artificial and not Cornish. In fact, some people might go as far as to argue that Kernewek Kemmyn has more in common with fictional artificial languages like Quenya[76] and Brithenig[77] than with traditional Cornish.

We do not have an agreed phonology of Cornish; reconstructions of Cornish phonology are at best conjectural. Consequently it would seem likely that theories concerning Cornish phonology will be in a state of flux for the foreseeable future. If one wants to revive a language like Cornish, it is necessary that there is consensus for a standardized form, even if there are uncertainties about the phonology. The introduction of Kernewek Kemmyn caused a split in the Revival movement that has resulted in three spelling systems in current use. Unified Cornish may have had shortcomings but at least everyone was using it. It is recommended that the standardization of Cornish orthography be based on that which is verifiable rather than on some speculative phonology or putative etymology.

There are alternatives to using an invented phonemic orthography to serve the Cornish language revival. One need not presuppose that there must be a direct correlation between phonemes and graphemes. There are other issues apart from phonology to be taken in account when standardizing the orthography of Cornish. Variations in spelling may contain useful clues to a word's etymology. If one wishes actually to be literate in a language, instead of merely conversational, it is not unreasonable that one understand more of words than simply their most common meaning and sound. Putative etymologies, however, should not be used as a basis for the respelling of place-names. One can standardize the spelling of Cornish by choosing one form for each lexeme from the forms attested in the texts using criteria similar to those being used for Central Ladin.[78] One then recommends a pronunciation for each word based on the best understanding that we have of Cornish phonology. Whilst it is not possible to recover the actual sounds of medieval Cornish, there are no significant grounds for rejecting Late Cornish as being corrupted by English, and Lhuyd[79] provides us with the clearest record of how Cornish was pronounced. Lhuyd[80] should, with some caution, provide the basis for recommendations on pronunciation.

NOTES AND REFERENCES

1. Ken George, *Gerlyver Kernewek Kemmyn*, Saltash, 1993.
2. Charles Penglaze, 'Authenticity in the Revival of Cornish', in Philip Payton (ed.), *Cornish Studies: Two*, Exeter, 1994; Ken George, 'Which Base for Revived Cornish', in Philip Payton (ed.), *Cornish Studies: Three*, Exeter, 1995. N.J.A. Williams, *Cornish Today: An Examination of the Revived Language*, Sutton Coldfield, 1995; N.J.A. Williams, ' "Linguistically Sound Principles": The Case against Kernewek Kemmyn' in Philip Payton (ed.), *Cornish Studies: Four*, Exeter, 1996; Bernard Deacon, 'Language Revival and Language Debate', in Philip Payton (ed.), *Cornish Studies: Four*, Exeter, 1996. Paul Dunbar and Ken George, *Kernewek Kemmyn: Cornish for the Twenty-First Century*, Saltash, 1997.
3. Paul Dunbar and Ken George, 1997, p. 40.
4. Ken George, *The Pronunciation and Spelling of Revived Cornish*, Torpoint?, 1986, p. 32.
5. George, 1986, p. 160.
6. Dunbar and George, 1997, p. 141.
7. George, 1986, p. 42ff. See also Douglas Bartlett Gregor, *Celtic: A Comparative Study of the Six Celtic Languages, Irish, Gaelic, Manx, Welsh, Cornish, Breton Seen against the Background of their History, Literature and Destiny*, Cambridge, 1980, Ch. 6, Cornwall, p. 73.
8. E. Lhuyd, *Archaeologia Britannica: Vol. I Glossography*, Oxford, 1707.
9. See also R.R.M. Gendall, *The Pronunciation of Cornish*, 2nd ed., Menheniot, Liskeard, 1991.
10. R. Williams, *Lexicon Cornu-Britannicum—Gerlyvr Cernewec*, London, 1865.
11. Whitley Stokes, 'Cornish Glossary', *Transactions of the Philological Society*, Oxford, 1869, pp. 137–250.
12. Whitley Stokes, 1869, p. 138.
13. L. Bonaparte, *Some Observations on the Rev. R. Williams' Preface to his Lexicon Cornu-Britannicum*, 1866.
14. J. Loth, 'Remarques et corrections au Lexicon Cornu Britannicum de Williams', *Revue Celtique: XXIII*, 1902.
15. R.R.M. Gendall, *A Students' Dictionary of Modern Cornish—Part 1, English–Cornish*, Menheniot, 1991, p. iii.
16. Henry Jenner, *A Handbook of the Cornish Language*, London, 1904.
17. Lhuyd, 1707.
18. Williams, 1865.
19. Henry Lewis, *Llawlyfr Cernyweg Canol: Handbook of Middle Cornish*, Wrecsam, 1923.
20. Robert Morton Nance, *Cornish for All*, St Ives, 3rd ed., 1958, p. v.
21. George, 1995, pp. 107–8.
22. Alfred Lord Tennyson (1991), 'The Charge of the Light Brigade', in Aidan Day (ed.), *Alfred Lord Tennyson: Selected Poems*, London, p. 289.
23. George, 1995, pp. 108, 121.
24. A.S.D. Smith (Caradar), *Cornish Simplified: Part Two*, ed. E.G.R. Hooper (Talek), Redruth, 1984, p. 38.

25. Lhuyd, 1707.
26. Lhuyd, 1707.
27. George, 1986, p. 6.
28. Steven Dodd and Jon Mills, 'Phonetics and Phenology', in R.R.K. Hartmann *Solving Language Problems: From General to Applied Linguistics*, Exeter, 1996, pp. 22–3.
29. George, 1995, p. 119.
30. George, 1995, p. 113.
31. Ken George, 'A Phenological History of Cornish', unpub. thesis, University of Western Brittany, 1984.
32. Kenneth Hurlstone Jackson, *A Historical Phonology of Breton*, Dublin, 1967.
33. Kenneth Hurlstone Jackson, *Language and History in Early Britain*, Edinburgh, 1953.
34. Dunbar and George, 1997, pp. 20ff.
35. George, 1995, pp. 109–10.
36. R.R.M. Gendall, 1991.
37. Lhuyd, 1707, p. 225.
38. Quoted in P. Berresford Ellis, *The Cornish Language and its Literature*, London, 1974, p. 194.
39. Abercrombie, *Elements of General Phonetics*, Edinburgh, 1967, p. 88.
40. Dunbar and George, 1997, pp. 74–5.
41. Dunbar and George, 1997, pp. 55–6.
42. R. Morton Nance and A.S.D. Smith, *An English–Cornish Dictionary*, 1934.
43. Dunbar and George, 1997, p. 134.
44. Dunbar and George, 1997, p. 134.
45. Dunbar and George, 1997, p. 134.
46. Dunbar and George, 1997, pp. 110ff.
47. George, 1995, p. 111.
48. George, 1986, pp. 110–13.
49. Lhuyd, 1707, p. 225.
50. Lhuyd, 1707, p. 2.
51. W. Borlase, *Antiquities Historical and Monumental of the County of Cornwall*, 2nd ed., London, 1769.
52. Lhuyd, 1707.
53. R. Brown, *Words and Things*, Glencoe, Ill., 1958; J.B. Carroll, *Language, Thought and Reality: Selected Writings of Benjamin Lee Whorf*, Cambridge, Mass., 1956; J.B. Carroll, *Language and Thought*, Englewood Cliffs, 1964, Ch. 7; D.I. Slobin, *Psycholinguistics*, London, 1971.
54. For a full discussion see Jon Mills, 'A Comparison of the Semantic Values of Middle Cornish *Luf* and *Dorn* with Modern English *Hand* and *Fist*', *Language Sciences: XVIII*, 1–2, 1996, pp. 71–86.
55. Ken George, 1993, p. 17.
56. Colin Smith, *The Collins Spanish Dictionary*, London, 1988.
57. Morton Nance, 1938.
58. George, 1993.
59. Morton Nance, 1952.

60. Morton Nance and Smith, 1934.
61. Lhuyd, 1707.
62. Borlase, 1769.
63. W. Pryce, *Archaeologia Cornu-Britannica; or An Essay to Preserve the Ancient Cornish Language; Containing the Rudiments of that Dialect, in a Cornish Grammar and Cornish-English Vocabulary, Compiled from a Variety of Materials Which Have Been Inaccesible to all other Authors Wherein the British Original of some Thousand English Words in Common Use is Demonstrated; Together with that of the Proper Names of most Towns, Parishes, Villages, Mines and Gentlemen's Seats and Families, in Wales, Cornwall, Devonshire, and other Parts of England*, Sherborne, 1790.
64. F. Jago, *English Cornish Dictionary*, London, 1887.
65. Lhuyd, 1707.
66. Pryce, 1790.
67. R. Delaporte, *Elementary Breton–English Dictionary: Geriadurig Brezhoneg–Saozneg*, Cork, 1979.
68. H. Meurig Evans and W.O. Thomas, *Y. Geiriadur Newydd: The New Welsh Dictionary*, Llandybïe, 1953.
69. George, 1993.
70. George, 1993.
71. *Domesday Book*.
72. In life of St Cadoc.
73. Fabio Ciocchetti and Fabio Pianesi, 'Language Standardisation and Linguistic resources: the Case of central Ladin (Dolomites)', *Proceedings of Workshop on Language Resources for European Minority Languages*, LREC First International Conference on Language Resources and Evaluation, Granada, Spain, May 27, 1998.
74. Robert Morton Nance, '*Origo Mundi*, unified transcription and English translation' unpublished ms. in the Royal Institution of Cornwall.
75. Keith Syed, *The Cornish Texts*, converted to Kernewek Kemmyn by Keith Syed, in Word for Windows vs. 6 format on 5¼" computer diskette, available from Kernewek dre Lyther, Sutton Coldfield.
76. J.R.R. Tolkien, *The Silmarillion*, London, 1977.
77. Andrew Smith, *The Page of Brithenig*, available http://www.earthlight. co.nz/users/andrew/brithenig/brithenig.html.
78. Ciocchetti and Pianesi, 1998.
79. Lhuyd, 1707.
80. Lhuyd, 1707.

'SAINT' IN CORNISH

N.J.A. Williams

TITLES WITH TERRITORIES AND TITLES IN APPOSITION
In traditional Cornish, terms like *myghtern* 'king', *myghternes* 'queen', *duk* 'duke' and *epscop* 'bishop' are frequently followed by a territorial or population name in genitival relation with them. As examples one might cite the following:

> *mygtern ethewon, myghtern yuthewon, myghtern yethewon,*
>   *myghtern yethewen* 'king of the Jews' PA 187d; PC 982,
>   1583, 2039, 2066, 2117, 2125, 2797, 2800, 2835
> *myghtern israel, myghtern ysrael* 'king of Israel' PC 276, 427,
>   2879
> *myghtern nef* 'king of heaven' RD 926, 1754, 2421, 2523
> *myghternes nef, myternes neff* 'queen of heaven' BM 154, 3134
> *duk bryten* 'duke of Brittany' BM 1
> *war thuk kernow* 'upon the duke of Cornouaille' BM 2396;
>   *Duk kernov* 'the duke of Cornouaille' BM 2397
> *epscop kernov, epscop kernow* 'bishop of Cornouaille' BM
>   2860, 2884, 2890
> *Ispak Kar-êsk* 'bishop of Exeter' AB: 222.

Compare also *chyff arluth rohan* 'chief lord of Rohan' BM 1936 and *Arlothas Kernow* 'the Duchess of Cornwall' BF: 31.

The same terms *myghtern, myghternes, duk* and *epscop* are also frequently used with a following personal name in apposition, e.g.:

> *mytern alwar* 'king Alwar' BM 2463
> *mytern casvelyn* 'king Casivellaunus' BM 2465

mytern connan 'king Conan' BM 223
the vyghtern dauid 'to king David' OM 1929; *Myterne Davith*
   'king David' TH 8a
myghtern erod 'king Herod' PC 1842
myghtern ihesu 'king Jesus' PC 2354
mytern lucius 'king Lucius' TH 51
mytern margh 'king Mark' BM 2464
mytern massen 'king Maximius' BM 3156
myghtern pharo 'king Pharaoh' OM 1479, 1712
myghtern salmon, *mytern Salamon* 'king Solomon' OM 2545;
   TH 31
duk conan 'duke Conan' BM 84
duk magus 'duke Magus' BM 3920; *duk nobyl magus* 'noble
   duke Magus' BM 3930
ebscop cayphas, *epscop cayphas* 'bishop Caiaphas' PA 88b;
   PC 1201, 1851.

Compare also *arluth costentyn* 'lord Constantine' BM 1739.

The second construction involving apposition rather than genitival relation is commoner in Cornish than the first. It would seem, however, to be the less native of the two. In all the Brythonic languages, when a proper noun follows a noun, it naturally acquires genitival force. Thus Breton *Barzhaz Breizh* means 'the Poesy of Brittany' and Welsh *Plaid Cymru* means 'the Party of Wales'. Similarly in Cornish *carek veryasek* BM 1072, for example, can only mean 'Meriasek's rock'. The expression *map dauid*, *map daueth* 'son of David' occurs at PC 271, 277, 419 and 423. Taken literally, therefore, *myghtern David* ought to mean 'David's king'—which makes no sense. The Cornish expression *myghtern David* 'king David' is clearly a calque on English 'King David' or Latin *rex David*. The same is true of *Duk Magus* 'duke Magus' and all the other titles in apposition cited above. Such expressions as *myghtern David*, *duk Magus* and *epscop Cayphas* do not conform to the natural tendency of the Brythonic languages to understand A + B (where B is a proper noun) as 'the A of B' rather than 'A, the B'.

'KING ARTHUR IS NOT DEAD'

In Welsh in order to express apposition with words meaning 'king', 'lord', etc., one originally inverted the word-order and lenited the title, e.g. *Arthur Frenin* 'King Arthur' and *Ioan Fedyddiwr* 'John the Baptist'. A similar word-order is also to be found in Irish, though without initial lenition, for example *Dáibhí Rí* 'King David', *Anraí Rí* 'King Henry' and *Íseáia Fáidh* 'the prophet Isaiah'. In contemporary

Welsh, however, the English word-order prevails, though the definite article precedes the title, e.g. *y Brenin Arthur* 'King Arthur', and *y Tywysog Siarl* 'Prince Charles'.

In Welsh the definite article cannot occur before a noun followed by a proper noun in genitival relation to it. This is because the first noun is already definite by reason of the following proper noun. In Welsh, therefore, one says *hanes Cymru* 'the history of Wales', not **yr hanes Cymru* and *Eglwys Loegr* 'the Church of England', not **yr Eglwys Loegr*. If the article is used, the noun and its following proper noun must be in apposition to each other. This is why the second noun in such phrases *y Brenin Arthur* and *y Twysog Siarl* cannot be understood as genitive. Since *y Brenin Arthur* with the definite article *y* before *Brenin*, cannot mean ***'Arthur's king' (which would be *brenin Arthur*), it can only mean the King, Arthur', i.e. 'King Arthur'. Similarly *y Tywysog Siarl* cannot possibly mean 'Charles's prince'. It can only mean 'The Prince, Charles', i.e. 'Prince Charles'.

In Welsh *Arthur Frenin* and Irish *Dáibhí Rí* the name comes first and the title second. A comparable syntax is sometimes found in Cornish, for example in the expressions *Walter Kembro* 'Walter the Welshman' (CPNE: 48) and *Charles Mightern* 'King Charles' in the Letter of King Charles.

I have noticed no precise parallel in Cornish for *y Brenin Arthur* 'King Arthur' involving the word *mytern* 'king'. The expressions *an emp[r]our costenten* 'the emperor Constantine' BM 1326, *then emperour costentyn* 'to the emperour Constantine' BM 3957 and *then vyternes helen* 'to queen Helena' BM 1158 are, however, exactly comparable. Similarly, the phrase *ov arluth costentyn* 'my lord Constantine' at BM 1527 can also be compared, since the first element *arluth* is rendered definite by the possessive adjective *ov* 'my' and the whole phrase is therefore unambiguous. It can only mean 'my lord, Constantine', i.e. 'my lord Constantine'.

The motto of the Federation of Old Cornwall Societies is *Nyns yu marow myghtern Arthur*. In view of *myterne Davith* 'king David', *myghtern Salmon* 'king Solomon', *mytern Connan* 'king Conan', *mytern Margh* 'king Mark', etc. in the texts, *myghtern Arthur* 'king Arthur' cannot be described as incorrect. Nonetheless *Nyns yu marow Arthur myghtern* (cf. *Charles Mightern*) or *Nyns yu marow an myghtern Arthur* (cf. *then emperour costentyn*) would have been even better Cornish.

THE SAINT'S NAME WITHOUT *SEN/SENT*

If *mytern David* 'king David' is based on English or Latin and is not Celtic in origin, it follows that expressions like *Sen Luk* 'St Luke', *Sent Powl* 'St Paul', etc., are similarly calques on English or Latin and are also non-Celtic. It is significant that *Sen/Sent* is common in Cornish only with foreign saints. Celtic saints and some of the commonest saints of the New Testament are usually referred to in Cornish by their Christian names alone.

As examples of the simple Christian name referring to the saint one might cite *Goluan* (<*gol *Yowan*) 'the feast of St John'; *bevnans meryasek* 'the Life of St Meriasek' BM 4550; *maria cambron* 'St Mary of Camborne' BM 2510; *Plêth Maria* 'Our Lady's tresses' AB: 245a; *myhall, sera* '[by] St Michael, sir' CW 599; *dugoll myhal, dugol myhall* 'the feast of St Michael, Michaelmas' BM 2077, 2201; *chear pedyr* 'the Chair of St Peter' TH 49 and *re Yîst, re Ist* 'by St Just' AB: 249. Some of these expressions will be discussed in greater detail below.

This use of the Christian name without *Sen* or *Sent* is customary in Cornish toponyms where the saint is a Celtic one. To exemplify this point I give below a brief selection of place-names. The toponyms consist of one of five toponymic elements: (A) *eglos* 'church'; (B) *fenten* 'well'; (C) *lan* 'enclosure'; (D) *merther* 'grave, burial place'; (E) *plu* 'parish' or (F) *porth* 'harbour; gateway', followed by the name of a Celtic saint:

A

Egglous Boryan 'St Burrian' PNWP: 43 and *Eglez Burian* BF: 27; *Eglosbudock* 'Budock' CLN5: 19; *Egloscraweyn* 'Crowan' CPNE: 91; *Egloscuri* 'Cury' CLN5: 21; *Egloscutbert* 'Cubert' CLN5: 21; *Egloserm* 'St Erme' CLN5: 21; *Egloslagek* 'Ladock' CLN5: 21; *Eglosmadern* 'Madron' CPNE: 91; *Egglostetha* 'St Teath' CPNE: 91; *Eglos Senor, Egglose Zennor* 'Zennor Churchtown' PNWP: 76

B

Fentyn Carensek = 'St Carantoc's well' CPNE: 97; *Ventongassick* = 'St Cadock's well'; *Ventonberron* = 'St Piran's well'; *Venton East* = 'St Just's well' PNWP: 79; *Ventonglidder* = 'St Clether's well'; *Fentonladock* = 'St Ladock's well'; *Ventontinny* < **fenten Entenin* = 'St Antoninus's well'

C

Lananta, Lalanta < *Anta* 'Lelant' PNWP: 57; *Lanberan* < *Piran* 'Perranzabuloe' CLN5: 17; *Lantinning* < *Entenin* 'St Anthony in Meneage' CLN5: 17; *Langustentyn* < *Costentyn* 'Constantine' CLN5: 17; *Langoron* 'Goran' CLN5: 17; *Lanhidrock* < *Ydroc* 'Lanhidrock' CLN5: 17; *Lanuah* 'St Ewe' CLN5: 17; *Lawenep* < *Gwenep* 'Gwennap' CLN5: 17;

Lanwethenek (also *Lodenek*) < *Gwethenoc* 'Padstow' CPNE: 277

D
Barrymaylor < *merther Maylor*; *Mertheruny*, *Mertherheuny* CPNE: 164 < *merther Euny*; *Merthersithny* CPNE: 164; *Menedarva* < *merther Derva*

E
Pelynt < **plu Nynt* CPNE: 187; *Plu-alyn* 'St Allen' CPNE: 295; *Plewe-Golen* 'Colan' CPNE: 295; *Plewgolom* '?St Columb Major' CPNE: 295; *Pluysie* 'St Issey' CPNE: 295; *plew Paule* 'Paul' BF: 38 and *pleu Paul* AB: 222; *pleu Yst* 'St Just in Penwith' AB: 222 and *Pleu Êst* JRIC 1886: 12; *Pluvogan* 'St Mawgan' CPNE 295; *plu vuthek* 'Budock' OM 2463

F
Porthia 'St Ives' < *porth Ya* CPNE: 299, *Poreeah* BF: 25; *Porthkea* = 'entrance to parish of St Kea'; *Porthleven* < *porth Elvan*; *Porthmawgan* 'St Mawgan in Pydar' CPNE: 300; *Porth Mellin* 'harbour of St Melyan'; *Porth Perane* 'Perranuthnoe' CPNE: 300; *Porthzennor Cove*; *Portsenen* 'Sennen Cove' < **porth Senen* PNWP: 68; *Priest Cove* < **porth Ust*, i.e. the cove of St Just PNWP: 65 (cf. *Porth East* at Gorran Haven PNWP: 26).

The above list could be considerably extended, particularly as far as toponyms in *Lan-* are concerned. Examples with different first elements include *Altarnun* < *alter Non* 'St Non's altar' and *Luxulyan* < *lok Sulyan* 'place of St Sulian'. This latter was also known as *Lansulien* (CLN5: 18). Some of the above may be uncertain; the important point to notice is that in none of them is the saint's name preceded by *Sen* or *Sent*.

'SAINT' IN WELSH AND IRISH
In Welsh, Celtic saints are usually referred to by the simple Christian name. If necessary the adjective *Sant* 'saint, holy' is added after the name, e.g. *Dewi Sant* 'St David'. Foreign saints are usually introduced by *Sant* before the Christian name. The practice in Welsh is described in the most recent English–Welsh dictionary as follows:

saint . . . attrib. *Sant* usua[lly]. precedes the names of saints
of the Roman and Greek calendars, and follows the name of
Celtic saints (WAD: S 1204).

The position is similar in Welsh toponyms. One finds the bare
Christian name with *llan* 'enclosure' (cf. Cornish *lan-*), for example, in
Llanfair < *Mair* 'Mary', *Llandudno* < *Tudno* and *Llanilltud* < *Illtud*.
Ty 'house' occurs with the bare name, for example, in *Tyddewi* 'St
David's'. Notice, however, that in most cases *Sant* before the saint's
name is most frequently *Sain* in place-names, e.g. *Sain Ffagan* 'St
Fagan's' and *Sain Nicolas* 'St Nicholas'. Welsh is thus broadly similar
to Cornish in this respect, since in neither does Welsh *Sant/Sain* or
Cornish *Sent/Sen* precede the Christian name of Celtic saints.

It is quite apparent that the use of the simple Christian name is a
common Celtic phenomenon and has its origins in the practice of the
Celtic church. In Irish, St Patrick, St Brigid and St Columba are
known as *Pátric/Pádraig*, *Brigit/Bríd* and *Colum Cille* respectively. We
thus find such expressions as *Bethu Phátric* 'the Life of St Patrick',
Teampall Phádraig 'St Patrick's Cathedral', *Bethu Brigte* 'the Life of St
Brigid', *Lá Fhéile Bríde* 'St Brigid's Day', *Betha Cholam Chille* 'the
Life of St Columba' and *Í Choluim Chille* 'Iona of St Columba'. If it is
necessary to distinguish Patrick the saint from a secular character, one
can say *Pádraig Naofa* 'Holy Patrick'—an expression reminiscent of
Dewi Sant in Welsh. The use of the Christian name was taken over into
Hiberno-English. St Brigid is sometimes called 'Biddy' and 17 March
is 'Patrick's Day' or even 'Paddy's Day'.

Foreign saints in Irish receive a prefixed *San* before their names,
e.g. *San Antaine* 'St Anthony', *San Froinsias* 'St Francis' and *San
Caitríona* 'St Catherine'. Even here *San* is not universal. SS Peter
and Paul, who are associated with the Apostolic See from the earliest
times, are known to the Catholic Irish as *Peadar* and *Pól.* respectively.
Certain other nativized saints are referred to without *San.* Thus 26
December, the feast of the protomartyr and a very important day in the
Irish calendar, is called *Lá Fhéile Stiofáin* 'Stephen's Feast Day'. St
Stephen's Green in Dublin is in Irish *Faiche Stiabhna* and indeed the
place is always referred to as 'Stephen's Green' by Dubliners.

There has been a tendency in Irish since the early seventeenth
century to prefix all saints' names with *Naomh* 'Saint', e.g. *Naomh
Pádraig*, *Naomh Eoin* 'St John' and *Naomh Pól* 'St Paul'. This practice
appears to have arisen first in litanies of the saints that were translated
from Latin. More recently English forms like St Patrick, St John,
etc., have reinforced the tendency. It is even now by no means universal, however. A branch of the Gaelic Athletic Association in South

Dublin is known as *Cumann Naomh Eoin* 'St John's Club' where *Naomh Eoin* 'Saint John' is a calque on English. On the other hand the all-Irish secondary school in Dublin bears the more authentic name *Coláiste Eoin.*

'SAINT' IN BRETON

Similarly in Brittany one finds toponyms in *Lan-*, e.g. *Lanndevenneg, Landudal,* and *Lannildud.* In Brittany the element *plou* 'parish' (cf. Cornish *plu, plew*) is common with the bare saint's name, e.g. *Plougouloum, Plouizi* and *Plouzeniel.* Further elements immediately followed in toponyms by the simple name include *kastell,* e.g. *Kastell Paol* 'St Pol-de-Léon'; *porzh* 'harbour', e.g. *Porzh-Pêr* 'Port-Saint-Pierre' and *lok* 'place', e.g. *Loctudy* and *Locmélar.* It would seem, then, that in Breton, as in Welsh and Cornish, Celtic saints were originally referred to by use of the Christian name by itself.

In Breton, however, there is a marked tendency, when the name is not preceded by any other element, to prefix Celtic saints' names with *Sant.* This occurs in prayer books, where one finds such expressions as *Sant Michœl Archœl* 'St Michael the Archangel', *Sant Jan-Badezour* 'St John the Baptist' and *an Ebestel Sant Pêr ha Sant Paul* 'the Apostles St Peter and St Paul' (CT: 263). It also occurs in toponyms, e.g. *Sant-Maodan, Sant Peran, Sant-Wenn* and *Sant-Yust.* Notice also that *Yann,* the equivalent of Cornish **Yowan,* appears with *Sant* in the place-names *Sant-Yann-ar-Biz* 'St Jean du Doigt' and *Sant-Yann-ar-C'houenon* 'St Jean-sur-Couesnon'. It should be noted further that in Breton, where male saints have *Sant,* female saints have *Santes, Santez* prefixed to their names. One thus finds forms like *Sanctez Cathell* 'St Catherine', *Buhez Santez Nonn* 'the Life of St Non' and even *Santes Mari* 'St Mary, the Blessed Virgin Mary'.

Collections of saints' lives were always popular in Brittany. In such works Celtic saints always receive *Sant* or *Santes* before their names. In BS, for example, one finds *s[ant] Gùénœl* 'St Gwenael' (3 Nov.); *s. Guénolé* 'St Gwenolé' (3 March); *s. Paul, escob a Léon* 'St Paul, bishop of Léon' (12 March); *s. Padern, quetan escob a Huénèd* 'St Paternus, first bishop of Vannes' (16 April) and *s. Mériadec, escob a Huéned* 'St Meriadec/Meriasek, bishop of Vannes' (7 June). Female saints in BS include *Sès Ninnoc, gùérhiès* 'St Ninnoc, virgin' (4 June) and *Stès Noal, gùérhiès* 'St Noal, virgin' (6 July).

The difference between *Sant* with male saints and *Santez* with female ones is reminiscent of Latin saints' names in *Sanctus* and *Sancta* respectively. It is likely, therefore, that the practice of prefixing the name of all saints, Celtic or foreign, with *Sant* or *Santez* is a Latin convention (reinforced no doubt by French *Saint* and *Sainte*) adopted

into Breton. A cursory glance at Breton works of popular piety indicates just how closely such Breton works follow Latin and French
models. In the litanies of the saints, for example, it is common to find
on one side of the page Latin invocations like the following:

> *Sancte Petre, ora pro nobis* 'St Peter, pray for us'
> *Sancte Paule, ora pro nobis* 'St Paul, pray for us'
> *Sancte Jacobe, ora pro nobis* 'St James, pray for us'
> *Sancte Joannes, ora pro nobis* 'St John, pray for us'
> *Sancte Toma, ora pro nobis* 'St Thomas, pray for us'
>> etc.

and the equivalent in Breton in the next column:

> *Sant Pêr, pedit evidomp* 'St Peter, pray for us'
> *Sant Paol, pedit evidomp* 'St Paul, pray for us'
> *Sant Jaques, pedit evidomp* 'St James, pray for us'
> *Sant Ian, pedit evidomp* 'St John, pray for us'
> *Sant Thomas, pedit evidomp* 'St Thomas, pray for us'
>> etc. (HBL: 659).

Notice that in the case of *Sant Pêr* and *Sant Ian* the form of the saint's
name was inherited from Latin in the early Christian period. With
neither would one expect *Sant*.

Female saints, when they occur in litanies, are prefixed by *Sancta*
in Latin and *Santes* in Breton. One thus finds the following equivalents, for example:

Latin	Breton
Sancta Agatha	*Santes Agata*
Sancta Lucia	*Santes Luç*
Sancta Agnes	*Santes Agnes*
Sancta Cæcilia	*Santes Aziliç*
Sancta Anastasia	*Santes Anastas*
	(HBL: 660–69).

If, then, Breton differs from Welsh and Cornish in using *Sant/Santez*
indiscriminately with all saints' names, it does so by analogy with
Latin. The Bretons, unlike either the Welsh or the Cornish, remained
uniformly Catholic at the Reformation. In consequence they maintained their devotion to the saints and were also exposed to a popular
piety mediated through Latin models. This is why the Breton treatment
of saints' names was so heavily influenced by Latin.

The Irish also remained Catholic and it is remarkable that the use of *Naomh* 'Saint' with all saints' names seems to begin in Ireland at the period of the Counter-Reformation.

THE SAINT'S NAME AS CORNISH TOPONYM

Not infrequently in Cornwall the saint's name is used by itself as the name of the parish. Examples of this use of the saint's name by itself from contemporary Cornish place-names include *Breage, Budock, Buryan, Colan, Constantine, Cubert, Degibna, Feock, Gerrans, Gluvian, Gulval, Gwennap, Gwinear, Gwithian, Kenwyn, Ladock, Mabe, Madron, Mawgan, Mawnan, Mylor, Paul, Phillack, Probus, Sithney, Stithians, Wendron* and *Zennor*.

The saint's name without *Sen* before it but with a descriptive element after occurs in *Perranarworthal < Peran *ar wothel* = 'St Piran facing the water ground'; *Perranuthnoe* = 'St Piran and St Gwethenoc'; *Perranzabuloe < Peran* + Latin *in sabulo* = 'St Piran in the sand' and *Petherwyn < Padarn wyn* 'Blessed St Paternus'.

The use of the name of the saint as name of the parish would seem to have its origins in the practice of Cornish speakers themselves. This can be seen from the following examples from the Cornish texts:

> *Kûz karna na huìla en Borrian* 'Cornawheely Wood in Buryan' BF: 18
> *Mean orrol en Madern* 'another stone in Madron' BF: 27
> *Tubmas Trythal, Proanter Sennen* 'Thomas Trythal, parson of Sennen' Ellis: 98
> *Drake Proanter East* 'Drake, the Parson of St Just' ACB & Ellis: 98
> *Dho Proanter Powle* 'the Parson of Paul' ACB
> *tha Pobl Bohodzhak Paull ha'n Egles nei* 'for the poor people of Paul and our church' BF: 57.

The name *Mevagissey* is for **Meva hag Issy* 'St Meva and St Issey', the two saints of the parish. The presence of the Cornish word *(h)ag* in the name would seem to indicate that **Meva hag Issy* was a living toponym while Cornish was spoken in the district.

SEN(T), SYNT 'SAINT'

As has been suggested, *Sen* or *Sent* is common only with foreign saints. Examples from the Cornish texts include the following:

> *S Ambros* TH 39, 47, 47a, 49; *S Ambrose* 45a; *S. Ambros* SA 62, 62a x 2, 66

Sent augustyn TH 37a; *S Austyn* TH 32; *S Austen* SA 59; *S. Austen* SA 64a, 65a, 66; *S austin* TH 32; *S Agustyn* TH 32a, 37, 56, 58; *S Agustin* TH 32a; *S Augustin* TH 48 x 2; *S Augustyn* TH 37a, 46

S Bartholomew TH 37a

S Basell TH 51a; *S Basyll* TH 45a

S Chrisostum TH 57

S Ciprian TH 39a, 42, 45; 48a, 56; *S Cyprian* TH 42a

S Cyrill TH 38a; *S Cirill* TH 57 x 2

s Ireneus TH 37; *S Yreneus* TH 19a

S Jherom TH 47; *S Hierom* TH 49

sen luk BM 391; *S Luk* TH 29a; *S luk* TH 38; *S. Luke* SA 64

S Mark TH 53

S mathew TH 31a; *S Mathew* TH 35a, 43a

sent sampson BM 2983

S Thomas SA 60a.

It is apparent from this list that the saints whose names are preceded by the title *Sen/Sent* (*Synt*) are almost invariably foreign ones. The only exception in the above list is the Breton saint Sampson of Dol referred to as *sent sampson* at BM 2983. The author of BM was almost certainly drawing at this point upon a Latin source which spoke of **ecclesia Sancti Sampson*. Moreover, as we have seen, the Bretons tended to use *Sant* with the name of all male saints. In either case the use of *sent* in this instance is not remarkable.

SEN/SENT IN TOPONYMS

We have very few examples from Cornish language texts of *Sen/Sent* in toponyms. Two examples known to me are the following:

Stean San Agnes an guella stean en Kernow 'The tin of St Agnes is the best tin in Cornwall' ACB: facing F f
Gûn St. Eler 'the moor of St Hilary' BF: 17.

In both cases the saints are foreign rather than Celtic ones.

One apparent exception is St Levan in Penwith, e.g. *En Termen ez passiez thera Trigaz en St. Levan; Dean ha Bennen en Tellar creiez cheir a Horr* 'In tyme that is passed, there Dwelt in St Levan a man & woman in a place called The House of a Ramm' (BF: 15, 19). St Levan is by *Volksetymologie* for *Seleven* < *Solomon* (Doble 1: 3). In the early twentieth century the place was still called *Seleven* by the older people. *St Levan* < *Seleven* is, despite appearances, a further example of the saint's name used by itself as a toponym.

SS JOVYN, MALAN AND GYLMYN

In the Cornish plays the unsympathetic characters not infrequently invoke the pagan 'saint' Jovin. The name occurs both with and without the prefix *synt* (a variant of *sent*):

> *ef a'n pren re synt iovyn* 'he'll pay for it by St Jovin' PC 368
>
> *syr cayfas re synt iouyn me a wra the gorhemmyn* 'Sir Caiaphas, by St Jovin, I'll do your command' PC 1363–4
>
> *synt iouyn whek re'n carro* 'may dear St Jovin love him' PC 1847
>
> *re synt iouyn* 'by St Jovin' PC 1962, 2858
>
> *re synt iouyn whek* 'by dear St Jovin' PC 2537
>
> *synt iouyn whek re'th caro* 'may dear St Jovin love you' PC 3016
>
> *me a'n te re synt iouyn* 'I swear it by St Jovin' RD 349
>
> *rak coske reys yv thy'mmo re synt iouyn* 'for I must sleep by St Jovin' RD 412–13.
>
> *mara'th caffaf re iovyn* 'if I catch you, by Jovin' OM 1532
>
> *rag henna thy's my a de gorthye iovyn beneges* 'therefore I swear to you to worship blessed Jovin' OM 1811–12
>
> *goef nep a worth jovyn* 'woe is him who worships Jovin' OM 1889
>
> *re iovyn arluth an beys* 'by Jovin, lord of the world' PC 449
>
> *re iovyn drok yv gyne* 'by Jovin, I'm sorry' PC 1292
>
> *wolcum cayphas re iouyn* 'welcome, Caiaphas, by Jovin' PC 1687
>
> *iouyn roy thy's bos den mas* 'may Jovin grant you to be a good man' PC 1706
>
> *me a'th pys gynes mar plek war iouyn gylwel mercy* 'I beg you please to call upon Jovin for mercy' PC 1896–7
>
> *kemmys na worthyo iouyn* 'as many as do not worship Jovin' PC 1917
>
> *a thev iouyn luen a ras* 'O god Jovin, full of grace' PC 2989
>
> *gorth quik iovyn ha soly* 'worship Jovin and Sol quickly' BM 1231
>
> *Thum du iovyn benygas me a offren iij bran vrays* 'to my blessed god Jovin I will offer three ravens' BM 3406–7.

The name *iouyn* is usually translated 'Jove' but it would seem to be a conflation of the oblique stem *Jov-* of *Jupiter* with *Jovinus* or *Jovinius*. The name *iouyn* is clearly a recent borrowing and as such would normally take *synt* before it. The reason for the inconsistency in the use of *synt* is presumably that the dramatists could not decide whether

Jovin was a Continental saint who required *synt* or a pagan god who did not.

Malan 'Belial, Beelzebub' (<?*Malignus*) is less well attested in the texts. He is both a saint: *rak why a scon ahanan the pilat re synt malan* 'for you will soon go to Pilate, by Saint Belial' PC 2340–1, and a god: *hou geiler abarth malan* 'ho! gaoler, in the name of Belial!' PC 2235; *gesough hy abart[h] malan yn morter skuat the gothe* 'let it fall, splat, into the mortise, in the name of Belial' PC 2815–16.

Synt gylmyn is a hapax legomenon: *syr arluth re synt gylmyn my a wra the worhemmyn* 'Sir Lord, by St Gylmyn, I will do your command' OM 2413–14. In view of the alternation seen in *synt iouyn/iouyn* and *synt malan/malan*, it is likely that the expression **re gylmyn* also occurred, although we have no instance of it. Since *re* 'by' (in oaths) lenites the following consonant, I suspect that we are really dealing with a basic form **Kylmyn*. This, with Lhuyd and Norris, I take to be the Cornish form of *Columbanus*, Irish *Colmán*. The basic form **re Gylmyn* 'by St Columbanus' has given rise to a form *Gylmyn* with permanent initial lenition. *Gylmyn* in turn has further been interpreted as a pagan deity.

The adverb *defry* 'indeed' is also made into a saint in the oath *re sent deffry* 'by Saint Truly' CW 606. This fictitious saint was believed to be of foreign origin, for he receives the element *sent* before his name.

SYNTA AS THE FEMININE OF *SENT/SYNT*

Synta has long been used by Cornish Revivalists as the feminine equivalent of *Sen/Synt*. Nance, for example, used the expression *Synta Brek* to render 'St Breage' (LPMS: 8–9). The element *Synta* is highly doubtful, however.

As far as can be ascertained, *Synta*, or *Synte*, occurs once only in the Cornish texts. In *Resurrexio Domini* St Thomas, doubting the resurrection of Christ, has already rebuked Peter, John and James for their foolish faith. Finally, he rounds on Matthew and says:

> *a synte mari mathew*
> *mara colyth ty a tew*
> > *gans the whethlow*
> *gul ges ahanaf a wreth*
> *marth yv gynef nath ues meth*
> > *ow keusel gow*

> 'By Saint Mary, Matthew
> if you will hearken, you will cease
> > your silly stories.

You are making fun of me.
I am astonished you are not ashamed
   to utter lies'
      (RD 1387–92).

Three things should be noticed here. In the first place, *synte mari* in this passage is not a specific reference to the Blessed Virgin Mary. St Thomas does not yet believe the resurrection and does not by implication accept the tenets of Christianity. He cannot therefore believe the mother of Jesus to be a saint. In the second place, the form is not Cornish, but French. *Synte mari* is the scribe's spelling of *Sainte Marie*, which is French, not Cornish. Since the present instance is the only example, we can conclude that *Synte, Synta* was never a productive formant in Cornish. In the third place, it is clear from *Stean Sen Agnes an guella stean en Kernow* 'The tin of St Agnes is the best tin in Cornwall', that the feminine form of *Sen* is *Sen*, not *Synta*.

Synta 'Saint' as a title for female saints is a ghost-word. *Sen* can be used with non-native saints, but when referring to female Celtic saints the Christian name by itself is sufficient. The toponym *Breage* itself indicates that the Cornish for St Breage was *Brek* or *Breg*. This is corroborated by the form *Eglosbrek* 'St Breage's church, Breage' from AD 1181 (CLN5: 19). Forms like *Synta Brek* 'St Breage', *Synta Ya* 'St Ives', etc. are not Cornish, and are best avoided in the revived language. If in Cornish one needs to indicate that Breg and Ya are saints, one can say *Breg Sans* and *Ya Sans* respectively.

ST JOHN

There are two forms of the name 'St John' in Cornish. The first was originally **Yowan* and is the direct reflex of Latin *Iohannes* 'John' adopted into the Brythonic languages in the early Christian period. It is therefore the exact equivalent of Welsh *Ieuan* (*Iwan, Ifan*) and Breton *Yann*. As far as I am aware, **Yowan* survives in only one place in Cornish, namely in the word *Golowan, Goluan* 'St John's day, Midsummer (24 June)', in the proverb *Guâve en Hâve terebah Goluan* (JRIC 1886: 11), where *Goluan* is from *gol* 'feast' (< Latin *vigilia*) + **Yowan* 'St John'. The loss of initial /j/ is quite regular here; compare *ezewon* 'Jews' PA 126a for *yethewon*; *eghas* 'health' TH 30a for *yehes* and *eyth* 'language' TH 1 for **yeth* (Welsh *iaith*). As in the case of *dugol Myhall* 'Michaelmas', the early formation *Goluan* renders the saint's name as the bare name without prefix.

The second form of the name 'St John' is *Sen Jowan, S Johan*. Here are some examples from the texts:

> *by sen iowan* BM 2878
> *sent Johan* TH 8; *Sent Johan* TH 23a
> *S Johan* TH 15, 42a, 43, 51a, 53 x 3, 57 x 2; *S Jowan* TH 39a
> *sen iowen baptyst* BM 4450
> *S Johan baptist* TH 8
> *S Johan evangelist* TH 8
> *S Johan an evangelest* TH 20a.

Notice also *Jowan baptist* without *S(ent)* at TH 43a and *Jowan* at TH 44. The form of the Christian name in *Sen Jowan, Jowan, S Johan* is identical with Lhuyd's *Dzhûan* 'John' and Boson's *Jooan* (BF: 16), where the initial is [dʒ]. Indeed Lhuyd is quite unequivocal that the initial of *Jowan* is [dʒ], for he says:

> In the *Cornish*, the Initial *I* before a Vowel, had two pronun-
> ciations: For in some words 'tis pronounced as in *English* in
> the word *Iew*: As *Jowan*, John; and some as *y*: For *yowynk*
> [young] must be read *yunk*, or *yynk* (AB: 228a)

and

> *ou* and *ow* in the *Cornish*, are also commonly Equivalent to *u*
> long; as *Gour an Chy* [The man of the House] is read *gûr an
> tshei*, and *Jowan* John, *Dzhûan* (AB: 228c).

The English use of 'by' in *by sen iowan* 'by St John' at BM 2878 is further evidence that *John* in English and *Jowan* in Cornish were considered interchangable.

The difference between *(Y)owan* and *Jowan* is the same as that between Welsh *Ieuan* and *Siôn*. *Ieuan* is the name of the saint, while *Siôn* is a secular name and never refers to the saint. Comparable also is the Irish *Eoin* (Scottish *Iain*, Manx *Ean*), the name of the saint and *Seán* (earlier *Seaán* < Old French *Jehan*), the boy's name. One thing is apparent, however: *Sen(t)* and *Yowan* never occur together in Cornish.

PETER, PAUL AND MARY

St Peter is, as far as one can ascertain, never referred to in Cornish as anything other than *Pedyr*. I have noticed the following examples from TH:

> *pedyr* TH 18 x 2, 24, 43 x 3, 44a x 7, 45, 45a. 46 x 3, 47a, 48, 49
> x 3
> *pedyr an apostell* TH 49

Pedyr TH 42a x 2, 43, 45, 45a x 2, 47a x 3
the pedyr TH 43 x 2, 43a x 3, 44 x 2, 44a x 2, 45, 45a, 46
the Pedyr TH 43
worth pedyr TH 43a
stall a pedyr 49.

Pedyr is a pre-Norman form of the saint's name. This can be seen by the internal *-d-*, which is the lenition product of original *-t-*. *Pedyr* is thus identical in origin with Welsh *Pedr* and Breton *Pêr* < *Pezr*. Had the name been borrowed from English it would have had an inter-vocalic *-t-*; cf. the common oath *Peter* in Chaucer.

St Paul the apostle is quite different. He is almost always referred to as *S(ent) Paul*. Here are some instances from the TH:

Sent powle TH 13
Sent powl TH 13
S paul TH 16a, 17a, 18a, 33, 53a x 2
S paule TH 18, 25, 32a, 33 x 2, 33a x 2, 34, 38, 39, 51a, 57a
S. Paule SA 66
S paull TH 18a, 41a, 45
S paulle TH 42 x 2
S pawle TH 14, 33
S Pawle TH 4a, 7a, 8
S poull TH 14, 31
S Poull TH 32
S poule TH 25
S poulle TH 31
S powle TH 33a, 34
S Powle TH 4a x 2.

The only instance in TH of the name of the saint without the prefix *S(ent)* occurs in the phrase *Pedyr ha powle* TH 48 where St Paul is linked with St Peter; cf. *Pedyr ha povle* BM 1689. As noted above, St Peter's name is never prefixed by *S(ent)*.

Just as there are two forms of the name of St John in Cornish, so there are two forms of the name St Paul. The apostle and author of the epistles is *Sent Powl*. The Celtic saint, Paul Aurelian (Doble 1: 10ff) gives his name to Paul in Penwith. In Cornish the toponym is either *plew Paule* (BF: 38), *pleu Paul* (AB: 222) or *pawl* (BF: 10, 12), *Paull* (BF: 57), *Paul* (BF: 60) or *Powle* (ABC). In either case this latter name lacks *Sen(t)*.

The Blessed Virgin Mary is a special case. 'Saint Mary' occurs but in many languages including English the mother of Jesus is frequently known as 'Our Lady', 'Notre Dame', etc., or 'the Blessed Virgin Mary'. Although the equivalent of 'Our Lady' is not usual in Cornish, the expression corresponding to English 'the blessed Virgin Mary' is well attested:

> *wyrhes ker maria* 'Blessed Virgin Mary' TH 12a
> *an wyrhes ker maria* 'the Blessed Virgin Mary' RD 154; TH 12a
> *an wyrhes maria* 'the Virgin Mary' TH 12a, 13, 13a, 52a
> *han wyrhes maria* 'and the Virgin Mary BM 756
> *in wyrhes maria* 'in the Virgin Mary' TH 13a
> *an werthias marya* 'the Virgin Mary' SA 59
> *an worthias maria* 'the Virgin Mary' SA 61
> *an Worthias Maria* 'the Virgin Mary' SA 61a
> *an werthias Marya* 'the Virgin Mary' SA 64a.

The name *Maria, Marya* is itself borrowed from Breton or Middle French *Marië*. The original name of the Blessed Virgin Mary direct from Latin *Maria* in the early Christian period would have been **Meyr*, **Myr* or **Mer* in Cornish. Although this is not attested in the literature, Padel suggests that *Venton Veor* (< *fenten ?*Veyr*) in Liskeard may conceivably contain the earlier name for Mary (CPNE: 97).

Maria, Marya in Cornish behaves as though it were an early Celtic name. This is perplexing, given that 'St Mary' is common in English expressions like 'St Mary the Virgin' (and indeed St Mary Magdalene, etc.). Moreover *Sancta Maria* and *Sainte Marie* are common in Latin and French respectively. In Cornish, however, *Marya* is never prefixed by *Sen(t)*. Instead one finds that her name alone is sufficient in such expressions as *plêth Marîa* 'lady's tresses' (AB: 245a), *chy maria* 'the house/church of Our Lady' BM 640 and even the oath *re Varîa* 'by Our Lady' (AB: 249c).

THE DATE OF THE TITLE *SYNT/SENT/SEN*
TH and SA for the most part use the abbreviation *S* or *S.* for the word meaning 'saint'. On occasion, however, TH writes *Sent*, e.g. *Sent augustyn*, *Sent powle* and *Sent powl*. BM writes *sen luk* but *sent sampson*. The *Ordinalia* have *synt iouyn* and *synt gylmyn*. It is not entirely clear, therefore, what was the pronunciation of *synt/sent/sen*. Given that *sen(t)*, *synt* would have been weakly stressed, it is likely that the title was most commonly pronounced [sən]. In more deliberate enunciation, however, the final group [nt] may well have been sounded. If this was so, we can be sure that the title *sent* was not adopted into Cornish until after the shift of final /nt < ns/. *Sent/Synt* is from Old

French *saint* or Middle English *saint*, the English itself being a borrowing from French. French *saint* is ultimately from Vulgar Latin *santus* < Classical *sanctus*. *Santus* was borrowed directly in British in the early Christian period and appears with assibilation of the final /nt/ as *sans* 'holy' in Middle Cornish. Cornish *sent/synt* 'saint' and *sans* 'holy' are thus doublets.

In the Old Cornish Vocabulary final /nt/ has already been assibilated to /ns/, for example in *dans* 'dens; a tooth' (cf. Welsh and Breton *dant*). Final /nt/ was already /ns/ in Cornish therefore by the first half of the twelfth century. It follows that the title *sent/synt* could not have been part of the Cornish language until the mid twelfth century at the earliest. By this period many of the Celtic toponyms of Cornwall were already in place. Any toponym involving a pre-Norman saint, therefore, would of necessity lacked the element *Sen(t)*. This is one reason that *Sen(t)* and *Yowan do not occur together.

'SAINT' IN THE ENGLISH FORMS OF TOPONYMS
There are a number of toponyms that present a striking contrast between the Cornish form without a word for 'saint' and the English form with it, e.g.

Cornish	English
Lanuste	*St Just in Penwith*
Plu-alyn	*St Allen*
Plugolom	*St Columb Major?*
Pluvogan	*St Mawgan in Meneage*
Pluyust, Pleu Yst	*St Just in Penwith*
Pluysie	*St Issey*
Porthia, Poreeah	*St Ives*
Porthkea 'entrance to St Kea'	*St Kea.*

Contrast also the Cornish name *Melyn Myhall* 'St Michael's Mill' from 1464 without the word for 'saint' with the Latin form of the same place-name from 1258, *Molendium Sancti Michaelis*, which contains *Sancti* 'saint' (Doble 1931: 67).

The majority of forms of the names for St Just in Penwith cited by Pool from historical documents contain the element 'Saint': *St Just* 1291, 1351, 1440; *St Yuste* 1523; *St Ewste* 1558 and *St Just/St Towst* 1581. The only form cited by him that does not contain the element 'Saint' is *Lanuste* from 1396 (PNWP: 54). It is nonetheless clear from the sixteenth-century form *Pluyust*, from Lhuyd's *Pleu Yst* and Pryce's *Pronter East*, that as long as Cornish survived, the name of the town in Cornish was *Lan Ust*, *Plu Ust* or plain *Ust*. The forms with a word for

'Saint' are from Latin and English documents (in particular registers of the bishops of Exeter). They should not be confused with genuine Cornish-language forms.

The same can be said of the attested names of St Ives. It is apparent from Nicholas Boson's *Poreeah* and indeed from earlier forms *Porthya* 1284; *Porthia* 1291, 1337; *Porthye* 1313 and *Porthea* 1472 (PNWP: 65), that *Porth Ya, Por' Ya* without the element 'Saint', was the Cornish form of the name. Yet the bulk of the forms cited by Pool contain 'Saint': *St Ya* 1283, 1468, 1523; *St Ye* 1283, 1327, 1473; *St Hye* 1342; *St Eye* 1380; *St Ies* 1503; *St Ia* 1540; *St Yes* 1550; *St Yees* 1576 and *St Yves* 1579 (PNWP: 54). These forms with 'Saint' are English, not Cornish.

The contrast between the forms used in English documents and the Cornish form of the same names should be constantly in the minds of Revivalists as they attempt to re-establish the Cornish toponymy of Cornwall. Unfortunately, the distinction appears to have been forgotten by some.

HENWYN TYLLERYOW KERNEWEK

In December 1995 the Cornish language magazine *An Gannas* published a supplement *Henwyn Tylleryow Kernewek* 'Cornish Place-names' (HTK). This consists of a list of over 500 Cornish toponyms in Cornish with the English equivalents. The spelling system and phonology used is Kernewek Kemmyn, a form of Revived Cornish devised by Ken George, one of the four authors of HTK. Kernewek Kemmyn or Common Cornish is the form of Revived Cornish currently preferred by *An Gannas*.

I have explained in detail in several places (Williams 1995, 1996, 1998 and forthcoming) why I believe the phonology and spelling of Kernewek Kemmyn to be mistaken.

The shortcomings of Kernewek Kemmyn can readily be seen from HTK. Noteworthy, for example, is the way 'wood, forest' is invariably written *koes*, the graph <oe> representing a long closed */o:/. Cornish never possessed a long */o:/ separate from an equivalent open vowel /ɔ:/. The vowel in the word for 'wood' was originally a diphthong /ui/ which developed via /oi/ into an undifferentiated long /o:/. In some western parts of the Cornish speaking area /ui/ developed as /u:/. In our surviving remains of Cornish, therefore, 'wood' is *coys* (e.g. *Coysbesek, Coyseglase, Coyse Laydock, Coysfala, Coyskentueles* CPNE: 257; *coys* BM 1618) or *cos* (e.g. *Cosesawsyn* CPNE: 257; *cosow* pl. CW 1495) in Middle Cornish, and *kûz* in Late and Western Cornish (e.g. *Kûz* BF: 18, 44). In some toponyms the dialectal form *cous* shortens to *cus-*

(e.g. *Cusgarne, Cusveorth* and *Cusvey*). Kernewek Kemmyn *koes* is without phonetic or orthographic justification.

HTK leaves much to be desired in other respects. Indeed, the faults of Kernewek Kemmyn itself are only one aspect of the problems in the work. The compilers seem in many places to have taken forms of toponyms occurring in Latin and English documents as genuine Cornish. Since the purpose of this article is to examine the way in which the English term 'Saint' is rendered in Cornish, I shall confine myself in my discussion of HTK to those toponyms with hagiographical connections only.

ANTHROPONYM AS TOPONYM

We have seen that in Cornish a saint's name was often used by itself as a place-name. As noted above, examples from Cornish language sources include *Pawl* 'Paul', *Borrian* 'Buryan' and *Sennen* 'Sennen'. In their recommendations for these three place-names in Cornish the compilers of HTK are oddly inconsistent. They suggest *Pawl* for 'Paul', *Eglosveryan* for 'Buryan' but *Sen Senan* for 'Sennen', i.e the simple name in the first, *Eglos* 'church' + the saint's name in the second but *Sen* + the saint's name, but without any toponymic element in the third. *Eglosveryan* is perhaps justified by the form *Egglous Boryan* from 1588, though *Burrian* from 1593 (PNWP: 43) is identical with the spoken form in Late Cornish (i.e. *Borrian*) and might have been preferable. *Sen Senan*, however, where the native saint has *Sen* before his name, seems wholly unmotivated. Presumably *Sen Senan* is recommended for 'Sennen' because *St Senane, St Senan* are attested in early documents (PNWP: 68). These forms are not in Cornish, however. They are English forms of the name, and as such are irrelevant to the establishment of the Cornish toponym.

St Paulus and *St Paulinus* are attested for the place-name 'Paul' from the thirteenth to fifteenth centuries (PNWP: 62). Doble tells us that the church of Paul is called both *Ecclesia S. Pauli* and *Ecclesia S. Paulini* in the registers of the bishop of Exeter (Doble 1: 33). It is difficult to understand therefore why the compilers of HTK did not recommend **Sen Pawl* as the Cornish form of the name. Perhaps they felt they really could not fly in the face of the evidence of our Late Cornish texts—which invariably call the place *Pawl* or *Paul*. Which being so, it is curious that they did not embrace spoken Cornish forms throughout and recommend *Senan* and *Beryan* as well.

It would appear, for example, from *Eglosveryan* < *eglos* + the saint's name that the compilers of HTK believe the simple name to suffice for Celtic saints in some contexts. Compare further the following place-names in *Eglos-* and *Lan-* from HTK (SN = saint's name):

Eglosalan < *eglos* + SN 'St Allen'
Eglosenoder < *eglos* + SN 'St Enoder'
Eglostedha < *eglos* + SN 'St Teath'
Eglostudi < *eglos* + SN 'St Tudy'
Lannentenin < *lan* + SN 'St Anthony'
Lannewa < *lan* + SN 'St Ewe'
Lannyust < *lan* + SN 'St Just in Penwith'.

In all these names the English form contains 'Saint' yet the Cornish form recommended by HTK appears tacitly to accept that after *Eglos-* and *Lan-* the saint's name by itself is used. In other toponyms they are prepared to use the saint's name without either *Sen* before it on the one hand or *Eglos-*, *Lan-*, or whatever is before it on the other. We have already noted *Pawl* in HTK. Other saints' names/toponyms from HTK without any element in front of them include *Pyran ar Woethel* 'Perranarworthal', *Pyran yn Treth* 'Perranzabuloe' and *Pyranudhno* 'Perranuthnoe'. Here St Piran, and in the last name, St Wethenoc, appear without the element *Sen*.

Given that the names of some Celtic saints recommended in HTK appear in unadorned form, it is difficult to understand why the compilers should insist on putting *Sen* before other names to produce a host of unwarranted forms: **Sen Endelyn* 'St Endellion'; **Sen Erven* 'St Ervan'; **Sen Gwenna* 'St Wenna'; **Sen Kolomm Veur* 'St Columb Major' and **Sen Mawgan* 'St Mawgan', for example. *Sen Kolomm Veur* is particularly unhappy when *Plewgolom* is attested from 1543 (CPNE: 295). Furthermore, in the light of *Pluvogan* (CPNE: 295) there seems to be little justification for **Sen Mawgan*.

Perhaps the compilers of HTK might explain their having added *Sen* to **Sen Endelyn*, **Sen Erven*, etc., by pointing out that in each case the English forms contain the element 'Saint'. This, however, does not justify *Sen* in **Sen Senan*, since there is no 'Saint' in the English form of the place-name. If **Sen Senan* 'Sennen' is unmotivated, so also are the following from HTK:

Sen Goedhyan 'Gwithian'
Sen Gwynnyer 'Gwinear'
Sen Ke 'Kea'
Sen Mowgan 'Mawgan
Sen Mownan 'Mawnan'
Sen Senar 'Zennor
Sen Sydhni 'Sithney'.

Here the English versions of the name lack 'Saint' and thus preserve the authentic Cornish forms. It is a pity that the compilers of HTK have added an unhistorical *Sen* to each of the toponyms. A transliteration of the current English place-names would have given a more authentic Cornish name.

TWO FURTHER NAMES IN HTK

We have seen that the place-name St Levan contains the name *Seleven* < *Solomon*. The original form of the name is thus the name of the saint by itself. It is noteworthy that *Selevan* is a form of the place-name recorded from 1523 (PNWP: 57). The same personal name is also to be found in the Penwith toponym *Bosliven* < *bos Seleven* 'the settlement of Solomon'. The first unstressed syllable in *Seleven* was subsequently reinterpreted as *Sen* 'Saint'. This in turn gave rise to the English form *St Levan*. Nance in his Unified Cornish version of *Jowan Chy an Horth* recommended *Plu Seleven* (CFA: 37). Though unattested, such a form would be unobjectionable. The compilers of HTK, however, recommend the remarkable form *Sen Seleven* (cf. LPMS: *passim*). In English this could be rendered literally as 'St St Levan'—a place of double sanctity!

The toponym St John is rendered by HTK as *Sen Yowann*. This combines the early form *Yowan* (which is attested only in *Goluan*) with the later element *Sen*. *St John* in Cornish, as we have seen above, is invariably *Sen(t) Jowan* with <J> [dʒ]. *Sen Yowann* is without historical basis and cannot possibly be justified.

HTK: CONCLUSION

HTK is doubly inauthentic. In the first place the orthography used is unsatisfactory. This is because the inventor of Common Cornish mistakenly believed that Middle Cornish was very close to Welsh and Breton and constructed his spelling in the light of this opinion. Breton in particular was the model both for the phonology and orthography of Common Cornish—with unfortunate results. In the second place, the hagiographical toponyms in HTK are inconsistent in themselves. In particular such place-names are vitiated by the compilers' unwarranted practice of equating 'Saint' in English with *Sen* in Cornish. The compilers take toponyms from non-Cornish sources that exhibit 'Saint' (or *Sancti, Sanctae*) and by translating 'Saint' as *Sen* appear to believe that they are producing a genuine Cornish place-name. It is also probable that Breton toponyms in *Sant* have served as a model for some of their recommended forms. Whatever the reasons for it, the policy of the compilers of HTK is ill considered. They would have been better advised to pay greater attention both to the toponyms that are actually attested in the Cornish texts on the one hand and to the Welsh, early Breton and other Celtic parallels on the other. As it stands, HTK is very unsatisfactory and cannot be recommended.

REFERENCES AND ABBREVIATIONS

AB = Edward Lhuyd, *Archaeologia Britannica*, London 1707, reprinted Shannon, 1971.

ACB = William Pryce, *Archaeologia Cornu-Britannica*, Sherbourne, 1790.

BF = O.J. Padel, *The Cornish Writings of the Boson Family*, Redruth, 1975.

BM = Whitley Stokes, *Beunans Meriasek: The Life of Saint Meriasek*, London, 1872.

BS = *Buhé er Saent, Vannes*, 1839.

CFA = R.M. Nance, *Cornish for All*, St Ives, 1949.

CLN5 = O.J. Padel, 'Cornish Language Notes: 5', *Cornish Studies* 4/5, 1976–7, pp. 15–27.

CPNE = O.J. Padel, *Cornish Place-name Elements*, Nottingham, 1985.

CT = *Catechis Treguer* published by authority of Augustin René-Louis Le Mintier, bishop of Treguier, Morlaix, 1783.

CW = Whitley Stokes, 'Gwreans an Bys: the Creation of the World', *Transactions of the Philological Society*, 1864, Part iv.

DOBLE 1 = G.H. Doble, *The Saints of Cornwall: Part One: Saints of the Land's End District*, Chattam, 1960.

Doble, G.H., *Saint Perran, Saint Keverne and Saint Kerrian*, Shipston-on-Stour, 1931.

Ellis = P. Berresford Ellis, *The Cornish Language and its Literature*, London, 1974.

HBL = *Heuryou Brezonec ha Latin*, Quimper, 1806.

HTK = Graham Sandercock, Julyan Holmes, Pol Hodge and Ken George, *Henwyn Tylleryow Kernewek: Place Names in our Cornish Language*, An Gannas, 1995.

JRIC = *Journal of the Royal Institution of Cornwall*.

LPMS = Mordon (R.M. Nance), *Lyver an Pymp marthus Seleven*, St Ives, 1939.

OM = 'Origo Mundi' in E. Norris, *Ancient Cornish Drama*, London, 1859, Vol. I, pp. 1–219.

PA = Whitley Stokes, 'Pascon agan Arluth: the Passion of our Lord', *Transactions of the Philological Society*, 1860–1, Appendix, pp. 1–219.

PC = 'Passio Domini Nostri Jhesu Christi', E. Norris, *Ancient Cornish Drama*, London, 1859, Vol. I, pp. 221–479.

PNWP = P.A.S. Pool, *The Place-names of West Penwith*, 2nd ed., Penzance, 1985.

RD = 'Resurrexio Domini Nostri Jhesu Christi' in E. Norris, *Ancient Cornish Drama*, London, 1859, Vol. II, pp. 1–199.

SA = *Sacrament an Alter*, the last sermon in the Tregear manuscript, ff 59–66a, pp. 38–45 in Bice's edition of TH.

TH = John Tregear, *Homelyes xiii in Cornysche*, British Library Additional

MS 46, 397 [quoted from Christopher Bice's cyclostyled text (no place [1969])].

WAD = Bruce Griffiths and Dafydd Glyn Jones, *Geiriadur yr Academi: The Welsh Academy English–Welsh Dictionary*, Cardiff, 1995.

Williams, N.J.A. *Cornish Today: An Examination of the Revived Language*, Kernewek dre Lyther, Sutton Coldfield, 1995.

Williams, N.J.A. '"Linguistically Sound Principles": The Case Against Kernewek Kemmyn', *Cornish Studies*: 4, pp. 64–87.

Williams, N.J.A. 'Nebbaz gerriau dro tho Curnoack', O'Donnell lecture given in Oxford, May, 1998.

Williams, N.J.A. (forthcoming), 'Middle and Late Cornish' in K. McCone, *Compendium Linguarum Celticarum*, Reichert Verlag.

REVIEW ARTICLE

'AN EVENT OF GREAT SIGNICANCE' [sic]: A REVIEW OF GEORGE'S *GERLYVER KRES*

Michael Everson

Ken George, *Gerlyver Kernewek Kemmyn: an Gerlyver Kres, Kernewek-Sowsnek Sowsnek-Kernewek. Cornish-English English-Cornish Dictionary*, 1998, 320 pp. [Bosprenn]: Kesva an Taves Kernewek. ISBN 0 907064 87 6, £14.99

INTRODUCTION

The publication of a new dictionary for a Celtic language is generally a cause for celebration. Ken George's new dictionary, appearing five years after his *Gerlyver Meur*, is rather a disappointment, as it is defective in two essential features: its form and its content.

FORM

Producing a dictionary is a formidable task: unlike most other books, a dictionary contains a very large number of paragraphs ('entries), each of which must adhere closely to the chosen style, and be as stylistically perfect as possible. Given the emphasis George places on computer-aided linguistics, one would expect a high degree of precision in the presentation of entries in his dictionary.

Precise they are: readable and attractive they are not. I find the typography of the *Gerlyver Kres* to be ugly and irritating, reflecting rather slipshod design parameters. In Part One, Cornish headwords are presented in **12-point Helvetica Bold,** with grammatical notes in *10-point Times Italic*, and English definitions in 10-point Times Plain.

Within an entry, Cornish subentrires are presented in **10-point Helvetica Bold**. References glossing 'homographs' (the usual word in lexicographical practice *homophones*) are given in <angle brackets> (which are normally used in linguistics to represent orthographic entities, rather than semantic ones); these are, inexplicably, not separated from the headword by a space.

Turning to Part Two, the English-Cornish half of the dictionary, one would expect that the same conventions would be applied. They are not. In Part Two, English headwords are given in **12-point Times Bold** (not **12-point Helvetica Bold**), and Cornish definitions in **10-point Helvetica Bold** (not 10-point Times Plain). Grammatical notes are still given in *10-point Times Italic*, and sub-articles in 10-point Times Plain. In some entries, additional comments are given in 9-point Times Plain with **9-point Helvetica Bold**. A bug in the conversion from database to dictionary text resulted in headwords beginning with a hyphen being set in plain text instead of bold (-iv, -oleth, -vann, -ya, instead of the expected **-iv, -oleth, -vann, -ya**).

This typography gives a totally different colour to the text of the two halves of the dictionary. The inconsistency is quite unacceptable, being confusing to the user, and without precedent in bilingual dictionary design. It appears to be the result of some kind of automated text-dump without sufficient attention to stylistic harmonization. It makes the dictionary hard to use. It draws the attention of the user to the typography, which is a cardinal sin in typesetting: the best typography is *always*, in lexicography at least, invisible.

In the entries, the plus sign is used to indicate a plural suffix added to the root (*ger, +yow* for *geryow*); the hyphen is used with plurals when some letters of the root are replaced (*triger, oryon* for *trigoryon*). This convention was also used in George's 1993 *Gerlyver Meur*. I cannot see that it has anything in particular to recommend it; at least in 12-point Helvetica Bold, the plus sign appears *very* large and black, leaping off the page at the reader. Nance did not find it necessary to make use of such a convention: he wrote *ger, -yow* for *geryow*, and *tryger, -goryon* for *trygoryon*. The practice is also unknown in Breton and Welsh dictionaries. It is possible that George may make some use of the +/- distinction in his database for purposes irrelevant to users of the *Gerlyver Kres*.

Let us take some sample entries, presented in actual size: first from George's dictionary. I chose this example only because it had showed all three of the features criticized above: varying sizes and faces of type, glosses in brackets attached to the headwords, and the use of the plus sign before the plural ending. I chose these examples before I looked at the equivalent entries in Nance's *Cornish-English Dictionary*.

les<plant> *m.* **+yow** plant, wort;
les an gog marigold; **les
densek** dandelion
les<profit> *m.* profit, advantage,
benefit; **dhe les** *adj.* useful,
interesting, worthwhile
les<width> *m.* width, breadth

Notice that no plural ending is given for the second and third
entries, though they are nouns (this makes those entries dependent
upon the first one), and that the <glosses> are completely redundant,
as the first word in the definitions gives *exactly* the same information.
Compare Nance:

> lēs, *m.*, breadth, width; landyard of 18 feet
> square, D. "lace": *trelles* (*trylles*), three
> times the width O.M. 393; *l. tyr* (*lace
> teere*), a "lace" of ground (Carew MS.,
> 1599, Hearne's *Curious Discourses*).
> lēs, *m.*, profit, advantage, behoof, interest,
> use, good, benefit, *hydh* Aelfric; to serve,
> be of use (of things): *nyns-yu dhe l.*, it is
> of no use; *myr dh'y l.*, watch over his
> interests; *oll rag agan l.* for the good of
> us all; **les-kemyn*, commonwealth; *ef a-
> drel dhyso dhe l.*, it will turn out
> profitable for thee; C.W. 739.
> †les, -les, *m.*, plant, -wort (in old
> compounds): see **losowen**, made from
> pl., **losow**.
> †les-an-gōk (C. Voc. *lesengoc*), *m.*,
> marigold, *solsaeve* Aelfric, lit. "cuckoo-
> flower"; see **cōk**.

A great deal more information is given in Nance than in George.
In fairness to George, however, note that the plural is not given clearly
for Nance's entries at all. I am not sure what to think about the fact
that Nance **lēs** for 'breadth' and 'profit' but **les** for 'plant' while George
gives only **les**. Either George considers the latter to have the same
vowel length as former, or he has forgotten to respell it **less** in his
orthography. The point size is considerably smaller (8.5-point type on
8-point leading where George has 12- and 10-point type on 10.5 point
leading); it is well to observe that George's dictionary would be far
shorter than it is, were it set like Nance's.

> **les**<plant> *m.* **+yow** plant, wort; **les an
> gog** marigold; **les densek** dandelion
> **les**<profit> *m.* profit, advantage, benefit;
> **dhe les** *adj.* useful, interesting,
> worthwhile
> **les**<width> *m.* width, breadth

And that means quantifiably shorter. Nance's English-Cornish letter L runs to 199.5 column centimetres and his Cornish-English letter N runs to 120.5 column centimetres. George's English-Cornish L runs to 216.5 column centimetres (8 per cent longer than Nance) and his Cornish-English letter N runs to 84.5 column centimetres (30 per cent shorter than Nance). But setting George at the same size as Nance would yield something like 149 column centimetres for L and 58 column centimetres for N, 25 per cent and 48 per cent shorter than Nance's L and N respectively. The *Gerlyver Kres* has about 200 pages of material in it page for page compared with Nance, though its typographical padding brings it to over 300 pages.

I was stunned by the headers and the footers of the dictionary. 'GERLYVER KRES . . . Kernewek - Sawsnek' and GERLYVER KRES . . . Sawsnek - Kernewek' appear, pointlessly, atop every page instead of the useful guide words one normally expects in a dictionary. The footers remind us that 'Dr Ken George' finalized the text of his dictionary in 'mis-Hedra 1998' on each page. People often use their wordprocessors to put this kind of information on draft documents, but one does not expect it to survive the publication process. Some uncorrected error resulted in the even-numbered page numbers in the Cornish-English half of the dictionary being inset 66 per cent into the footer, instead of being centred as are all other page numbers in the dictionary.

The English in the two pages of front matter appears not to have been proofed: 'never-endingtask' on page 2 should have been 'never-ending task'. For 'asonderstondya' on page 3 read 'as *onderstondya*'. The terms 'English-Cornish' and 'Cornish-English' are written with 'space en-dash space' ('English – Cornish') where a simple hyphen would have sufficed. The dust jacket proudly announces that the publication of this dictionary 'is an event of great signcance [sic] in the development of the language'.

Typographically, this dictionary is a disaster. It looks as though it were prepared by people who neither cared for, nor understood the noble art of lexicography.

CONTENT
The title of the dictionary is difficult to ascertain, as the book has a number of titles. On the title page: '*Gerlyver Kernewek Kemmyn: An Gerlyver Kres. Kernewek-Sowsnek Sowsnek-Kernewek. Cornish-English English-Cornish dictionary*'; on the spine and dust jacket: '*The New Standard Cornish Dictionary. An Gerlyver Kres. Cornish-English English-Cornish*'. If George thinks we shall consider '*Gerlyver Kernewek Kemmyn*' to be an acceptable translation equivalent for

'*The New Standard Cornish Dictionary*', he should think again. '*New Standard Cornish Dictionary*' in Kernewek Kemmyn is '*Gerlyver Savonek Nowydh a'n Tavas Kernewek*'. '*An Gerlyver Kres*' could also mean '*the Middle Dictionary*', '*the Dictionary of Faith*', or '*the Dictionary of Peace*'. What does the author intend us to understand? Just that this dictionary is smaller than the *Gerlyver Meur* of 1993? The learner of Cornish will certainly be confused.

The front matter comprises just two pages, which is a bit scant. The list of abbreviations omits symbols such as <AV>, <CN>, <IJ>, etc., although these appear with some frequency. The information contained in these codes is redundantly entered in the dictionary, and it is often possible to decipher them. My objection is that the user of a dictionary should not be presented with such material nor required to perform decipherment. Consider:

as- *pref.* re-

-as<-ful> *suff.* **-asow** -ful

-as<VN> *v.* (VN ending)

-as<33> *v.* (3rd sg. pret. ending)

es<PV> *v.* thou wast

ha<IJ> *int.* ha

ow<-ing> *ptl.* -ing

ow<my> *adj.* my

-ow *suff.* (pl. ending)

One can guess VN to be 'verbal noun', and suppose PV to be 'personal verb' (or something), but I will not hazard a guess at decoding '33'. Is there a 30, 31, 32? Note that for *-as* VN is given not only in brackets, but also in the definition—though VN does not appear in the list of abbreviations. Neither does *sg* or *pret.* or *ptl.* or *pl*—though *plur.* does. The list also gives *int.* 'interjection', though *interj.* is more usual in dictionaries in opposition to *intr.* 'intransitive'. Redundant or not, it looks as though, in generating the dictionary from the database, the information was exported from the same field as the glosses which also appear within brackets. A database structured so that grammatical information and glosses appear to be in the same field is certainly something to wonder about.

I suppose if one is going to go to the trouble to gloss *es* as 'thou wast' instead of 'you were', one should also give 'thou wert'.

Non-penultimate stress is not indicated in the *Gerlyver Kres*. Non-penultimate stress is unpredictable; it must be indicated in a Cornish dictionary. Nance used the middle dot to indicate this. Does George not use it because his database and his comparison programs are unable to handle headwords so marked? That would be one explanation for not showing stress in the headwords. Otherwise, there is no excuse. Either way the dictionary is faulty. The dust jacket states that it is 'an essential volume for beginner and scholar alike', but this fault alone reduces the dictionary's usefulness for either.

Regarding the coverage of the dictionary, the blurb on the dust jacket claims: 'This New Standard Dictionary contains all known words of the traditional language, except the English borrowings for which there are perfectly good Cornish alternatives, plus the [sic] new words for the 21st. [sic] century'. The front matter, however, asserts that 'the master-files include practically all the words found in tradional Cornish, and many more words introduced into Cornish in the 20th century, especially by R. Morton Nance'. Why exactly do the 'master-files', the basis for all of George's work, not include *exhaustively* all the words found in the corpus of traditional Cornish? Exactly what percentage has not been included, and why?

In any case, neither claim is true. An assertion that a dictionary contains 'all known words' is extravagant and easily checked. But let us look just at the loan words which George finds offensive. Taking a list of 513 borrowed verbs ending in -*a* and -*ya* found in *Pascon agan Arluth, Origo Mundi, Passio Christi, Resurrexio Domini, Beunans Meriasek*, John Tregear's *Homilies, Sacrament an Altar*, and *Creation of the World*, we must first note that 191 of these (37 per cent) are *only* found in Tregear's texts and cannot be expected to be found in Nance 1938. Of the 322 words remaining, 48 (15 per cent) are missing from Nance as headwords in the dictionary. I have not checked the provenance of these 48 words. Some may also have been unavailable to him; some may be errroneous omissions. One does not suspect Nance to have withheld Cornish words from publication.

In George's dictionary, of these 513 words borrowed into traditional Cornish, 270 (53 per cent) do not appear as headwords in the *Gerlyver Meur*. One could be tempted to believe the front matter's claim, which explains that '[s]ome of the words in the traditional corpus, such as *onderstandya*, [which] have not found favour with Cornish speakers' have therefore been omitted, but an investigation of the loanwords included and omitted makes one wonder what criteria George used in order to make his determination of which words Cornish speakers liked and which they did not. Of the 191 words from Tregear unavailable to Nance, but available to George, 143 (75 per cent) have been omitted by George. Why omit *glorifya* when *glori* and *gloryus* are included as headwords? Why omit *rebellya* but not *rebellyans*? Why omit *kreatya* when *kreador* is included? Under the English headword **creator**, *furvyer, gwrier*, and *kreador* are given, while under **create**, only *gwruthyl* is cited. Why are *furvya* and *kreatya* omitted under the verb? English admits the synonyms '*form*', '*make*', and '*create*'. Surely Cornish may also be as rich. Why include *confessya, ordena*, and *marya*, but not *confyrmya*? Why is *comondya* (found in *Origo Mundi, Beunans Meriasek*, John Tregear's *Homilies, Sacrament an Altar*, and *Creation of the World*) omitted, but *comendya* (found only in *Beunans Meriasek*) included? Why is *remembra* omitted in favour of *perthi kov* 'bear in mind' when it is found frequently in *Beunans Meriasek*, John Tregear's *Homilies, Sacrament an Altar*, and *Creation of the World*? *Perthi kov* cannot be used in a phrase such as *remember vy dhe'th whor* 'remember me to your sister'.

Nance's 1955 English-Cornish dictionary recognized the importance of Tregear, remarking that his homilies gave 'by far the longest run of Cornish prose'. Tregear's Cornish must be considered to be authentic, regardless of the proportion of loanwords it contains; and what loanwords it does contain must be considered to be authentic Cornish. Traditional Cornish of all periods contains loanwords from other languages.

The front matter states that some of the doubtful borrowings are 'included in the English-Cornish section (printed in light print) because no suitable alternatives have yet been found for them' and asks readers with ideas for such alternatives to inform the editor. Possibly this is an excuse for the questionable typography. In any case, paging through the English-Cornish section, I found 21 such doubtful words. I give them below, with traditional Cornish sources in parentheses.

contentious kavillek (OM 2784), **controversy** kontroversita (TH 19, 37, 38), **domineer** lordya (CW 456), **hobby-horse** hobihors (BM 1061), **implore** konjorya (PC 1321), **inheritance** eritons (BM 2452, TH 41), **installation** installashyon (*recte* Kernewek Kemmyn *stallashyon* BM 3017), **interlude** ynterlud (Nance < Lhuyd *antarlick*), **justify** justifia (TH 9 x 2), **perfume** perfumya (possibly an error for *perfumyas* TH 21a 'performed' *perfumya* 'to perform' TH 51a, cf. *performya* TH 52 with the same sense), **persecute** persekutya (TH 22), **pertain** pertaynya (TH 10 x 2, 22, 26a, 43), **petition** petyshyon (BM 4300), **precept** presept (TH 10), **pronounce** prononsya (TH 54), **protest** protestya (SA 64a), **radish** redigenn (*redic* OCV), **second (2ⁿᵈ)** sekond (OM 17, BM 2198, CW 51, CW 80, TH x 16), **suppress** suppressya (TH 28a, 42, 42a), **swerve** swarvya (TH 18a, 38), **usurp** usurpya (TH 31a).

I do not know what objections George has to *kavillek* or *redigenn*. But the rest of these are perfectly authentic. All of these words come from traditional Cornish texts, so it is hard to see why they are so disfavoured. Nevertheless, hiding problematic words in 'light type' is not how one should elicit comment on them. One should publish an article discussing them, or, if such doubtful words must appear in the dictionary, one should place them all together in an annex for easy access and discussion.

It would appear that George's dictionary is intended to solidify in some way the authority of George's orthography by offering the Cornish market a replacement for Nance's dictionaries. In terms of the lexicon presented, however, he has failed to do so. I took for comparison the letter L (chosen at random) in the English-Cornish half and the letter N (also chosen at random) in the English-Cornish half of both books. Allowing for certain editorial differences in arranging headwords and subheadwords, and for possible errors on my part made during the attempt to locate words in the two different orthographies, I found the following.

Out of a total number of 261 English headwords, Nance has 84 headwords which George omits:

labial, laboratory, laburnum, lad, laden, Lammas, languid, languish, languor, lapse, larch, lass, lassitude, latten, latter, launch, launder, lavatory, lavender, lavish, lea, league, leal, leaven, leavings, lechery, ledge, leer, lees, legate, legislate, leisure, lenient, lest, lethargic, leveret, Leviathan, Levite, lexicon, liar, libel, lilac, limber, limbo, limp, linden, linger, linseed, lint, lintel, lissom, litany, literal, lithe, loafer, loath, locomotive, locust, lodge, logan-berry, logan rock, loll, loneliness, locquacious, lounge, lovely, lozenge, lubber, lucid, lucrative, ludicrous, lug, lugworm, lullaby, lullay, lumber, lunacy, lurch, lurid, lustre, lusty, lute, lying-in, lymph.

Out of a total number of 342 English headwords, George has 70 English headwords which Nance does not; 11 of these begin with *long-*:

laceration, lacking, lamp-chill, lamp-post, lamp-wick, lancet, landing, land-surveyor, langoustine, lapse-rate, lardy, large-footed, laryngitis, lathe, latitudinal, Launceston, laurels, law clerk, lawn-mower, lay-by, leading, lead pencil, lectionary, ledger, left-overs, leniently, leper-hospital, letter-box, ley, ley-land, liaise, liaison, LibDem, life-style, light-bulb, liken, lime-juice, limp, limpid, limpidity, line-drawing, linguistics, Liskeard, lisper, litigation, litter-bin, liver-fluke, locate, Lombardy, long-beaked, long-distance, long-eared, longitude, longitudinal, long-lasting, long-limbed, long-muzzled, long-nosed skate, long-sight, long-standing, long-stone, long-tongued, Looe, lorry, Lostwithiel, loudspeaker, lowering, Loyalist, luggage-rack, luminosity.

One cannot say anything against the publication of Cornish words for useful terms like *laryngitis, lawnmower, ledger, leftovers* . . . but one must ask why useful words like *laboratory, lavatory, languish, lavender, launch, launder, league, ledge, legislate, leisure,* and *lethargic* do not appear as headwords.

Out of a total number of 168 Cornish headwords, Nance has 27 headwords which George omits:

na fors, namma, nappa, nasya, nasyon, na-vē, navyth, na-whāth ('nevertheless'; George glosses 'not yet'), *neb-ür, nedha, negesa, negeth, negh, neghy, nep-dēn, nep-part, nep-plas, nep-pow, nep-tra, nessa, nomber, nowedhyans, nowedhynsy, nowyjyans, nowys, noys, nȳthowa.*

Out of a total number of 165 Cornish headwords, George has 52 English headwords which Nance does not:

nadh, nadha, naturel, nawmen, naw-ugens, nebreydh, negysya, negysydh, nerthegeth, nerv, nervenn, nervus, neskar, nester, -neth, neusynn, neuvell, neuvella, neuvelladow, neuvwisk, neuvyer, neves, nevesek, nevra, -ni, nijys, nivel, niverenn, niverieth, niveronieth, niverus, niwlgorn, niwllaw, niwl-ster, niwlwias, Normanek, north-west, noskan, noswara, noswikor, noswikorek, noswikorieth, notenn, noter, notyans, nowedhys, nowydhadow, nowydhses, Noy, nuk, nuklerek.

In all fairness to George, it has to be said that the additions in his Cornish headwords are good ones, and the omissions from Nance are not particularly alarming. All the *nep* words are more or less predictable compounds. They are still worth listing in a dictionary, however.

In general, though, I find the wordlist in the English-Cornish part to be quite weak. Its selection seems rather *ad hoc*; I think that a learner, for instance, would find this dictionary rather frustrating to use due to its omissions. No mention is made of dictionaries or works presumably consulted (such as English, Welsh, Breton, or other Cornish dictionaries) in selecting the headwords.

George has been recognized by many Cornish speakers as an authority on spelling. This recognition, merited or not, does not confer upon him authority in lexicography. The lexical content of the *Gerlyver Kres*, especially in terms of its exclusion of loanwords found in traditional Cornish, calls into question the scope of his 'master-files'.

KERNEWEK KEMMYN

I do not like Common Cornish (Kernewek Kemmyn), but my criticisms on the form and content of the *Gerlyver Kres* stand on their own merits regardless of the spelling used. Nevertheless, the fact that the dictionary *is* a dictionary of Kernewek Kemmyn calls the whole enterprise into serious question.

The front matter states that the Kernewek Kemmyn 'orthography was criticized by N. Williams in his book *Cornish Today*, but his criticisms are largely unfounded, as shown by Paul Dunbar and the present editor in their reply *Kernewek Kemmyn: Cornish for the 21st Century*'.

It is understandable that George might consider Dunbar and George[1] to be an adequate response to the criticisms made by Williams in *Cornish Today*[2], but few Cornish speakers and even fewer Cornish scholars would take that dialogue seriously.

In *Cornish Today*, Williams presented a cogent analysis of the Cornish language situation as he saw it: Unified Cornish (Kernewek Unyes) as an orthography with some failings, Modern Cornish (Curnoack Nowedga) as an orthography with too many ambiguities and too many differences from Medieval Cornish, Breton, and Welsh to be practical, and Common Cornish (Kernewek Kemmyn) as an orthography derived from unsuccessful respelling of traditional Cornish orthographic forms on the basis of a mistaken phonemic theory. Dunbar and George try to show that Williams is wrong, but one is so put off by the sniggering schoolboy tone of the discourse that in the end one prefers to reject the work *in toto*. It cannot be taken to be a serious reply to Williams' criticisms.

In any case, it is important to note that many of the arguments in Dunbar and George's book are based on George's proprietary 'master-files' and graphemic analysis algorithms. Since these files are not in the public domain, one does not know either how complete they are or whether they are trustworthy.

George's arguments for a phonemic orthography for Cornish are questionable for a number of reasons.

(1) George's phonemic analysis has always been suspect. Williams, as early as 1987, showed that George's introduction of the *dj/tj* distinction was erroneous, and George withdrew it in 1989. Williams has shown quite clearly that George's understanding of Cornish vocalic length is mistaken, though George says that he does not believe him.

(2) The whole nature of the Kernewek Kemmyn reform is based on George's assertion that phonemic orthographies are better than historical ones based on quasi-phonemic and other traditional conventions (he gives the usual tiresome complaint about English orthography, which was dealt with far more comprehensively by Axel Wijk in 1959[3]). George maintains that it is difficult to implement phonemic reform where the size of the populations using competing orthographic practices is large. But this is not true to the facts. Reforms in many languages occur quite regularly, for very large populations. Languages with millions of speakers like Norwegian *bokmål* and *nynorsk* routinely implement reforms. Other languages have successfully implemented complete revisions of their orthographies: Azerbaijani changed officially from the Cyrillic alphabet to the Latin in 1992; when Irish Gaelic shifted from Gaelic script to Roman this was done in conjunction with spelling simplifications in the 1940s and 1950s.

(3) George posits that because the population of Cornish speakers is small it did no harm to introduce a radically different system as opposed to making simple corrections of the existing system, regardless of the merits of the system. I disagree: the harm done has been considerable.

(4) George maintains that real and proportionally significant grass-roots consensus had been achieved with regard to Kernewek Kemmyn when the Cornish Language Board adopted it in 1987; this is not the case, as the continuing language debate attests.

Kernewek Kemmyn was a sociolinguistic disaster. It split the Cornish Revival in two. It encouraged Richard Gendall into further splitting the community with his Modern Cornish. (Gendall, it must be re- membered, is acknowledged by Nance for reversing the *Cornish-English Dictionary* of 1939 which became the basis for Nance's 1955 *English-Cornish Dictionary*.) Williams approach, based on his genuine concern for the future of the Revival, was to go back to first principles and suggest corrections to the errors in Unified Cornish. Unified Cornish Revised,[4] as Williams himself admits, will not be the last word in that process—but it is the best way forward. Unified Cornish Revised was made in the spirit of the Norwegian orthographic reforms —an incremental step towards perfecting the orthography, correcting known errors in Nance's orthography. Future revisions will be taken on their merits with true consensus of academic and non-academic experts alike.

CONCLUSION

The *Gerlyver Kres* is certainly no substitute for Nance's 1938 and 1955 dictionaries, as it omits much which can only be found in them. Its claims to comprehensiveness are unfounded. Its appearance at this time does little to advance the Cornish language revival, not least because it is presented in the experimental orthography known as Common Cornish (Kernewek Kemmyn), a form that has experienced sustained criticism from Celtic scholars and must be regarded as flawed.

NOTES AND REFERENCES

1. Paul Dunbar and Ken George, *Kernewek Kemmyn: Cornish for the Twenty-First Century*, 1997, ISBN 0-907064-71-X.
2. Nicholas J.A. Williams, 1995, *Cornish Today: An Examination of the Revived Language*, Sutton Coldfield: Kernewek dre Lyther.
3. Axel Wijk, *Regularized English: An Investigation into the English Spelling Reform Problem with a New, Detailed Plan for a Possible Solution*, (Acta Universitatis Stockholmiensis: Stockholm Studies in English; 7) Stockholm, 1959.
4. Nicholas J.A. Williams, *Clappya Kernowek: An Introduction to Unified Cornish Revised*, Redruth, 1997.

NOTES ON CONTRIBUTORS

Catherine Brace is a Lecturer in the Department of Geography at the University of Exeter. She is a historical cultural geographer and her research focuses on the representation of regional landscapes and identities in art, literature and popular culture. She is currently undertaking research on the construction and representation of Cornwall through the work of writers who have lived and worked there, such as Arthur Caddick and Denys Val Baker. A member of the Directors of the Landscape Research Group, Catherine Brace is especially interested in forging interdisciplinary links between scholars interested in the study of landscape and representation.

Brian Elvins, a native of Mevagissey, was formerly Head of the VIth Form at the Kings of Wessex Upper School in Cheddar, Somerset, and is a member of the New Cornish Studies Forum. He is an authority on the politics of nineteenth-century Cornwall, on which he has written widely.

Michael Everson is director of Everson Gunn Teoranta (EGT), a Dublin-based company which specializes in minority-language software localization, fonts and publishing. He is a linguist by training, an expert in writing systems, and works as Irish national representative in a number of International and European Standardization com- mittees whose emphasis is on linguistic and cultural adaptability in information technology. In 1995 EGT published his *Breton Grammar*, an English translation and adaptation of Roparz Hemon's *Grammaire Bretonne*.

Jim Hall teaches literature, media and culture studies at Falmouth College of Arts in Cornwall. He writes on new media and literary topics. Recent publications include work on Saul Bellow and Edith Wharton. He is currently researching the vicissitudes of Cornish identity from the late medieval period to the present.

John Hurst was formerly Senior Tutor in the University of Exeter's Department of Continuing and Adult Education (today's Department of Lifelong Learning) in Truro, Cornwall, for whom he now lectures on a part-time basis. He contributed a chapter on 'Literature in Cornwall' to Philip Payton (ed.), *Cornwall Since The War* (1993), and his article 'Voice From a White Silence: The Manuscripts of Jack Clemo' appeared in *Cornish Studies: Three* (1995).

Patrick Laviolette trained as a geographer in his home city of Montreal. He then completed an M.Sc. in Human Ecology at the University of Edinburgh, where he worked as a teaching assistant for a year until becoming a Ph.D. candidate in the Department of Anthropology at University College London. Presently, he is undertaking ethnographic field research in Cornwall, examining the ways in which landscape icons act as items of material culture which shape cultural identities and premise the character of environmental experiences in the peninsula.

Jon Mills is a Lecturer in Linguistics in the Department of Linguistics at the University of Luton. His research interests include lexicography, computational linguistics and Cornish linguistics. His published work includes 'Phonetics and Phonology' in R.R.K. Hartmann (ed.), *Solving Language Problems: From General to Applied Linguistics* (1996); 'Lexicon Based Critical Tokenisation: An Algorithm' in *EURALEX '98 Proceedings* (1998); 'Lemmatisation of the Corpus of Cornish' in *Proceedings of the LREC Workshop on Language Resources for European Minority Languages* (1998); and 'Cornish Lexicography in the Twentieth Century: Standardisation and Divergence' in *Bulletin Suisse de Linguistique Appliquée*, 69/1 (1999).

William A. Morris was born and brought up in Cornwall, later moving to Wales and London in the field of semiconductor physics. He is a Bard of the Cornish Gorsedd and was a founder member of the Cornish Language Board. He studied community history as part a B.A. degree course, and his publications include *Osborn of Zennor* (1999). He is a member of the New Cornish Studies Forum.

Ronald Perry is a founder member of the New Cornish Studies Forum, and was formerly Head of the Faculty of Management at Cornwall College. A pioneer of the 'new Cornish social science', he wrote (with Ken Dean, Bryan Brown and David Shaw) the important *Counter-urbanisation: International Case Studies of Socio-economic Change in Rural Areas* (1986), a volume which underpins our current understanding of the nature of social, economic and demographic change in post-war Cornwall. More recently, Ronald Perry has shifted his research attentions to the socio-economic and cultural conditions of late-Victorian and Edwardian Cornwall.

Sharron Schwartz is a postgraduate student at the Institute of Cornish Studies, University of Exeter, where she is currently writing a Ph.D. thesis on the Cornish in Latin America. She is also Director of the Cornish Global Migration Programme at Murdoch House, Redruth, and is a member of both the New Cornish Studies Forum and the Cornish History Network. Amongst her published work is her widely acclaimed *Lanner: A Cornish Mining Parish* (1998), co-authored with Roger Parker, a volume which has established a new standard of scholarship in the writing of Cornish local history.

Garry Tregidga is Assistant Director of the Institute of Cornish Studies, University of Exeter. His research interests are centred on the political experience of Cornwall since the 1880s, and his *Decline, Dormancy & Rebirth: The Liberal Party in South West Britain after 1918* is shortly to be published by the University of Exeter Press. He is also preparing an edited collection of the corres- pondence of Sir Francis and Lady Eleanor Acland from 1906 to 1939, to be published by the Devon and Cornwall Record Society, and he is founder of the Cornish History Network whose *Newsletter* he edits.

N.J.A. Williams is Lecturer in Irish at University College Dublin, and he has also taught Celtic Studies at Queen's University Belfast and in the University of Liverpool. He is a Bard of the Cornish Gorsedd and has won first prize for Cornish poetry in the Gorsedd competitions on several occasions. His handbook of Unified Cornish Revised *Clappya Kernowek* was published in 1997, and in 1998 he delivered the O'Donnell Lectures at the University of Oxford on the Manx and Cornish languages.